Fodor's
NINTH
New
EDITION

Vienna &
the Danube
Valley

W9-BIA-844

Reprinted from *Fodor's Austria*

Fodor's Travel Publications, Inc.
New York and London

Fodor's Vienna & the Danube Valley

Editor: Jillian Magalaner
Contributors: George Hamilton, Tara Hamilton, Alan Levy, Marcy Pritchard, George Sullivan
Art Director: Fabrizio La Rocca
Cartographer: David Lindroth
Illustrator: Karl Tanner
Cover Photograph: Franklin/Magnum

Design: Vignelli Associates

Contents

Maps

Foreword

We would like to thank the directors of the Austrian National Tourist Offices in Vienna and New York, especially Gabriele Wolf and the New York staff, for their generous and considerable assistance in preparing this new edition.

We also wish to thank Austrian Airlines and Tom Fredo for their help.

While every care has been taken to ensure accuracy of the information in this guide, tourism in Austria is a dynamic industry and changes will occur; consequently, the publisher can assume no liability for errors.

All prices and opening times quoted in this guide are based on information supplied to us at press time. Hours and admission fees may change; call ahead to avoid disappointment. Fodor's wants to hear about your travel experiences, both pleasant and unpleasant. When a hotel or restaurant fails to live up to its billing, let us know, and we will investigate the complaint and revise our entries where warranted.

Send your letters to the editors of Fodor's Travel Publications, 201 E. 50th St., New York, NY 10022.

Highlights and Fodor's Choice

Highlights

Austria—and in particular, Vienna—has become the undisputed center of East–West activity following the collapse of communism in the East. Until 1918 those lands were part of the vast Habsburg empire, and despite language differences, ties are still fairly strong: Every Viennese is said to have an aunt in Prague (and every Czechoslovak an aunt in Vienna). The influence of East European cuisine is evident on every Viennese menu.

Politics and the Economy Long the "last outpost" of Western Europe, Austria today is struggling with the concept of integration with the European Community. The country wants to be a part of the bigger show, but it is not about to give up its claim to being the center of East–West trade. Many Western multinational companies use Vienna as a coordination center for their sales activities in the East, and the city is becoming the focal point for East–West financing. The airport is being expanded, new office complexes built, communications improved. Vienna is fighting to maintain its competitive edge as Eastern cities such as Budapest and Prague open up.

A formal application to join the EC was filed in 1990 and could be acted upon as early as 1994. A wave of liberalization has brought much legislation into line with European Community practice in anticipation of membership; old monopolies are disappearing and more competition is being encouraged, particularly in sectors (such as finance) once dominated by state-owned industry.

Austria this year expects an economic growth rate among the highest in Europe as a consequence of flourishing exports and tourism. The manufacturing side is led by production of parts and components for the German automotive industry. The nation's increased prosperity is reflected in the quality of goods (and their price ranges) in shop windows.

Travel Tourism has regained its position as the number one industry, and the emphasis is increasingly on quality. Planners, seeing limits to the number of tourists and tourist facilities, propose to preserve the country's virtues: sensational scenery, unpolluted air and water, and easy accessibility. Last year the railroads adopted a new schedule system that better coordinates trains between all parts of the country and speeds up many long-distance routes while tour bus traffic in Vienna is being restricted in order to make the environment more pleasant.

For travelers headed to Austria from Canada or the northeastern United States, a new Singapore Airlines service flies Toronto–Vienna via Amsterdam twice weekly. Air transportation within Austria is improving, with more competition on several routes. While this has resulted in greater frequency of services, domestic fares remain high.

Hotels have traditionally been independent enterprises in Austria, but an increasing number are joining reservation and referral groups such as Best Western or affinity organizations such as Romantik-Hotels, which groups hotels of unusual charm; Silencehotels, which are set in a particularly quiet environment; and Schlosshotels, which offer accommodation in castles and former palaces. Hotels affiliated with the referral and affinity groups continue under private management. The quality of accommodations has improved greatly in recent years, resulting in an upgrading of formerly lower-priced facilities; bargain accommodations are becoming harder to find in Vienna, while prices in the country remain low by any measure.

Travelers who depend on credit cards for payment may lose some of this convenience in Austria. Many hotels and restaurants and virtually all travel agents canceled their contracts with credit card companies in 1991 in protest over high discount rates and often slow payment. At midyear the issue was in negotiation, with neither side showing an inclination to compromise.

The Arts Annual music events begin with the **New Year's Concert** and a performance of Beethoven's Ninth symphony, both in Vienna on New Year's Day. **The Festival Weeks** is from mid-May to mid-June. For many people summer ends officially on September 1, when the **opera** in Vienna resumes its season after a two-month holiday.

The near future should see a resumption of the "noble" balls, recently canceled in deference to the international crisis in the Gulf. The Philharmonic Ball will take place in late January, in the Musikverein, and the noblest of all, the Opernball, in the very end of February in the Opera. *Fasching*, the carnival season between New Year's and Lent, concludes with a great parade around the Ring.

Special markets abound throughout the year. Of the many Christmas markets, one of the nicest is that on Freyung in Vienna in the weeks before the holiday, with many handmade goods.

Fodor's Choice

No two people will agree on what makes a perfect vacation, but it can be fun and helpful to know what others think. We hope you'll have a chance to experience some of Fodor's Choices yourself while visiting Austria. For detailed information on individual entries, see the relevant sections of this guidebook.

Times to Remember

A night at the Opera

High Mass on Sunday in the Augustinerkirche

A ride on the Prater's Giant Wheel at dusk

Works of Art

Bosch's *Last Judgment*

Brueghel's *Hunters in the Snow*

Cellini's gold salt cellar

Klimt's *The Kiss*

Schiele's *The Family*

Vermeer's *Allegory of the Art of Painting: the Artist in his Studio*

Museums

Belvedere Palace

Historisches Museum der Stadt Wien (Museum of Viennese History)

Kunsthistorisches Museum (Museum of Art History)

Taste Treats

Sampling wine at a romantic *Heuriger*

Wiener schnitzel practically anywhere

A snack from the *Wurstelstand* in the Albertinaplatz

The appetizer cart at Drei Hussaren

Architectural Gems

Ferstel Palace and Café Central

Gloriette (Schönbrunn Palace Gardens)

Hundertwasserhaus

Looshaus

Secession building

Hotels

König von Ungarn

Palais Schwarzenberg

Pension Zipser

Restaurants

Glacisbeisl

Römischer Kaiser

Cafés

Central

Hawelka

Schwarzenberg

Churches and Abbeys

Karlskirche

St. Peter's

St. Stephen's

Parks and Gardens

Belvedere

Burggarten

Schönbrunn

Stadtpark

Austria

...kag.

Franz Josefs Kai

Obere Donaustrasse

Danube Canal

Hollandstrasse

Taborstr.

Praterstrasse

...ertorg.

Heinrichsg.

Rudolfs-pl.

Golsdorfg.

Salztorg.

Salzgries

Salztorbr.

Morzin-pl.

Marc-Aurel-Str.

Sterng.

...lvatorgasse

...lingerstr.

...pl.

Hoher

Juden G.

Raben Steig

Markt

Rotg.

Landskrong.

Bouermmkt.

Brandstätte

Jasomirg. Str.

Goldschm.g.

Rotenturmstr.

Lugech

Köllnerhofg.

Fleischmarkt

Sonnenfelsg.

Bäckerstr.

Stephanspl.

Wollzeile

Domg.

Schulerstr.

Zedlitzg.

Blutg.

Kumpfg.

Grünangerg.

Riemerg.

Singerstr.

Rauhensteing.

Lilieng.

Weihburgg.

Ball g.

Himmelpfortg.

Seilerstätte

Schellingg.

Johannesg.

Fichteg.

Annag.

Krugerstr.

Walfischg.

Schwarzenbergstr.

Hegelg.

Schubert Ring

...ahlerstr.

e Kärntner Ring

Akademie...

Musikverein

Karlsplatz

...Argentinier-str.

Prinz Eugenstr.

Rennweg

Schwedenbr.

Schwedenpl.

Danube Canal

Franz Josefs Kai

Aspernbr.

Untere Donaustr.

Radetzkystr.

Juluis-Rabb-Pl.

Laurenzer-berg

Postg.

Wiesingerstr.

Dominikanerbastei

Georg-Coch-Pl.

Falkestr.

Biberstr.

Postg.

Dr. Karl Luegerpl.

Stuben Bastei

Stuben Ring

Hint. Zollamtsstr.

Vord. Zollamtsstr.

Weiskchr.-str.

Bahnhof Wien-Mitte

Park Ring

Liebenbgg.

Landstrasser Hauptstrasse

Invalidenstr.

Stadtpark

Johannesg.

Lothringerstr.

Am Heumkt.

Salesianerg.

Beatrixgasse

Rechte Bahngasse

Konzerthaus

Schwarzenberg-pl.

Neuer Markt

...danog.

...rasse

N

0   1/4 mile

0   1/4 km

World Time Zones

Numbers below vertical bands relate each zone to Greenwich Mean Time (0 hrs.).
Local times frequently differ from these general indications,
as indicated by light-face numbers on map.

Algiers, **29**	Berlin, **34**	Delhi, **48**	Istanbul, **40**
Anchorage, **3**	Bogotá, **19**	Denver, **8**	Jerusalem, **42**
Athens, **41**	Budapest, **37**	Djakarta, **53**	Johannesburg, **44**
Auckland, **1**	Buenos Aires, **24**	Dublin, **26**	Lima, **20**
Baghdad, **46**	Caracas, **22**	Edmonton, **7**	Lisbon, **28**
Bangkok, **50**	Chicago, **9**	Hong Kong, **56**	London (Greenwich), **27**
Beijing, **54**	Copenhagen, **33**	Honolulu, **2**	Los Angeles, **6**
	Dallas, **10**		Madrid, **38**
			Manila, **57**

Introduction

by George Sullivan

George Sullivan is a freelance writer whose expertise lies in the art history and the life of European cities.

It was, as the Viennese say of a particularly successful funeral, *eine schöne Leich'*—a beautiful corpse. The mourners filled St. Stephen's Cathedral, in the heart of the city. The Imperial deceased had lived to the age of 97 and possessed some 100 living descendants, so the royal contingent was especially large and impressive. The various peoples of Central Europe were widely represented as well, for at its height the Austro-Hungarian Empire had extended to present-day Austria, Hungary, Czechoslovakia, Poland, the Ukraine, Romania, Yugoslavia, and Italy.

After the service, a horse-drawn hearse carried the plain coffin, draped with the Imperial standard, through the inner city. Many thousands of people lined the streets, watching as the procession slowly made its way through the Graben, along Kohlmarkt to the Imperial Palace, past the Augustinerkirche and the Albertina, and into Neuer Markt. There the procession stopped at the entrance to the Imperial Burial Vault, and a member of the royal entourage, chosen for his long and faithful devotion to the deceased, stepped forward. He carried a black stick with a silver handle, and rapped three times on the closed door, signalling the beginning of an ancient ritual.

"Who is it?" came the response from inside.

"Her Imperial and Royal Majesty, Zita, Empress of Austria, Queen of Hungary, Queen of Bohemia, Queen of Croatia. . . ." Several dozen titles followed, mapping out the farthest reaches of the Empire.

"We know her not," answered the doorkeeper. The door remained shut.

Three more raps on the door followed.

"Who is it?"

"Her Imperial and Royal Majesty, Zita, Empress of Austria and Queen of Hungary." This time the long list of titles was conspicuously absent.

"We know her not," came the adamant response. Again the door remained shut.

Once more the silver-handled stick rapped three times.

"Who is it?" "Your sister Zita, a humble sinner."

"She may enter."

The door opened, and the coffin passed through. The deceased, Zita of Bourbon–Parma, was the widow of Karl I, the last emperor of the Austro–Hungarian Empire, who abdicated at the end of World War I and died four years later. The empress survived her husband by 67 years. The funeral took place on April 1, 1989.

Vienna is a city that deeply loves its past. For many centuries it was one of the great capitals of Europe, home to the Habsburg rulers of the Austro–Hungarian Empire. Today the Empire is long gone, but many reminders of the city's Imperial heyday remain, carefully preserved by the tradition-loving Viennese. Most of Vienna's renowned 18th- and 19th-century buildings have been preserved as well, attesting to a brilliant architectural past that few cities can match.

From the late 18th century until World War I, Vienna's culture—particularly its musical culture—was famous throughout Europe. Haydn, Mozart, Beethoven, Schubert, Brahms, Strauss, Mahler, and Bruckner all lived in the city, producing music that is still played in concert halls all over the world. And at the tail end of the 19th century the city's artists and architects—Gustav Klimt, Egon Schiele, Oskar Kokoschka, Josef Hoffmann, Otto Wagner, and Adolf Loos among them—brought about an unprecedented artistic revolution, a revolution that swept away the past and set the stage for the radically experimental art of the 20th century.

At the close of World War I the Austro-Hungarian Empire was dismembered, and Vienna lost its cherished status as the seat of Imperial power. Its influence was much reduced, and (unlike most of Europe's other great cities) its population began to decline, from around 2 million to the current 1.5 million. Today, however, the city's future looks bright, for with the collapse of the Iron Curtain Vienna may at long last regain its traditional status as the hub of central Europe.

For many first-time visitors, the city's one major disappointment is the Danube River. The inner city, it turns out, lies not on the river's main stream but on one of its narrow offshoots, known as the Danube Canal. As a result, the sweeping river views expected by most newcomers fail to materialize.

The Romans are to blame, for when Vienna was founded as a Roman military encampment around AD 100, the walled garrison was built not on the Danube's main stream but rather on the largest of the river's eastern branches, where it could be bordered by water on three sides. (To this day the outline of the Roman walls, a lopsided square, can be seen in the street plan of the inner city: Naglergasse and the Graben to the southwest, Kramergasse and Rotgasse to the southeast, Salzgasse to the northeast, and Tiefer Graben to the northwest.) The wide present-day Danube did not take shape until the late 19th century, when its various branches were rerouted and merged to prevent flooding.

The Romans maintained their camp for some 300 years (the emperor Marcus Aurelius is thought to have died there in AD 180) and finally abandoned it around AD 400. The settlement survived, however, and by the 13th century growth was sufficient to require new city walls to the south. According to legend, the walls were financed by the English: In 1192 the local duke kidnapped King Richard I, who was on his way home from the Third Crusade, and held him prisoner for two years until he was expensively ransomed.

Vienna's third set of walls dates from 1544, when the existing walls were improved and extended. The new fortifications were built by the Habsburg dynasty, who ruled the Austro–Hungarian Empire for an astonishing 640 years, beginning with Duke Rudolph I in 1278 and ending with Emperor Karl I in 1918. The walls stood until 1857, when Emperor Franz Josef finally decreed that they be demolished and replaced by the famous Ringstrasse ("Ring Street").

During medieval times the city's growth was relatively slow, and its heyday as a European capital did not begin until 1683, after a huge force of invading Turks laid siege to the city for two months and were finally routed by an army of Habsburg allies. Among the supplies left behind by the fleeing Turks were sacks filled with coffee beans. It was these beans, so the story goes, that gave a local entrepreneur the idea of opening the first public coffeehouse. Cafés remain a Viennese institution to this day.

The passing of the Turkish threat produced a Viennese building boom, and the Baroque style was the architectural order of the day. The style had originated in Italy around 1600, when a group of brilliantly inventive Italian architects began to embroider and transform the classical motifs that the High Renaissance had copied from ancient Rome. Architects in other countries throughout Europe followed suit, and during the 17th century England, France, and Austria all developed Baroque styles that were very much their own. Austrian Baroque possessed a special grace, described in detail in the walking tours to follow, and it is this grace that gives Vienna the distinctive architectural character that sets the city so memorably apart from its great rivals London, Paris, and Rome.

1 Essential Information

Before You Go

Government Tourist Offices

by George W. Hamilton

A longtime resident of Vienna, George Hamilton writes on travel and tourism in Eastern Europe.

In the United States the primary source of information for anyone planning a trip to Austria is the **Austrian National Tourist Office,** 500 5th Ave., 20th floor, New York, NY 10110, tel. 212/944–6880; 11601 Wilshire Blvd., Suite 2480, Los Angeles, CA 90025, tel. 213/477–3332; 1300 Post Oak Blvd., Suite 960, Houston, TX 77056, tel. 713/850–9999; 500 N. Michigan Ave., Suite 1950, Chicago, IL 60611, 708/644–5556. These offices have detailed material on all kinds of specific holiday offerings, so indicate what you most want to do or see. They can also tell you about snow and ski conditions at various resort centers.

In Canada the tourist offices are at 2 Bloor St., Toronto, Ontario M4W 1A8, tel. 416/967–3348; 1010 Sherbrooke St. W, Suite 1410, Montreal, Quebec H3A 2R7, tel. 514/849–3709; 200 Granville St., Suite 1380, Granville Square, Vancouver, BC V6C 1S4, tel. 604/683–5808 or 683–8695. For current snow conditions, tel. 416/967–6870.

In the United Kingdom, check with the tourist office at 30 George St., London W1R 0AL, tel. 071/629–0461. Ask for the *Holiday Hotline* for the latest resort and price information.

Tour Groups

If you want to see the best and most of Austria in a limited time, then consider an escorted tour. Imaginative itineraries abound, hitting out-of-the-way places you might not be able to get to on your own as well as the traditional tourist spots. Because Austria is a major travel destination, a number of operators offer packages covering every conceivable interest. These packages also tend to save you money on airfare and hotels. If group travel is not your thing, look into independent packages (described below). Here, too, variety abounds. You can design your own itinerary by stringing together mini hotel packages in various cities, taking a self-drive tour, castle-hopping, riding the rails, or whipping up a unique combination of all of the above.

Nearly all operators offer both general and special-interest tours year-round. For specifics, see below or check with one of the Austrian National Tourist Offices, major international airlines, and, of course, travel agents.

When evaluating any tour, be sure to find out exactly what expenses are included (particularly tips, taxes and service charges, side trips, additional meals, and entertainment); ratings of all hotels on the itinerary and the facilities they offer; the policy regarding complaints, tour-interruption insurance, and cancellation by either you or the tour operator; the number of travelers in your group; and, if you are traveling alone, the cost for a single supplement. Note whether the tour operator reserves the right to change hotels, routes, or even prices after you've booked.

Listed below is a sampling of operators and packages to give you an idea of what is available. Most tour operators request that bookings be made through a travel agent—there is no additional charge for doing so.

General-Interest Tours   **Adriatic Tours** (691 W. 10th St., San Pedro, CA 90731, tel. 213/548–1446 or 800/272–1718) offers a nine-day escorted tour that includes Vienna, Salzburg, and Innsbruck.

For shorter stays, **Hapag Lloyd Tours** (1640 Hempstead Tpke., East Meadow, NY 11554, tel. 516/794–1253 or 800/334–2724) offers eight-day tours. **Intropa International** (1066 Saratoga Ave., San Jose, CA 95129, tel. 408/247–5574 or 800/468–7672) specializes in music tours of Austria. At the upper end of the price spectrum, **Abercrombie & Kent** (1420 Kensington Rd., Oak Brook, IL 60521, tel. 708/954–2944 or 800/323–7308) has a seven-day luxury rail and road tour through Austria.

Tour operators that combine Austria with other Alpine destinations include **American Express Vacations** (Box 5014, Atlanta, GA 30302, tel. 800/241–1700 or 800/282–0800 in GA), **Trafalgar Tours** (21 E. 26th St., New York, NY 10010, tel. 212/689–8977 or 800/854–0103), **Globus Gateway** (150 S. Los Robles Ave., Pasadena, CA 91101, tel. 818/449–0919 or 800/556–5454), **Olson-Travelworld** (100 N. Sepulveda Blvd., Suite 1010, El Segundo, CA 90245, tel. 213/615–0711; 800/421–2255; in CA 800/421–5785), and **TWA Getaway Vacations** (tel. 800/438–2929).

Special-Interest Tours   From the United States, you can book ski tours, rail tours, self-drive tours, ballooning tours, Vienna-only tours, Danube cruise tours, and budget tours, among others. Fly/drive tours combining Austria with the southern part of Germany, northern Italy, or Switzerland are a popular way of seeing more than one country.

Value Holidays (10224 N. Port Washington Rd., Mequon, WI 53092–5755, tel. 414/241–6373 or 800/558–6850) sells a Royal Castle Vacation, which includes seven nights or more in romantic castles or historic hunting lodges in Austria and unlimited use of a rental car.

The Bombard Society (6727 Curran St., McLean, VA 22101, tel. 703/448–9407 or 800/862–8537) will get you to Austria and above it on any of several ballooning tour packages that include lodging and meals.

For Britons   Austria has long been a popular destination for British travelers, so a great many tour operators—about 75 in fact—have vacation packages for all seasons. These cover every interest from guided art tours to excellent budget ski trips. With so many firms offering good Austrian package tours, only a few can be listed here; for a full list, check with the Austrian National Tourist Office or your travel agent.

Austria Travel (46 Queen Anne's Gate, London SW1H 9AU, tel. 071/222–2430), run by the Anglo-Austrian Society, is one of the best sources of well-organized tours that are good value. As you might suspect, the society arranges economical packages to encourage more Britons to visit Austria. The tours take in the countryside as well as the major cities, and side trips to Budapest and Prague can be arranged.

DER Travel Service (18 Conduit St., London W1R 9TD, tel. 071/408–0111) offers two-center stays in Austrian cities, resort holidays in the Tirol, and 10-night Christmas and New Year packages.

GTF Tours (182–186 Kensington Church St., London W8 4DP, tel. 071/792–0311) offers city breaks in Vienna, fly/drive holidays, and Danube river cruises.

Page & Moy (136–140 London Rd., Leicester LE2 1EN, tel. 0533/552521) offers an eight-day Austria and Switzerland Alpine trip that takes in Innsbruck and St. Anton, art and music holidays in Vienna, and tours of Austrian cities and the Salzkammergut region.

Prospect Music & Art Ltd. (454–458 Chiswick High Rd., London W4 5TT, tel. 081/742–2323) has art tours and opera and music tours in Vienna.

Shearings Holidays (Miry La., Wigan, Lancashire WN3 4AG, tel. 0942/824824) and **Wallace Arnold Tours** (Gelderd Rd., Leeds LS12 6DH, tel. 0532/310739) have a selection of coach tours around Austria.

Swan Hellenic (77 New Oxford St., London WC1A 1PP, tel. 071/831–1616) provides guided art and culture tours with lectures by eminent scholars and Oxford and Cambridge dons.

Tyrolean Travel (10–18 Putney Hill, London SW15 6AX, tel. 081/789–6555) is an Austrian specialist with a wide range of tours and resort-based vacations. Its 15-day Grand Austrian Tour, for example, covers all major tourist regions and cities.

Package Deals for Independent Travelers

Independent travel usually costs more than going in a group, but you will have far more flexibility in terms of what you can see and how you spend your time; it may be a good idea in a country like Austria, with so much tempting variety. And you will get far better value for money when dining on your own. Many of the independent packages that include lodging will work out to be less expensive than the flight alone would be if you booked a regular economy fare. American Express or your travel agency can also assist with rail passes, Danube river boats, and other surface transportation; airline packages tend to get you to one city and leave you there, which is fine if you'll be on a ski holiday, less useful if you want to see more of Austria.

Austrian Airlines (*see* above), offers a series of air/hotel packages in Vienna and Salzburg ranging from five to nine days. **Pan Am Holidays** (tel. 800/843–8687) provides special rates at select hotels when you fly round-trip to Vienna on Pan Am; stay for just one night or as many as you choose. Pan Am also serves up fly/drive packages.

American Airlines Fly Away Vacations (tel. 817/355–1234 or 800/433–7300) lets you design your own fly/drive itinerary, choosing from among dozens of hotels in all price ranges, rental cars, and rail passes. **TWA Getaway Vacations** (tel. 800/438–2929) has three-night and six-night Vienna packages.

Travel Bound (599 Broadway, New York, NY 10012, tel. 212/334–1350 or 800/223–6243) offers both fly/drive and Eurail packages, which include six nights' hotel accommodations and either seven days' use of a rental car or a rail pass.

Jet Vacations (888 7th Ave., New York, NY 10106, tel. 212/247–0999 or 800/538–0999) has preferred nightly rates at hotels in

Vienna. Sightseeing in a chauffeured Mercedes limo or sedan can be arranged.

When to Go

Austria has two main tourist seasons. The weather usually turns glorious about Easter to mark the start of the summer season and holds until about mid-October, often later. Because much of the country remains "undiscovered," you will usually find crowds only in the major cities and resorts. May and early June, September, and October are the pleasantest months for traveling around; there is less demand for restaurant tables, and hotel prices tend to be lower.

An Italian invasion takes place over the long Easter weekend, and hotel rooms in Vienna are at a premium, but otherwise July and August and when the main festivals take place are the most crowded times.

Climate Austria has four distinct seasons, all on the whole fairly mild. But because of altitudes and the Alpine divide, temperatures and dampness vary considerably from one part of the country to another; for example, northern Austria in winter is often overcast and dreary, while the southern half of the country basks in sunshine. In winter it's wise to check with the automobile clubs for weather conditions, since mountain roads often get blocked and ice and fog are hazards.

Average daily maximum and minimum temperatures in Vienna:

Jan.	34F	1C	May	66F	19C	Sept.	68F	20C
	25	- 4		50	10		52	11
Feb.	37F	3C	June	73F	23C	Oct.	57F	14C
	27	- 3		57	14		45	7
Mar.	46F	8C	July	77F	25C	Nov.	45F	7C
	34	1		59	15		37	3
Apr.	59F	15C	Aug.	75F	24C	Dec.	37F	3C
	43	6		59	15		30	- 1

Current weather information for more than 750 cities around the world may be obtained by calling **WeatherTrak** information service at 900/370–8728 (the cost is 95¢ per minute). A taped message will tell you to dial the three-digit access code for the destination you're interested in (either SAL or VIE in Austria). For a list of all access codes, send a stamped, self-addressed envelope to Cities, 9B Terrace Way, Greensboro, NC 27403. For further information, phone 800/247–3282.

Festivals and Seasonal Events

Jan. 1 The **New Year** opens in Vienna with the world-famous concert by the Vienna Philharmonic Orchestra (tickets from Vienna Philharmonic, Musikverein, Bösendorferstr. 12, A–1010 Vienna, tel. 0222/505–6525; they may be charged to your credit card, but you may need to write a year—or more—in advance). Those who can't get into the Philharmonic concert try for one of the performances of the Johann Strauss operetta *Die Fledermaus* in the State Opera and Volksoper (tickets from Bundestheaterverband, Goethegasse 1, A–1010 Vienna, by credit card; tel. 0222/513–1513) or for Beethoven's Ninth (Choral) Symphony by the Vienna Symphony Orchestra (tickets by credit card from Konzerthaus, Lothringerstr. 20, A–1030 Vienna, tel. 0222/712–1211). Those who want to dance their way into the new year can do so at the Kaiserball in the elegant rooms of the Hofburg (information and tickets: WKV, Hofburg, Heldenplatz, A–1014 Vienna, tel. 0222/587–3666–14).

Early Mar. **Viennale** in Vienna shows films ranging from the latest of the avant-garde to retrospectives (tickets, information: Wiener Festwochen Viennale, Uraniastr. 1, A–1010 Vienna, tel. 0222/753285).

May 30 **Corpus Christi** is a religious holiday celebrated throughout Austria with colorful processions and parades.

Mid-May–mid-June **Wiener Festwochen** takes place in Vienna—a festival of theater, music, films, and exhibitions (tickets: Wiener Festwochen, Lehargasse 11, A–1060 Vienna, tel. 0222/586–1676).

June 21 **Midsummer Night** is ablaze with bonfires throughout the country, with the liveliest celebrations taking place in the mountains of Tirol and in the Wachau region along the Danube in Lower Austria.

July–Aug. **Musical Summer** in Vienna gives you a choice every night of a recital in one of the city's many palaces or an orchestral concert in the courtyard of the city hall. (Tickets and information: Musikalischer Sommer, Friedrich Schmidt-Platz 5, A–1082 Vienna, tel. 0222/4000–8400).

Sept. 1 Marks the start of the **theater and music season** in Vienna, and life gets back to normal for the Viennese. (Information from the Wiener Fremdenverkehrsverband, Obere Augartenstr. 40, A–1020 Vienna, tel. 0222/211–1400).

Early Sept. The **Autumn Trade Fair** packs Vienna during the first weeks of the month; the international event promotes everything from Eastern Europe's heavy machinery to canned goods, wine, and office supplies from almost everywhere.

The **International Bruckner Festival** makes Linz come alive: theater, concerts, fireworks, and art exhibits spread to the St. Florian monastery, where the composer Anton Bruckner worked and is buried (tickets and information: Untere Donaulände 7, A–4010 Linz, tel. 0732/775230).

Nov. 11 **St. Martin's Day** is as good as a holiday; restaurants throughout the country serve traditional roast goose and red cabbage in honor of the patron saint of publicans and innkeepers. Called *Martinigansl*, or *Ganslessen* ("Martin's goose," or "goose eating"), it's much more than just a feast of goose; people celebrate with parties and processions, church services, and village parades.

Nov. 15 On **St. Leopold's Day,** the name day of the ruler Leopold III (1075–1136), a splendid folk and religious festival takes place at Klosterneuburg, outside Vienna, where the saint is buried in the great monastery.

Dec. 6 On **St. Nicholas's Day** the patron saint of children is honored at *Christkindl* (Christchild) festivals, open-air markets throughout the country selling toys, favors, decorations, and food.

Dec. 24 The **Christmas Eve midnight mass** in St. Stephen's cathedral in Vienna is an impressive if crowded event; get an entrance pass at the cathedral in advance.

What to Pack

Clothing The Austrians are conservative in dress; slacks on women are as rare as loud sports shirts are on men. Jeans are ubiquitous in Austria as everywhere, but are considered inappropriate— even the designer versions—at concerts (other than pop) or formal restaurants.

If concerts and opera are on the schedule, women may want a skirt or dress, men a jacket, and both, dress shoes. Even in the summer, gala performances at even the small festivals tend to be dressy affairs. And since an evening outside at a *Heuriger* (wine garden) may be on your schedule, be sure to take a sweater or light wrap. Unless you're staying in an expensive hotel or will be in one place for more than a day or two, take hand-washables; laundry service gets complicated. And pack sturdy, comfortable shoes. Austria is a walking country, in the cities or the mountains. The most interesting sections of many cities are now pedestrian zones, and you'll need flat heels to cope with the cobblestones.

Miscellaneous An extra pair of glasses, contact lenses, or prescription sun-glasses is always a good idea. Consider packing a small folding umbrella.

Austria, like the rest of Europe, runs on 220V electric current, so if you pack a hairdryer or other appliance, bring along a converter and the appropriate adapter plugs.

Carry-on Luggage Airlines generally allow each passenger one piece of carry-on luggage on international flights from the United States. The bag cannot exceed 45 inches (length + width + height) and must fit under the seat or in the overhead luggage compartment. Experienced travelers often include essential personal-care items in the carry-on bag as insurance against their checked luggage getting lost.

Checked Luggage Passengers are generally allowed to check two pieces of luggage (or one piece in addition to skis), neither of which can exceed 62 inches (length + width + height) or weigh more than 70 pounds. Baggage allowances vary slightly among airlines, so be sure to check with the carrier or your travel agent before departure. If you're going to ski, ask the airline about appropriate packing for your skis, poles, and boots.

Taking Money Abroad

Traveler's checks and major U.S. credit cards are widely accepted, but in 1991 a dispute with the credit card organizations made many hotels, restaurants, and travel agencies in Austria unwilling to take credit cards. Yet some hotels whose stated policy is "No credit cards" may be announcing their reluctance, not a refusal, to accept the cards, and in some circumstances they may take them. Cards are more welcome in major tourist centers. Whether or not this situation continues in 1992, the prudent consumer will confirm a facility's credit card policy before using its services.

You will need cash for some of the smaller restaurants and shops, for snacks and coffee, for taxis, and for museum admissions. Although you won't get as good an exchange rate at home as abroad, it's wise to change a small amount of money into Austrian schillings before you go; lines at airport currency-exchange booths can be long. Most U.S. banks will convert dollars into schillings. If your local bank can't provide this service, you can exchange money through **Thomas Cook Currency Services** (29 Broadway, New York, NY 10006, tel. 212/635–0515).

For safety and convenience, it's always best to take traveler's checks. The most recognized ones are American Express, Barclays, Thomas Cook, and those issued through major commercial banks, such as Citibank and Bank of America. Some banks will issue the checks free to established customers, but most charge a 1% fee. Buy part of the traveler's checks in small denominations for the end of your trip, to save you from having more foreign money left than you need; but note that in Austria, all banks and exchange offices have a base fee for cashing a check of any size, which could eat up 15% or more of a small check. (Hold on to your receipts after exchanging your traveler's checks in Austria; it's easier to convert leftover foreign currency back into dollars if you have the receipts. You can exchange any surplus schillings as you are leaving Austria and will probably get a better rate than you will through your bank at home.) You can also buy traveler's checks in West German deutschemarks, which have a fixed exchange rate of 1:7 to the Austrian schilling. Traveler's checks in deutschemarks are a good idea if the American dollar is falling and you want to lock in the current rate. Remember to take the addresses of offices where you can get refunds for lost or stolen traveler's checks and be sure to keep a list of the check numbers separate from the checks themselves.

In Austria, you will get the best exchange rate at one of the larger banks or, if you're carrying American Express checks, at American Express offices. Shops, hotels, and smaller banks and exchange offices often charge a higher fee and may not offer as favorable a rate.

Getting Money from Home

There are at least four ways to get money from home:

(1) Have it sent through a large commercial bank that has a branch where you are staying. The only drawback is that you must have an account with the bank; if not, you'll have to go through your own bank, and the process will be slower and more costly.

(2) Have it sent through American Express. If you are an American Express credit-card holder, you can cash a personal check or a counter check at American Express offices for up to $1,000; $200 will be in Austrian schillings and $800 in traveler's checks (which you can immediately cash if you need the funds). There is a 1% commission on the traveler's checks. You can also obtain up to $10,000 in cash through an American Express MoneyGram. It works this way: You call home and ask someone to go to an American Express office or an American Express MoneyGram agent located in a retail outlet, and fill out a MoneyGram form. It can be paid for in cash or with any major

credit card. The person making the payment is given a reference number and telephones that number to you. The MoneyGram agent calls an 800 number and authorizes the transfer of funds to the American Express office or participating agency where you are staying. In most cases, the money is available immediately on a 24-hour basis. You pick it up by showing identification and giving the reference number. Fees vary with the amount of money sent. For $300, the fee is $30; for $5,000, the fee is $195. For the American Express MoneyGram location nearest your home and to find the Austrian locations, call 800/543–4080. You do not have to be a cardholder to use this service.

(3) Present your MasterCard or Visa card at one of the participating banks in Austria (in Vienna, at any branch of the Zentralsparkasse) and ask for schillings. You will receive the cash, sometimes minus a fee, and your card account will be billed in dollars just as though you had made a purchase. Be aware, though, that interest at your own bank's regular rate will begin immediately and accrue until you repay the advance.

(4) Have money sent through Western Union. If you have MasterCard or Visa, you can have a friend in the United States call 800/325–6000 and have money sent for any amount up to your credit limit. If not, have someone take cash or a certified check to a Western Union office. The money will be delivered to a bank where you are staying. Fees vary with the amount of money sent and the location of the recipient.

U.K. citizens holding a Eurocheque card and the Eurocheques themselves—obtainable from a bank—can write checks for up to AS2,500 a day and receive cash at virtually any bank. The checks may also be used for purchases, although no single check can be written for more than AS2,500.

All major British banks have correspondents in Austria and can arrange for a telex transfer of cash usually overnight.

Cash Machines American Express has cash machines in Vienna at the airport and at its office at Liebenberggasse/Parkring 10, A–1010 Vienna. More such machines are appearing. For U.K. citizens, the possibility exists that by 1992, Eurocheque cards can be used to obtain schillings from any of the Bankomat cash machines throughout the country.

Austrian Currency

The Austrian unit of currency is the schilling (AS), subdivided into 100 groschen. At this writing, the exchange rate was about AS11.7 to the dollar, AS20.7 to the pound sterling. These rates can and will vary. The schilling is pegged to the West German deutschemark at a 7-to-1 ratio that remains constant.

There are Austrian coins for 5, 10, and 50 groschen and for 1, 5, 10, and 20 schillings. The paper notes have AS20, AS50, AS100, AS500, AS1,000 and AS5,000 face value. There is little visible difference between the 100- and 500-schilling notes, so be careful, since confusion could be expensive!

Foreign currency and Austrian schillings may be taken in and out of the country in any amount. Legally, foreign exchange is limited to licensed offices (banks and exchange offices); in practice, the rule is universally ignored.

What It Will Cost

Austria remains one of Europe's best buys. Indeed, this is the reason behind the annual invasion of Italians, Germans, and Dutch, in particular; a holiday in Austria for them is relatively inexpensive. The Austrians, in turn, are shocked by prices in neighboring countries. Inflation in Austria is negligible, so prices go up slowly if at all. Generally, costs directly related to tourism (hotels, restaurants, ski lifts, and such) increased less, despite high taxes, than in other major tourist countries.

Vienna and Salzburg are the expensive cities in Austria, followed by Innsbruck, but many attractive places—Graz, Linz, Krems, Hallstatt, Feldkirch, Dürnstein, and Steyr, to name but a sampling—offer almost as much history and some notable architecture at a much lower cost. The high-priced resorts are Kitzbühel, Lech, St. Anton, Seefeld, Badgastein, Bad Hofgastein, Bad Kleinkirchheim, Velden, Saalbach, Zell am See, and Pörtschach.

Ample bargains can be found off the beaten path and in rural areas. You can also cut your vacation costs by staying in one place for at least a week and making it a base for daily excursions. Many hotels of all classes offer special weekly rates, although not all of them during the high season. In many resort areas, a longer stay will entitle you to a Visitor's Card, carrying substantial reductions at local swimming pools, saunas, ski lifts, bowling alleys, and such.

In many localities, including the expensive resort towns, you can cut costs by taking an apartment or a bungalow. And if your German is up to it, you can find room and board in the kind of alpine-style farmhouse that's the original model for every balconied inn and luxury country hotel in Austria (*see* Lodging, below).

Off-season travel is recommended if you are willing to pass up the big events that take place in—or create—the peak season. Air travel and hotel rates are lower out of season. The hotel reductions, especially for full-board, can amount to one-third or more.

Taxes Austrian prices include 20% VAT (value-added tax) on most items, 10% on some goods and services. If you buy goods totaling AS1,000 or more in one shop, ask for the appropriate papers *when you make the purchase*, and you can get a refund of the VAT either at the airport when you leave or by mail. You can have the refund credited to your credit card account and not have to worry about the exchange rates. In Austria tax upon tax is piled onto beverages, but don't worry about it—they are all included automatically in the prices. In some resorts, a small local hotel-room tax is added to the bill.

Sample Costs A cup of coffee in a café will cost about AS22; a half-liter of draft beer, AS27–30; a glass of wine, AS32; a Coca-Cola, AS22; an open-face sandwich, AS20; a mid-range theater ticket AS200; a concert ticket AS250; an opera ticket AS600; a 1-mile taxi ride, AS27. Outside the hotels, laundering a shirt costs about AS30; dry cleaning a suit costs around AS100; a dress, AS70. A shampoo and set for a woman will cost around AS400, a manicure about AS60; a man's haircut (without shampoo) will cost about AS120.

Passports and Visas

Americans All U.S. citizens need a passport to enter Austria. Application for your first passport must be made in person; renewals can be obtained in person or by mail. First-time applicants should apply at least five weeks in advance of their departure date to one of the 13 U.S. Passport Agency offices. In addition, local county courthouses, many state and probate courts, and some post offices accept passport applications. Necessary documents include (1) a completed passport application (Form DSP–11); (2) proof of citizenship (birth certificate with raised seal or naturalization papers); (3) proof of identity (unexpired driver's license, employee ID card or any other document with your photograph and signature); (4) two recent, identical, two-inch-square photographs (black-and-white or color) with a white or off-white background; (5) $42 application fee for a 10-year passport (those under 18 pay $27 for a five-year passport). When you pay in cash, you must have the exact amount; no change is given. Passports should be mailed to you in about 10 working days, but it can take longer in the early summer.

To renew your passport by mail, you'll need to complete Form DSP–82 and submit two recent, identical passport photographs, your current passport (less than 12 years old), and a check or money order for $35.

A visa is not required to enter Austria for a stay of up to three months. For longer stays, check with the Austrian Embassy (2343 Massachusetts Ave. NW, Washington, DC 20008, tel. 202/232–2674) or the nearest Austrian Consulate General.

Canadians All Canadians need a passport to enter Austria. Send your completed application (available at any post office or passport office) to the Bureau of Passports (Suite 215, West Tower, Guy Favreau Complex, 200 Rene Levesque Blvd. W, Montréal, Québec H2Z 1X4). Include $25, two photographs, a guarantor, and proof of Canadian citizenship. Applications can be made in person at the regional passport offices in Edmonton, Halifax, Montreal, Calgary, St. John's (Newfoundland), Victoria, Toronto, Vancouver, or Winnipeg. Passports are valid for five years and are nonrenewable.

A visa is not needed by Canadians to enter Austria for stays of up to three months.

Britons British subjects do not need a visa to enter Austria, but they do need a valid passport or a British Visitor's Passport. Application forms are available from most travel agents and major post offices or from the Passport Office (Clive House, 70 Petty France, London SW1H 9HD, tel. 071/279–3434). The cost is £15 for a standard 32-page passport, £30 for a 94-page passport. British Visitor's Passports are valid for one year only, cost £7.50, and are nonrenewable. All applications must be accompanied by two photographs and be countersigned by your bank manager or by a solicitor, a barrister, a doctor, a clergyman, or a justice of the peace.

Customs and Duties

On Arrival Austria follows the general European regulations, with the honor system of green and red gates ("Nothing to Declare" or "Goods to Declare") at the airports. If you are entering by highway, officials may ask what you are bringing into the country. In general, though, there is no need to worry about the letter of the regulations. Customs officials are as a rule so overworked that they are not too concerned whether you have 400 or 420 cigarettes with you. Travelers over 17 *coming from European countries*—regardless of citizenship—may bring in duty-free 200 cigarettes *or* 50 cigars *or* 250 grams of tobacco, two liters of wine and one liter of spirits, one bottle of toilet water (approx. 300 ml), and 50 milliliters of perfume. *Travelers from all other countries* (such as those coming directly from the United States or Canada) may bring in *twice* these amounts.

If you take into Austria any foreign-made equipment from home, such as cameras, it's wise to carry the original receipt with you or register it with U.S. Customs before you leave (Form 4457). Otherwise you may end up paying duty on your return.

On Departure You may take any reasonable quantity of goods with you when you leave, but you may need an export permit for certain art objects and some antiques. The shop where you bought the goods will advise you and help with any formalities.

U.S. Customs U.S. citizens may bring home duty-free up to $400 worth of foreign goods, as long as they have been out of the country for at least 48 hours and haven't made an international trip in 30 days. Each member of a family is entitled to the same exemption, regardless of age, and exemptions may be pooled. For the next $1,000 worth of goods, a flat 10% is assessed; above $1,400 the duty varies with the merchandise. Travelers 21 years or older may include in the duty-free allowance one liter of alcohol, 100 cigars (non-Cuban), and 200 cigarettes. Only one bottle of perfume trademarked in the United States may be imported. Anything exceeding these limits will be taxed at the port of entry and may be taxed additionally in the traveler's home state. There is no duty on original works of art or on antiques over 100 years old. Gifts valued at under $50 may be mailed to friends or relatives at home duty-free, but you may not send more than one package per day to any one addressee, and packages may not include tobacco, liquor, or perfumes costing more than $5.

Canadian Customs Exemptions for returning Canadians range from $20 to $300, depending on length of stay out of the country. For the $300 exemption, you must have been out of the country for one week. In any given year, you are allowed only one $300 exemption. You may bring in duty-free up to 50 cigars, 200 cigarettes, 2.2 pounds of tobacco, and 40 ounces of liquor, provided these are declared in writing to customs on arrival and accompany you in hand or checked-through baggage. Personal gifts should be mailed labeled "Unsolicited Gift—Value under $40." Obtain a copy of the Canadian Customs brochure *I Declare* for further details.

U.K. Customs Returning to the United Kingdom, those who are 17 years or older may bring home duty-free: (1) 200 cigarettes or 100 cigarillos or 50 cigars or 250 grams of tobacco; (2) two liters of still table wine and, in addition, (a) one liter of alcohol over 22% by volume (most spirits) or (b) two liters of alcohol under 22% by volume (fortified or sparkling wines) or (c) two more liters of still table wine; (3) 60 milliliters of perfume and 250 milliliters of toilet water; (4) other goods to the value of £32, but not more than 50 liters of beer or 25 lighters.

In addition, *no animals or pets of any kind* may be brought into the United Kingdom. The penalties for doing so are severe and the regulation strictly enforced; there are *no* exceptions. Similarly, fresh meats, plants and vegetables, controlled drugs, and firearms and ammunition may not be brought into the United Kingdom.

For further information, contact **HM Customs and Excise** (Dorset House, Stamford St., London SE1 9PS, tel. 071/620–1313).

Traveling with Film

If your camera is new, shoot and develop a few rolls of film before leaving home. Pack some lens tissue and an extra battery for your built-in exposure meter. Invest about $10 in a skylight filter; it will protect the lens and reduce haze, particularly if you're taking pictures at high altitudes.

Film doesn't like hot weather, so if you're driving in summer, don't store it in the glove compartment or on the shelf under the rear window. Put it on the floor behind the front seat on the side opposite the exhaust pipe.

On a plane trip, never pack unprocessed film in check-in luggage; if your bags get X-rayed, say goodbye to your pictures. Always carry undeveloped film with you through security and ask to have it inspected by hand. (It helps to have your film in a plastic bag, ready for quick inspection.)

The old airport scanning machines, still in use in some countries, administer heavy doses of radiation that can turn a family portrait into an early morning fog. The newer models used in all U.S. airports are safe for many more scans, depending on the speed of your film. But the effects are cumulative; you can put the same roll of film through several scans without worry. After five scans, however, you're asking for trouble.

If your film gets fogged and you want an explanation, send it to the National Association of Photographic Manufacturers (550 Mamaroneck Ave., Harrison, NY 10528), which will try to determine what went wrong. The service is free.

Language

German is the official national language in Austria. In larger cities and in most resort areas, you will have no problem finding people who speak English; hotel and restaurant staffs in particular speak it reasonably well. Most young Austrians speak at least passable if not fluent English.

Staying Healthy

No health certificate or special shots are required before visiting Austria, but if you will be cycling or hiking through the eastern or southeastern parts of the country, get inoculated against encephalitis; it can be carried by ticks.

If you have a health problem that may require the purchase of prescription drugs, have your doctor write a prescription using the drug's generic name, as brand names vary from country to country.

Water throughout Austria is safe and drinkable unless marked *"Kein Trinkwasser"* (not drinking water).

The **International Association for Medical Assistance to Travelers (IAMAT)** is a worldwide organization that offers a list of approved physicians and clinics meeting British and American standards. For a list of Austrian physicians and clinics that are part of this network, contact IAMAT (417 Center St., Lewiston, NY 14092, tel. 716/754–4883; in Canada, 40 Regal Rd., Guelph, Ontario N1K 1B5; in Europe, 57 Voirets, 1212 Grand-Lancy, Geneva, Switzerland). Membership is free.

Insurance

We recommend strongly that you take out adequate insurance to cover you in three areas, where applicable: health and accident, lost or stolen luggage, and trip cancellation. First review your existing insurance policies; some health plans cover you while traveling, some major-medical plans cover emergency transportation, and some homeowner policies cover the theft or loss of luggage.

Travel-accident insurance and extra coverage against baggage loss or damage are often included in the price of a ticket when paid for with American Express, Visa, or another major credit card.

In the United Kingdom, for free general advice on all aspects of holiday insurance, contact the **Association of British Insurers** (Aldermary House, 10–15 Queen St., London EC4N 1TT, tel. 071/248–4477). A proved leader in the holiday-insurance field is **Europ Assistance** (252 High St., Croydon, Surrey CR0 1NF, tel. 081/680–1234).

Health and Accident Several companies offer coverage designed to supplement existing health insurance for travelers:

Carefree Travel Insurance (Box 310, 120 Mineola Blvd., Mineola, NY 11501, tel. 516/294–0220 or 800/323–3149) provides coverage for emergency medical evacuation and accidental death and dismemberment. It also offers 24-hour medical advice by phone.

International SOS Assistance (Box 11568, Philadelphia, PA 19116, tel. 215/244–1500 or 800/523–8930), a medical assistance company, provides emergency evacuation services, worldwide medical referrals, and optional medical insurance.

Travel Assistance International (1133 15th St. NW, Suite 400, Washington, DC 20005, tel. 202/331–1609 or 800/821–2828) provides emergency evacuation services and 24-hour medical referrals.

Travel Guard International, underwritten by Transamerica Occidental Life Companies (1145 Clark St., Stevens Point, WI 54481, tel. 715/345–0505 or 800/782–5151), offers emergency evacuation services and reimbursement for medical ex-penses with no deductibles or daily limits.

Wallach and Company, Inc. (243 Church St., Suite 100D, Vienna, VA 22180, tel. 703/281–9500 or 800/237–6615) has comprehensive medical coverage, including emergency evacuation services worldwide.

WorldCare Travel Assistance Association (1150 S. Olive St., Suite T-233, Los Angeles, CA 90015, tel. 213/749–0909 or 800/ 666–4993) provides unlimited emergency evacuation, 24-hour medical referrals, and an emergency message center.

Lost Luggage Before you go, itemize the contents of each bag in case you need to file an insurance claim. Be certain to put your business address and telephone number on and inside each piece of luggage, including carry-on bags. If your luggage is lost or stolen and later recovered, the airline will deliver it free of charge.

On international flights, airlines are responsible for lost or damaged property to a limit of $9.07 per pound (or $20 per kilo) for checked baggage and up to $400 per passenger for unchecked baggage. If you're carrying valuables, either take them with you on the plane or buy additional insurance for lost luggage. Some airlines sell extra luggage insurance on request when you check in, but many do not. You can buy insurance for lost, damaged, or stolen luggage through travel agents or directly from various insurance companies. Luggage loss is usually part of a comprehensive travel-insurance package that includes personal accident, trip cancellation, and sometimes default or bankruptcy.

Two companies that offer luggage insurance are **Tele-Trip** (Box 31685, 3201 Farnam St., Omaha, NE 68131, tel. 800/228–9792), a subsidiary of Mutual of Omaha, and **The Travelers Insurance Corporation** (Ticket and Travel Dept., 1 Tower Sq., Hartford, CT 06183, tel. 203/277–0111 or 800/243–3174). Tele-Trip operates sales booths at airports and also sells insurance through travel agents. Tele-Trip will insure checked luggage for up to 180 days; rates vary according to the length of the trip. The Travelers will insure checked or hand luggage for $500 to $2,000 valuation, also for a maximum of 180 days. Rates for $500 coverage for one to five days are $10; for 180 days, $85. Some other companies whose comprehensive policies cover loss of luggage are **Access America Inc.,** a subsidiary of Blue Cross-Blue Shield (Box 11188, Richmond, VA 23230, tel. 800/334–7525 or 800/284–8300); **Near Services** (450 Prairie Ave., Suite 101, Calumet City, IL 60409, tel. 708/868–6700 or 800/654–6700); **Carefree Travel Insurance** and **Travel Guard International** (*see* Health and Accident Insurance, above).

Trip Cancellation This is usually included in combination travel-insurance packages available from most tour operators, travel agents, and insurance agents.

Renting and Leasing Cars

Car-rental firms, both local and international, will supply self-drive and chauffeured cars, which you can pick up at an airport, rail station, or hotel in large cities. You will need a valid license; for U.S. or Canadian residents, an international driver's license is preferred.

It is considerably cheaper to arrange car rental in the United States than to wait until you get to Austria; the variety of rates and packages—prepaid and deposit-only, daily and weekly, "Supersaver" and "Super-value"—offers you a multitude of choices. Two companies that give good value are Kemwel (800/ 678–0678) and Europcar, an affiliate of National (800/227– 3876), both of which have one-week packages on a two-door manual-shift hatchback with unlimited mileage for well under $200 plus tax (price guaranteed in schillings). You can choose to take the rental company's insurance, which will add about $8–$10 per day to the cost, or you can charge the rental to a major credit card, which will become your primary insurer in case of an accident.

The approximate cost of a comparable car rented locally is $500 per week, plus 23¢ per km, insurance extra. In either case the tax is 20%, so it may be cheaper to hire the car in a neighboring country (Switzerland has no tax, for example), and drive it into Austria even if there's a one-way charge. Shop around, as rates and tax vary widely. Among the cheapest local rental firms is **Autoverleih Buchbinder** (Schlachthausgasse 38, A–1030 Vienna, tel. 0222/71750, 0222/717–5021, and offices throughout Austria).

Car leasing in Austria is practical only if you will be using a car for six months or longer; when you need a car for more than one or two weeks, make a deal with one of the regular rental firms.

Rail Passes

The **EurailPass,** valid for unlimited first-class train travel through 17 countries including Austria, is an excellent value if you plan on traveling around the Continent. The pass must be bought from an authorized agent before you leave for Europe. Apply through your travel agent or through **Rail Europe** (610 5th Ave., New York, NY 10020, tel. 800/345–1900). It does not cover Great Britain and is not available to people who live in Europe or North Africa.

In Austria, the pass is good on the extensive rail network, on Danube river boats of the DDSG (Erste Donau-Dampfschiffahrts-Gesellschaft) Company between Passau and Vienna, on the steamers on Wolfgangsee, and on the Puchberg am Schneeberg/Hochschneeberg cog railway. The ticket can be bought for periods of 15 days ($390), 21 days ($498), one month ($616), two months ($840), and three months ($1,042). When two or more people travel together, a 15-day rail pass costs each of them $298. Between April 1 and September 30, you need a minimum of three in your group to get this discount. For discount travel within Austria, *see* Getting Around, By Train, below.

For those 25 or younger, the **Eurail Youthpass** is good for one or two months' unlimited second-class travel for $425 or $560. And travelers who like to spread out their train journeys may opt for the **Eurail Flexipass.** With the 15-day pass ($230), you get five days of unlimited travel within the 15 days; a 21-day pass gives you nine days of travel ($398), and a one-month pass gives you 14 days ($498).

Student and Youth Travel

The **International Student Identity Card** (ISIC) entitles full-time students of any age to rail passes, special fares on local transport, student charter flights, and discounts at museums, theaters, sports events, and many other attractions. If bought in the United States, the $14 cost of the ISIC card also includes $3,000 in emergency medical coverage, $100 a day for up to 60 days of hospital coverage, as well as a phone number to call collect in case of emergency. Apply to the Council on International Educational Exchange (CIEE, 205 E. 42nd St., New York, NY 10017, tel. 212/661–1414 and 35 W. 8th St., New York, NY 10011, tel. 212/254–2525). In Canada, the ISIC is available for $CN12 from **Travel Cuts** (187 College St., Toronto, Ontario M5T 1P7, tel. 416/979–2406).

Travelers under age 26 can apply for a **Youth International Educational Exchange Card** (YIEE) issued by the Federation of International Youth Travel Organizations (FIYTO, 81 Islands Brugge, DK–2300 Copenhagen S, Denmark). It provides services and benefits similar to those of the ISIC card. The YIEE card is available in the United States from CIEE (*see* above) and in Canada from the Canadian Hosteling Association (CHA, 1600 James Naismith Dr., Suite 608, Gloucester, Ont. K1B 5N4, tel. 613/748–5638).

An **International Youth Hostels Federation** (IYHF) membership card is the key to inexpensive dormitory-style accommodations at more than 5,000 youth hostels in 75 countries around the world. Hostels aren't only for young travelers on a budget, though; many have family accommodations. Hostels provide separate sleeping quarters for men and women at rates ranging from $7 to $20 a night per person and are situated in a variety of facilities, including converted farmhouses, villas, restored castles, even lighthouses, as well as specially constructed modern buildings. IYHF memberships, which are valid for 12 months from the time of purchase, are available in the United States through the CIEE (*see* above) or **American Youth Hostels** (AYH, Box 37613, Washington, DC 20013, tel. 202/783–6161). The cost of a first-year membership is $25 for adults 18 to 54; renewal is $15. For those under 18, the rate is $10; for seniors (55 and older), the rate is $15; and for families of two adults and two children, it's $35. Every national hostel association arranges such benefits as discounted rail fares and free bus travel, so be sure to ask for an international concessions list when you join.

In Austria, youth hostels are coordinated through the **Jugendherbergverband** (Gonzagagasse 22, A–1010 Vienna, tel. 0222/533–5353), which can help you plan a hostel holiday of hiking, cycling, or camping.

Council Travel, a CIEE subsidiary, is the foremost U.S. student travel agency, specializing in low-cost charters and serving as the exclusive U.S. agent for many student airfare bargains and student tours. CIEE's 80-page *Student Travel* catalogue and *Council Charter* brochures are available free from any Council Travel office in the United States (enclose $1 postage if ordering by mail). In addition to the CIEE headquarters and branch office in New York City (*see* above), there are Council Travel offices in Berkeley, La Jolla, Long Beach, Los Angeles, San Diego, San Francisco, and Sherman Oaks, CA; Boulder, CO; New Haven, CT; Washington, DC; Atlanta, GA; Chicago and Evanston, IL; New Orleans, LA; Amherst, Boston, and Cambridge, MA; Minneapolis, MN; Durham, NC; Portland, OR; Providence, RI; Austin and Dallas, TX; Seattle, WA; and Milwaukee, WI.

The **Educational Travel Center** (438 N. Frances Street, Madison, WI 53703, tel. 608/256–5551) is another student travel specialist.

ÖKISTA-Reisen (Türkenstr. 4, A–1090 Vienna, tel. 0222/317526 or 318681, with a branch at Karlsgasse 3, A–1040, tel. 0222/505–0128) is a leader in organizing student travel and cheap charters in Austria. It arranges for standby and other inexpensive flights and weekend excursions to Budapest, Prague, and other eastern European cities.

Students who want to work abroad should contact CIEE's Work Abroad Department (205 E. 42nd St., New York, NY 10017, tel. 212/661–1414, ext. 1130) for information on paid and voluntary jobs overseas for up to six months. CIEE also sponsors study programs in Europe, Latin America, Asia, and Australia and publishes such books as *Work, Study, Travel Abroad: The Whole World Handbook* ($10.95 plus $1 book-rate postage or $2.50 first-class postage) and *Volunteer! The Comprehensive Guide to Voluntary Service in the U.S. and Abroad* ($6.95 plus $1 book-rate postage or $2.50 first-class postage).

The Information Center at the **Institute of International Education** (IIE, 809 UN Plaza, New York, NY 10017, tel. 212/984–5413) has reference books, foreign-university catalogues, study-abroad brochures, and other materials, free for consultation.

Traveling with Children

Publications *Family Travel Times* is a newsletter published 10 times a year by Travel With Your Children (TWYCH, 80 8th Ave., New York, NY 10011, tel. 212/206–0688). A one-year subscription costs $35 and includes access to back issues and a phone number you can call for specific advice.

Hotels Most hotels in Austria happily welcome children and will arrange special beds and baby-sitters. There's even a hotel in Carinthia named **Austria's First Baby Hotel** (Trebesing Bad 1, A–9852 Trebesing, tel. 04732/2350) where parents accompany the babies instead of the other way around! Ask for the brochure on hotels with special facilities for children at any of the Austrian National Tourist Offices. Many of the smaller holiday hotels are family-run and have special programs for younger guests that leave parents free.

Getting There On international flights, children under 2 years of age not occupying a seat pay 10% of adult fare. Various discounts apply to children aged 2–12, so check with your airline when booking. Reserve a seat behind the bulkhead of the plane, since there's usually more leg room and enough space to fit a bassinet, which the airline will supply. At the same time, ask about special children's meals and snacks; most airlines offer them. See TWYCH's "Airline Guide," published in the February 1990 and 1992 issues of *Family Travel Times* (and scheduled again for February 1992) for a rundown on the services for children offered by 46 airlines. Ask in advance if you can bring aboard your child's car seat. For the booklet "Child/Infant Safety Seats Acceptable for Use in Aircraft," contact the Federal Aviation Administration (APA–200, 800 Independence Ave. SW, Washington, DC 20591, tel. 202/267–3479).

Home Exchange Exchanging homes is a surprisingly low-cost way to enjoy a vacation abroad, especially a long one. The largest home-exchange service, **International Home Exchange Service** (Box 190070, San Francisco, CA 94119, tel. 415/435–3497), publishes three directories a year. Membership, which costs $45, entitles you to one listing and all three directories. Photos of your property in the listing cost an additional $10, and including a second home costs $10.

A good choice for domestic home exchange, **Vacation Exchange Club, Inc.** (Box 820, Haleiwa, HI 96712, tel. 800/638–3841) publishes three directories a year as well as updated, late listings. Annual membership, which includes your listing in one book, a newsletter, and copies of all publications, is $50.

Loan-a-Home (2 Park La., 6E, Mount Vernon, NY 10552, tel. 914/664–7640) is popular with the academic community on sabbatical and businesspeople on temporary assignment. There's no annual membership fee or charge for listing your home; however, one directory and a supplement costs $35. Loan-a-Home publishes two directories (in December and June) and two supplements (in March and September) each year. All four books cost $45 per year.

Baby-sitting Services Children are generally welcome in Austrian hotels, and concierges can arrange reliable baby-sitting. But make your request a day in advance; don't expect baby-sitters at a moment's notice. In Vienna, you can call on the **Babysitter** of the Austrian Academic Guest Service (Mühlgasse 20, A–1040, tel. 0222/587–3525), or the **Babysitterzentrale** (Herbststr. 6–10, A–1160, tel. 0222/951135). Since both organizations draw mainly on students for their sitters, you can arrange for someone who speaks English.

Hints for Disabled Travelers

The Austrian National Tourist Office nearest you can provide a guide to Austrian hotels that are accessible to disabled visitors, and the tourist office in New York City also has a guide to Vienna for the disabled, a special map of the city that locates accessible sights, and a booklet on Vienna's hotels with facilities for the disabled. The Hilton, InterContinental, and Marriott chain hotels plus a number of smaller ones are accessible to handicapped travelers. The railroads are both understanding and helpful. If prior arrangements have been made, taxis and private vehicles are allowed to drive right to the train platform; railway personnel will help with boarding and leaving trains; and with three days' notice, a special wheelchair can be provided for getting around train corridors.

Once in Austria, check with the Österreichischer Zivilinvalidenverband (Lange Gasse 60, A–1080 Vienna, tel. 0222/408–5505) for more information. The **Sozialamt der Stadt Wien** (Schottenring 24, A–1020, tel. 0222/531140) and the **Vienna Tourist Office** (Obere Augartenstr. 40, A–1020, tel. 0222/211140) also have the booklet on Vienna hotels and the city guide for the disabled. The biggest problem in Vienna is the subway system; a number of stations have only stairs or escalators, no elevators.

The **Information Center for Individuals with Disabilities** (Fort Point Pl., 1st floor, 27–43 Wormwood St., Boston, MA 02210, tel. 617/727–5540; TDD 617/727–5236) is good at problem solving and has lists of travel agents who specialize in tours for the disabled.

Moss Rehabilitation Hospital Travel Information Service (1200 W. Tabor Rd., Philadelphia, PA 19141, tel. 215/456–9600; TDD 215/456–9602) provides information on tourist sights, transportation, and accommodations in destinations around the world for a small fee.

For a $15 per person annual membership fee, the **Travel Industry and Disabled Exchange** (TIDE, 5435 Donna Ave., Tarzana, CA 91356, tel. 818/368–5648) provides a quarterly newsletter and a directory of travel agencies and operators of tours to Europe, Canada, Great Britain, New Zealand, and Australia, who specialize in travel for the disabled.

Mobility International USA (Box 3551, Eugene, OR 97403, tel. 503/343–1284) has 500 affiliated members. For a $20 annual fee, it coordinates exchange programs for disabled people around the world and offers information on accommodations and organized study programs.

In the United Kingdom, excellent guides, *Holidays and Travel Abroad* and *Holidays in the British Isles*, published by the **Royal Association for Disability and Rehabilitation** (25 Mortimer St., London W1N 8AB, tel. 071/637–5400), can be ordered for £3 each from W. H. Smith bookseller or direct from RADAR, with no charge for postage or packing.

Hints for Older Travelers

Austria itself has so many senior citizens that facilities almost everywhere cater to the special needs of older travelers, with concessions like smaller portions in restaurants and discounts for rail travel and museum entry. Check with the nearest branch of the Austrian National Tourist Office to find what form of identification is needed for various advantages.

The **American Association of Retired Persons** (AARP, 1909 K St. NW, Washington, DC 20049, tel. 202/872–4700), open to anyone 50 or older for an annual membership fee of $5 per person or couple, has a Purchase Privilege Program that gives discounts on hotels, airfare, car rentals, RV rentals, and sightseeing to the member and member's spouse or another person who shares the member's household. The AARP Travel Service (800/227–7737) also arranges group tours, including apartment living in Europe, through **AARP Travel Experience from American Express** (Box 5850, Norcross, GA 30091, tel. 800/927–0111).

When using an AARP or other identification card, ask for the reduced hotel rate at the time you make your reservation, not when you check out. At restaurants, show your card to the maître d' before you're seated, since discounts may be limited to certain set menus, days, or hours. When renting a car, remember that economy cars, priced at promotional rates, may cost less than cars available with your discount ID card.

Elderhostel (75 Federal St., 3rd floor, Boston, MA 02110, tel. 617/426–7788) is an innovative educational program for people 60 years and older. Participants live in dorms on some 1,200 campuses around the world. Mornings are devoted to lectures and seminars, afternoons to sightseeing and field trips. Fees for two- to three-week trips, including room, board, tuition, and round-trip transportation, range from $1,800 to $4,500.

National Council of Senior Citizens (925 15th St. NW, Washington, DC 20005, tel. 202/347–8800) is a nonprofit advocacy group with some 5,000 local clubs across the country. Annual membership is $12 per person or per couple. Members receive a monthly newspaper with travel information and an ID card for reduced-rate hotels and car rentals.

Saga International Holidays (120 Boylston St., Boston MA 02116, tel. 800/343–0273) specializes in group travel for people 60 and over, with a selection of variously priced tours.

Further Reading

Edward Crankshaw, *The Habsburgs* (Weidenfeld & Nicolson, 1972): a good and brief history of the royal house that ruled Austria from 1278 to 1918.

Vienna: The Image of a Culture in Decline (Macmillan, 1938; out of print, check your library).

Sarah Gainham, *Night Falls on the City* (Collins, 1967; out of print): an extraordinary novel about the struggle of an actress to hide her Jewish husband from the Nazis in wartime Vienna.

Henriette Mandl, *Vienna Downtown Walking Tours* (Ueberreuter, 1987): an excellent and compact guide to seeing Vienna on foot.

Christian Nebehay, *Vienna 1900* (Brandstätter, 1984): a set of profusely illustrated guides to architecture and painting, music, and literature in turn-of-the-century Vienna.

Richard Rickett, *A Brief Survey of Austrian History* (Heinemann, 1983): a good overview, and *Music and Musicians in Vienna* (Heinemann, 1973): a compact guide to those musicians who helped make Vienna the musical capital of the world.

Arriving and Departing

From North America by Plane

When booking a flight, air travelers will want to keep in mind the distinction between *nonstop flights* (your destination is the only scheduled stop), *direct flights* (one or more stops are scheduled before you reach your destination), and *connecting flights* (you'll stop and change planes before you reach your destination).

Airports and Airlines Scheduled international flights from North America all fly into Vienna's Schwechat airport, about 12 miles southeast of the city. Other Austrian cities with international service—but not from North America—are Linz, Salzburg, Innsbruck, Graz, and Klagenfurt. Airlines specifically serving Austria from major U.S. cities (usually New York) include the following:

Austrian Airlines (tel. 800/843–0002) offers nonstop service Wednesday–Monday from New York/JFK.

Pan Am (tel. 212/687–2600) flies three times weekly from New York/JFK, once nonstop, twice via Budapest.

Tarom/Romanian Airlines (tel. 212/687–6013) has, depending on the season, one or two nonstop flights weekly from New York/JFK.

Air Canada (tel. 416/925–2311 or 800/268–7240) flies from Toronto via Frankfurt or Zurich three times a week.

Singapore Airlines (tel. 416/323–1911) flies Toronto–Vienna via Amsterdam three times weekly.

Flying Time From New York, a nonstop flight to Vienna takes just over eight hours. From Toronto, a direct flight takes about 11 hours.

Enjoying the Flight If you're lucky enough to be able to sleep on a plane, it makes sense to fly at night. Many experienced travelers, however, prefer to take a morning flight to Europe and arrive in the evening, just in time for a good night's sleep. Because the air on a plane is dry, it helps, while flying, to drink plenty of nonalcoholic beverages; alcohol contributes to jet lag, as does eating heavy meals on board. Feet swell at high altitudes, so it's a good idea to remove your shoes at the beginning of your flight. Sleepers usually prefer window seats to curl up against; those who like to move about in the cabin ask for aisle seats. Bulkhead seats (located in the front row of each cabin) have more legroom, but seat trays are attached rather awkwardly to the arms of the seat rather than to the back of the seat ahead. Bulkhead seats are generally reserved for the disabled, the elderly, or parents traveling with babies.

Discount Flights As a rule, the farther in advance you buy an airline ticket, the less expensive it is, but these tickets carry certain restrictions. An APEX (advance-purchase) ticket must be bought in advance (usually 21 days); it limits your travel, usually with a minimum stay of seven days and a maximum of 90; and it penalizes you severely (up to 100%) for changes—voluntary or not—in your travel plans. But if you can work around these drawbacks (and most travelers can), they are among the best values. For example, you can fly round-trip New York–Vienna in peak periods for around $700, versus $1,800 on regular coach or $4,400 in first class.

Other discounted fares can be found through consolidators, companies that buy blocks of tickets on scheduled airlines and sell them at wholesale prices—up to 50% below APEX fares. Seats are limited on any one flight, so passengers must have flexible travel schedules. Here again, you can lose all or most of your money if you change plans, but you will be on a regularly scheduled flight, with less risk of cancellation than on a charter. As an added precaution, you might want to purchase trip-cancellation insurance. Once you've made your reservation, call the airline to confirm it. Among the best-known consolidators to Europe are **UniTravel** (Box 12485, St. Louis, MO 63132, tel. 314/569–2501 or 800/325–2222) and **Access International** (101 W. 31st St., Suite 1104, New York, NY 10001, tel. 212/465–0707 or 800/825–3633). Others advertise in Sunday newspaper travel sections.

Another option is to join a travel club that offers special discounts to its members. Several such organizations are **Discount Travel International** (114 Forrest Ave., Narberth, PA 19072, tel. 215/668–7184), **Moment's Notice** (425 Madison Ave., New York, NY 10017, tel. 212/486–0503), **Travelers Advantage** (CUC Travel Service, 49 Music Sq. W, Nashville, TN 37203, tel. 800/548–1116), and **Worldwide Discount Travel Club** (1674 Meridian Ave., Miami Beach, FL 33139, tel. 305/534–2082). These cut-rate tickets should be compared with APEX tickets on the major airlines.

Travelers willing to put up with some restrictions and inconvenience, in exchange for substantially reduced airfares, may be interested in flying as air couriers, to accompany shipments between designated points. For a telephone directory listing courier companies by the cities to which they fly, send $5 and a self-addressed, stamped business-size envelope to **Pacific Data Sales Publishing** (2554 Lincoln Blvd., Suite 275–F, Marina del Rey, CA 90291). For "A Simple Guide to Courier Travel," send $14.95 postpaid to the **Carriage Group** (Box 2394, Lake Oswego, OR 97035). For more information call 800/344–9375.

Smoking On long-distance flights where smoking is still permitted, U.S. carriers are required to find seats in a nonsmoking section for travelers who request them on the day of the flight and meet check-in time restrictions. But the best move for nonsmokers may be to request a nonsmoking seat when you book your ticket.

From the United Kingdom by Plane, Car, Train, and Bus

By Plane **British Airways** (tel. 071/897–4000), **Austrian Airlines** (tel. 071/439–0741), and **Lauda Air** (tel. 071/494–0702) have nonstop services from London to Vienna. There are at least four flights daily to Vienna from London Heathrow, a trip of a little more than two hours, and nonstop service three days a week to Salzburg on Austrian Airlines (about two hours).

Austrian Air Transport, a subsidiary of Austrian Airlines, has daily "scheduled charter" service to Vienna. **DanAir** and **British Airways** have additional scheduled charter flights. You can book these flights through **GTF Tours** (tel. 071/792–0311); **Austria Travel** (tel. 071/222–2430), the travel arm of the Anglo-Austrian Society; or a travel agent or charter operator. Scheduled charter flights must be booked well in advance, and you can't change your plans without losing your money, but the round-trip fares start at about £100, instead of £180 for APEX or £460 for business class. Several bucket shops also offer flights to Austria; check the ads in *Time Out* and the Sunday papers.

By Car The best way to reach Austria by car from England is to take one of the North Sea/Cross Channel ferries to Oostende or Zeebrugge in Belgium or Dunkirk in northern France. Then take the toll-free Belgian motorway (E5) to Aachen, and head via Stuttgart to Innsbruck and the Tirol (A61, A67, A5, E11, A7) or east by way of Nürnberg and Munich, crossing into Austria at Walserberg and then on to Salzburg and Vienna. Total distance to Innsbruck is about 1,100 km (650 mi); to Vienna, about 1,600 km (1,000 mi). The most direct way to Vienna is virtually all on the autobahn via Nürnberg, Regensburg, and Passau, entering Austria at Schärding. In summer, border delays are much shorter at Schärding than at Salzburg.

If this seems like too much driving, in summer you can put the car on a train in s'Hertogenbosch in central southern Netherlands, on Thursday, or in Schaerbeek (Brussels) on Friday, for an overnight trip, arriving in Salzburg early the following morning and in Villach three hours later. **DER Travel Service** (18 Conduit St., London W1R 9TD, tel. 071/408–0111) has details of fares and schedules.

By Train There's a wide choice of rail routes to Austria. You can take the *Oostende Wien* direct link from London to Vienna, leaving London at 9:15 AM and arriving in Vienna at 9:40 AM the next day. If you don't mind changing trains, you can travel more comfortably via Paris, where you catch the *Arlberg Express* at 10:40 PM for Vienna via Innsbruck. First- and second-class sleepers and second-class couchettes are available as far as Innsbruck.

When you have the time, a strikingly scenic route to Austria is via Cologne and Munich; after an overnight stop in Cologne, you take the EuroCity Express *Johann Strauss* to Vienna.

Fares represent reasonable value for money. One-way London–Vienna costs around £150 first class, £105 second class. **Eurotrain** (52 Grosvenor Gardens, London SW1W 0AG, tel. 071/730–3402) and **Transalpino** (71–75 Buckingham Palace Rd., London SW1W ORE, tel. 071/834–9656) both offer excellent deals for those under 26. Otherwise, book through **British Rail Travel Centers** (tel. 071/834–2345). For additional information, call **DER Travel Service** (071/408–0111) or, in the United States, **GermanRail** (747 3rd Ave., New York, NY 10017, tel. 212/308–3100).

By Bus There are no direct bus services from the United Kingdom to Austria; the closest you can get is Munich, and from there, the train is your best bet. **International Express** (Coach Travel Center, 13 Lower Regent St., London SW1Y 4LR, tel. 071/439–9368) operates daily in summer, leaving London's Victoria coach station in mid-evening and arriving in Munich about 23 hours later.

Staying in Vienna

Getting Around

By Plane Austria has domestic air service, but the fares are high. The train is much cheaper and, in most cases, about as convenient as flying. **Austrian Airlines** or its subsidiary **Austrian Air Services** has flights connecting Vienna with Linz, Salzburg, Graz, and Klagenfurt. **Tyrolean** flies between Vienna and Innsbruck, and it has a fly/drive combination with Avis that can save you money. Tyrolean also connects to points outside Austria, and Rheintalflug flies between Vienna and Altenhausen, in Switzerland, just over the border from the province of Vorarlberg. Winter schedules on all domestic lines may vary, depending on snow conditions. There is helicopter service between St. Anton and St. Christoph, which can be combined with ski tours in the high mountain regions of the Arlberg. For private charter flights contact **Alpenair** (tel. 0222/945228), **Jetair** (tel. 0222/533–6033), or **Polsterer Jets** (tel. 0222/71110–2077).

By Train Austrian train service is excellent: it's fast and, for Western Europe, relatively inexpensive, particularly if you take advantage of the discount fares. The main intercity lines run at fixed intervals, so trains usually run hourly and leave at set times after or before each hour. Although speeds are improving, trains on the mountainous routes are slow. But driving is no faster. And what difference does it make that the 580-km (360-mi) run from Vienna to Innsbruck, for example, takes 5½ hours? The scenery is gorgeous! Many of the remote rail routes will give you a look at traditional Austria, complete with alpine cabins tacked onto mountainsides and a backdrop of snowcapped peaks even in summer.

Your hotel desk can often provide a train schedule, but in any case, planning a train trip is simple. In every station and in many hotels, you will find large posters labeled *Abfahrt* (departures) and *Ankunft* (arrivals). Look through the Abfahrt glisting for a train to your destination. You'll find the departure time in the main left-hand block of the listing and, under the train name, details of where it stops en route and the time of each arrival. There is also information about connecting trains and buses, with departure details.

Austrian Federal Railways trains are identifiable by the letters that precede the train number on the timetables and posters. The *Ex* and *D* trains are fastest, but a supplement of AS30 is automatically included in the price of the ticket. All tickets are valid without supplement on *Eilzug* (fast) and local trains. Seat reservations are required on some trains; on most others you can reserve for a small extra charge up until a few hours before departure. Be sure to do this on the major trains at peak holiday times.

The difference between first and second class on Austrian trains is mainly a matter of space. First- and second-class sleepers, and couchettes (six to a compartment) are available on international runs, as well as on long trips within Austria.

If you're driving and would rather watch the scenery than the traffic, you can put your car on a train in Vienna and take it to Salzburg, Innsbruck, Feldkirch, or Villach. You relax in a compartment or sleeper for the trip, and the car is unloaded when you arrive.

The railroad also has an arrangement whereby you can rent a bicycle for AS80 per day at any one of many stations and leave it at another. You don't have to be a rail passenger to take advantage of this scheme, but if you are, the rental is half the price. Virtually all the major stations—well over 100 of them—will take credit cards.

Discount Fares   Even if you'll be in Austria for only a short time, you can save money on one of the discount rail fares. For AS200 and a passport photo, senior citizens (women 60 years, men 65) can obtain a *Seniorenpass*, which carries discounts up to 50% on rail tickets. The pass is also accepted as identification for reduced-price entry into museums and has a host of other useful fringe benefits. Most rail stations can give you information.

Travelers under 26 should inquire about discount fares under the Billet International Jeune (BIJ). The special one-trip tickets are sold by **Eurotrain International** (no connection with Eurailpass) at its offices in London, Dublin, Paris, Madrid, Lisbon, Rome, Zurich, Athens, Brussels, Budapest, Hanover, Leiden, Vienna, and Tangier and at travel agents, main-line rail stations, and youth-travel specialists.

The **Rabbit Card** is good on any four days within a 10-day period for unlimited travel on any rail route, including the private lines, the cog railways, and the Wolfgangsee ships. It carries a 50% reduction on ships on Lake Constance run by the railroad and 30% off on any one of the 10 days on the DDSG Danube river boats. The Rabbit Card costs AS1,390 first class, AS950 second class. If you're 27 or under, prices are AS860 first class, AS590 second. (The rates are scheduled to be higher in 1992.) You'll need identification when you buy the ticket. But unless you'll be confining your rail travel to Austria, the *Eurailpass* (*see* Rail Passes, above) will probably be cheaper.

A *Bundesnetzkarte* (full-network pass) gives you unlimited travel for a month (AS4,650 for first class, AS3,100 second class) or a year (check on current prices) and will allow you a 50% reduction on Austrian intercity buses and private rail lines. The ticket is also good on the suburban rail system (*S-Bahn*) around Vienna and ships on the Wolfgangsee. Apply for a *Bundesnetzkarte* at any large rail station, and expect the cost to be higher in 1992. You will need a passport photo.

Zonenkarten, or regional tickets, both first class (AS500) and second class (AS400), are available for some 18 different areas and are good for any four days within a 10-day period. Again, you'll need a passport photo when you buy the ticket. Note that the *Zonenkarten* may be discontinued and that prices are likely to be higher in 1992.

You can buy regular rail tickets through travel agents and at any station, but for the special passes and tickets, you'll usually have to go yourself to a train station.

Railroad enthusiasts and those with plenty of time can treat themselves to a ride on narrow-gauge lines that amble through alpine meadows; some even make flower-picking stops in season. A few lines still run under steam power, and summertime steam excursions are becoming more frequent. Local stations have descriptive brochures with dates, points of origin, and fares.

By Bus Where Austrian trains don't go, buses do, and you will find the yellow railroad and post-office buses in some of the remotest outposts you might imagine, carrying passengers as well as the mail. You can get tickets on the bus itself, and in the off season there is no problem getting a seat, but on routes to favored ski areas and during holiday periods reservations are essential. Most towns with bus service have a ticket office, or tickets can be booked with a travel agent. In most communities, the bus routes begin and end at or near the railroad station, making transfers easy. Increasingly, coordination of the bus service with that of the railroads means that many of the discounts and special tickets available for trains apply to the buses as well. Bus services also tie together the outskirts of many Austrian cities, both with circumferential and crosstown routes.

By Car The Austrian highway network is excellent, well maintained, and well marked. Secondary roads may be somewhat narrow and winding, but these are so shown on maps. The main through routes (autobahn) are packed during both Austrian and West German school holidays, and weekends in summer can also be hectic. As a nod to the ecology, less salt is being used on highways in winter, but few drivers seem to take heed of the greater hazard. In bad weather you will need snow tires and often chains in winter, even on the well-traveled roads. Austrians are fairly poor drivers, inclined to take chances and aggressive; defensive driving is the best policy.

Tourists from European Community countries may bring their cars to Austria with no documentation other than the normal registration papers and their regular driver's license. A Green

Card, the international certificate of insurance, is recommended for EC drivers and compulsory for others. All cars must carry a first-aid kit and a red warning triangle (obtainable at border crossings or from the Automobile Club—*see* below) to use in case of accident or breakdown.

A set of eight excellent detailed roadmaps is available at a nominal price from the **Austrian Automobile Club/ÖAMTC** (Schubertring 1–3, A–1010 Vienna, tel. 0222/711–9955), at most service stations, and at many bookstores. The maps supplied without charge by the Austrian National Tourist Office are adequate for most needs, but if you will be covering much territory, the better ÖAMTC maps are a worthwhile investment.

The minimum driving age in Austria is 18, and children under 12 years must ride in the back seat. Passengers in the front seats must use seat belts. Vehicles coming from the right have the right of way, except that at unregulated intersections, streetcars coming from either direction have the right of way. No turns are allowed on red.

Unless otherwise marked, the speed limit on autobahns is 130 kph (80 mph), although this is not strictly enforced, as you will discover. On other highways and roads, the limit is 100 kph (62 mph), 80 kph (49 mph) for RVs or cars pulling a trailer weighing more than 750 kilos (about 1,650 lbs). In built-up areas, a 50 kph (31 mph) limit applies and is likely to be taken seriously.

Gasoline is readily available, but remember that on Sunday, rural stations may be closed. Virtually all stations now carry unleaded (*bleifrei*) gas, both regular and premium (*Super*). Diesel fuel may not be easy to find off the beaten path. Gasoline prices are the same throughout the country, slightly lower at discount filling stations and self-service stations. Expect to pay about AS10 per liter for regular, AS11.50 for premium. If you're driving into Austria, consider tanking up on the other side of the border, particularly if you're entering from West Germany, where gasoline is consistently cheaper. Oil in Austria is expensive, retailing at AS50–AS80 per liter.

Austria has two automobile clubs, ÖAMTC and ARBÖ, both of which operate motorist service patrols. You'll find emergency phones along all the key highways. Otherwise, if you have problems, call ARBÖ (tel. 123) or ÖAMTC (tel. 120) anywhere in the country. No area or other code is needed for either number. Both clubs charge nonmembers for emergency road service.

Along the autobahns, the roadside food services run by the **Rosenberger** chain are excellent. They are well designed, and the food is good and varied, with a salad bar and children's menus.

By Boat For leisurely travel between Vienna and Linz or eastward across the border into Czechoslovakia or Hungary, consider taking a Danube boat. More than 300 km (187 mi) of Austria's most beautiful scenery awaits you, as you glide past romantic castles and ruins, medieval monasteries and abbeys, and lush vineyards. One of the high spots, particularly in spring, when the apricot and apple trees are in blossom, is the Wachau valley near Vienna.

The trip from Passau (West Germany) to Vienna takes two days, including an overnight stop in Linz (on board, if you like), and runs from late June to late September. The boat leaves Passau at 3 PM, arriving at Linz at 8 PM and departing the next morning at 10 for arrival in Vienna at 8:15 PM. Check for current fares with your travel agent or, in Austria, with the **DDSG/Danube Steamship Company** (Handelskai 265, A–1020 Vienna, tel. 0222/217100). Fares vary according to the type of accommodation and the ship itself; the new river cruiser *Mozart*—complete with swimming pool—is in the luxury category.

Day trips are also possible on the Danube, and in the Wachau, you can use the boats to move from one riverside community on or across to the next. The Eurailpass includes the DDSG network.

Daily hydrofoil services run from Vienna to Bratislava in Czechoslovakia and to Budapest in Hungary. You need no visa for these trips, but be sure to have your passport with you. Both routes offer on-board, duty-free shopping. If you want adventure, you can travel via the Danube to the Black Sea and back on river passenger ships flying the Soviet or Romanian flag.

Telephones

Austria's telephone service is in a state of change as the country converts to a digital system. We make every effort to keep numbers up to date, but do check—particularly in Innsbruck, Linz, and Vienna—if you have problems getting the connection you want. All numbers given here include the city or town area code; if you are calling within that city or town, dial the local number only.

Basic telephone numbers in Austria consist only of numerals, of three to seven digits; longer numbers are the basic number plus a direct-dial extension of two to four digits.

Coin-operated pay telephones are numerous and take a one-schilling piece for local calls. Drop in the coin, pick up the receiver and dial; when the party answers, push the indicated button and the connection will be made. If there is no response, your coin will be returned into the bin to the lower left.

If you plan to make many calls from pay phones, a *Wertkarte* is a convenience. At any post office you can buy an electronic credit card for AS95 or AS48 that allows AS100 or AS50 worth of calls from any *Wertkartentelephon*. You simply insert the card and dial; the cost of the call is automatically deducted from the card.

Calls within Austria are one-third cheaper between 6 PM and 8 AM on weekdays and from 1 PM on Saturday to 8 AM on Monday.

International Calls You can dial direct to almost any point on the globe from Austria. The international access code for the United States and Canada is 001, followed by the area code and number. For Great Britain, first dial 0044, then the city code *without the usual "0"* (71 or 81 for London), and the number. Other country and many city codes are given in the front of telephone books (in Vienna, in the *A–H* book). By 1992, reduced off-peak rates may be in effect for out-of-country calls, but at press time, these calls are all billed at the same rate no matter when you phone.

Don't make long-distance calls from your hotel room without first checking carefully on the cost of the call. Hotels in Austria, as in many countries, frequently add several hundred percent to such calls. AT&T's USA Direct plan enables you to charge the call to your card or call collect. The access number, 022–903011, is a local call all over Austria. You can also make a quick call asking the called party to phone you back at the number in Austria. All post offices in Austria have public telephone facilities, and you can get assistance in placing a long-distance call. In large cities, these centers are open around the clock.

Operators and Information For information on local calls, dial 16; for assistance with long-distance service, dial 09; and for information on direct dialing out of Austria, call 08.

Mail

Postal Rates Within Europe, all mail goes by air, so there's no supplement on letters or postcards. A letter of up to 20 grams (about ¾ ounce) takes AS7, a postcard AS6. To the United States or Canada, a letter of up to 20 grams takes AS9 minimum, plus AS1.50 per 5 grams for airmail. If in doubt, mail your letters from a post office and have the weight checked. The Austrian post office also adheres strictly to a size standard; if your letter or card is outside the norm, you'll have to pay a surcharge. Postcards via airmail to the United States or Canada need AS7.50. Post offices have air-letter (aerogram) forms for AS11 to any overseas destination.

Receiving Mail When you don't know where you'll be staying, **American Express** mail service is a great convenience, with no charge to anyone either holding an American Express credit card or carrying American Express traveler's checks. (American Express: Kärntner Str. 21–23, A–1015 **Vienna,** tel. 0222/515400; Mozartplatz 5, A–5020 **Salzburg,** tel. 0662/842501; Brixner Str. 3, A–6020 **Innsbruck,** tel. 0512/582491; Bürgerstr. 14, A–4021 **Linz,** tel. 0732/669013.) You can also have mail held at any Austrian post office, but the letters should be marked *Poste Restante* or *Postlagernd.* You will be asked for identification when you collect mail. In Vienna, this service is handled through the main post office (Fleischmarkt 19, A–1010 Vienna, tel. 0222/512–76810), now temporarily located at Postgasse/Barbaragasse 2 until renovations on the Fleischmarkt building are completed.

Tipping

Although virtually all hotels and restaurants include service charges in their rates, tipping is still customary, but at a level lower than in the United States. Tip the hotel doorman AS10 per bag, and the porter who brings your bags to the room another AS10 per bag. In very small country inns, where the staff doubles in a number of jobs, such tips are not expected but are appreciated. Tip the hotel concierge only for special services or in response to special requests. Room service gets AS10 for snacks or ice, AS20 for full meals. Maids normally get no tip unless your stay is a week or more or service has been special.

In restaurants, round up the bill by AS5 to AS50, depending on the size of the check and the class of the restaurant. Big tips are not usual in Austrian restaurants, since 10% has already been included in the prices. Hat-check girls get AS7–AS15, depending on the locale. Washroom attendants get about AS2–AS5. Wandering musicians and the piano player get AS20, AS50 if they've filled a number of requests.

Round up taxi fares to the next AS5 or AS10; a minimum AS5 tip is customary. If the driver offers (or you ask for) special assistance, such as carrying your bags beyond the curb, an added tip of AS5–AS10 is in order.

Opening and Closing Times

Banks in most cities are open weekdays from 8 to 3, on Thursday until 5:30 PM. Smaller bank offices close from 12:30 to 1:30. All are closed on Saturday, but you can change money at various locations (such as American Express offices on Saturday morning and major railroad stations around the clock) at other than bank hours.

Museum hours vary from city to city and museum to museum; if there's a closing day, it will usually be a Monday. Few Austrian museums are open at night.

In general, you'll find shops open weekdays from 8:30 or 9 AM until 6 PM, with a lunchtime closing from noon to 1 or 1:30. In smaller villages, the midday break may run until 3 PM. Many food stores, bakeries, and small grocery shops open at 7 or 7:30 AM and, aside from the noontime break, stay open until 6:30 PM. Shops in large city centers take no noon break. On Saturday, shops stay open until noon or 1 PM, except on the first Saturday of the month, when (except for food stores) they stay open until 5, a few until 6 PM. Barbers and hairdressers traditionally take Monday off, but there are exceptions.

All banks and shops are closed on national holidays: Jan. 1; Jan. 6, Epiphany; Apr. 19–20, Easter Sunday and Monday; May 1, May Day; May 28, Ascension Day; June 7–8, Pentecost Sunday and Monday; June 18, Corpus Christi; Aug. 15, Assumption; Oct. 26, National Holiday; Nov. 1, All Saints' Day; Dec. 8, Immaculate Conception; Dec. 25–26, Christmas. Museums are open on most holidays and closed on Good Friday and Dec. 24.

Shopping

You'll find specific shopping tips in the individual chapters, but in general, such locally produced goods as textiles, crystal, porcelain figurines, leather goods, wood carvings, and other handicrafts are good value. Prices are similar throughout the country, but higher, of course, in the major tourist centers. Shops will ship your purchases, but if you can, take them with you. If you do ship goods, be sure you know the terms in advance, how the items will be sent, when you can expect to receive them, *and get all these details in writing.*

All purchases made in Austria are subject to a 20% value-added tax (VAT). You can get this refunded on goods you personally take or have shipped out of the country, when the purchases amount to AS1,000 or more from one shop and the shop will handle the necessary paperwork. Ask for details on the spot. The refund can be arranged and later credited to your credit card by the shop, or you can present the papers at the Post Office window at the airport upon departure (look for "VAT Refund" signs) and get an immediate cash refund. (The banks at the airports usually slap on a healthy handling fee, which may cancel out a substantial chunk of your refund.) You may be asked to show the purchases at Customs as you depart, so don't pack them in the bottom of the suitcase you have just checked through!

Sports and Outdoor Activities

Austria is one of the most participant-sports-minded countries anywhere. At a snowflake's notice, half the population will take to their skis; in summer, water sports are just as popular. But new attractions are appearing; golf, for example, is becoming more common. The National Tourist Offices have information on many specific sports.

Ballooning Get details of the sport for the whole country from the **Austrian Ballooning Club** (Endresstr. 65, A–1230 Vienna, tel. 0222/ 888222); **Austrian Aero-Club** (Prinz Eugen-Str. 12, A–1040 Vienna, tel. 0222/505–1028); or from the **Vienna Ballooning Club** (tel. 0222/692913, 692916, or 883–0353).

Bicycling Cyclists couldn't expect much more than the new cycle track that runs the length of the Danube or the many cycling routes that crisscross the country, major cities included. You can rent a bicycle for AS80 per day (AS40, if you've a rail ticket in your hand) at any of about 100 railroad stations throughout the country and return it to another. Special brochures available from the national tourist offices have details, including maps and hints for trip planning and mealtime and overnight stops. Ask for the booklet *Radfahren in Österreich*, or contact **Austria Radreisen** (A–4780 Schärding, tel. 07712/2409), which organizes cycling tours.

Boating and Sailing You can rent a rowboat on almost all of Austria's lakes and on the side arms of the Danube (Alte Donau and the Donauinsel) in Vienna. Information is available from the **Österreichischer Segel-Verband,** the Austrian Yachting Club (Grosse Neugasse 8, A–1040 Vienna, tel. 0222/587–8688).

Camping You'll find more than 400 campsites throughout the country, usually run by regional organizations, a few private. Most have full facilities, often including swimming pools and snack bars or grocery shops. Charges range from about AS30 to AS40 per person per day, depending on the range and quality of services offered, plus AS30–AS40 for car parking. For details, check with the **Österreichischer Camping Club** (Johannesgasse 20, A–1010 Vienna, tel. 0222/512–5952) about sites, prices, and availability and with the tourist offices of the individual Austrian provinces. Camping is not restricted to the summer season; some sites are open year-round, with nearly 80 specifically set up for winter camping.

Fishing The Danube, Steyr, Traun, Enns, Krems, and Alm rivers also provide good fishing. Ask the Austrian National Tourist Office for the guidebook "Fishing in Austria"; it includes details of licensing. Unfortunately for anglers, the rights along many of the best streams have been given, meaning that no additional licenses will be issued, but ask at the local tourist office.

Gliding If you're set for adventure, from May to September you can glide solo or learn to glide at one of Austria's schools. At Wien-Donauwiese (Vienna), there are two-seater gliders, for instructor and passenger; at the other airfields you're on your own. For details, contact the **Austrian Aero Club** (Prinz Eugen-Str. 12, A–1040 Vienna, tel. 0222/505–1028).

Golf Austria is changing quickly from a golfing no-man's-land into a place where golfers can now find more than 50 courses. Most of them are private, but for a greens fee, you can arrange a temporary membership. Several of the courses are associated with hotels, so package arrangements can be made. The Austrian National Tourist Offices have special golfing brochures, or you can write **Golf Green Austria** (Panzaunweg 1g, A–5071 Wals, tel. 0662/851355).

Hiking and Climbing With more than 50,000 km—that's about 35,000 miles—of well maintained mountain paths through Europe's largest reserve of unspoiled landscape, the country is paradise for hikers. Three long-distance routes traverse Austria: E-4, the Pyrenees-Jura-Neusiedler See route, ending in Burgenland on the Hungarian border; E-5 from Lake Constance in Vorarlberg to the Adriatic; and E-6 from the Baltic, cutting across mid-Austria via the Wachau valley region of the Danube and on to the Adriatic. Wherever you are in Austria, you will find shorter hiking trails requiring varying degrees of ability. Routes are well marked and maps are readily available. Hikers' maps on a scale of 1:20,000 or 1:25,000 will be the most useful.

Skiing Austrians lean toward downhill skiing, though in recent years a number of cross-country routes have been developed. Depending on the local terrain, most ski resorts now have some cross-country trails, but you'll have to look harder to find them.

Ski areas offer a weekly pass for use on all lifts, cable cars, and usually swimming pools, at 20%–30% reductions. Your hotel or the local tourist office will have details. Many resorts, including several of the more expensive and fashionable towns, offer all-inclusive weekly rates, sometimes including ski schools and lifts. Not surprisingly, the Austrian National Tourist Office will overwhelm you with detailed information on the various packages.

Student ski trips are organized in the December–April period by the **Büro für Studentenreisen,** the Office for Student Tours (Schreyvogelgasse 3, A–1010 Vienna, tel. 0222/533–3589) and by two other student-travel organizations: **ÖKISTA** (Türkenstr. 4, A–1090 Vienna, tel. 0222/347526) and its partner **OS-Reisen** (Reichstratstr. 13, A–1010 Vienna, tel. 0222/408–7821).

Water Sports and Swimming There are hundreds of places to swim throughout Austria, and with very few exceptions, the water is unpolluted. All the lakes in the Salzkammergut, Carinthia, and Tirol have excellent swimming, but all are crowded in the peak season. In the Vienna area, the Alte Donau and Donauinsel arms of the Danube are accessible by public transportation and are suitable for families, so it's best to go early to avoid the crowds on hot summer weekends. The Alte Donau beaches have changing rooms and checkrooms.

Spectator Sports Soccer is a national favorite. Every town has at least one team, and rivalries are fierce. Matches are held regularly in Vienna. There's horse racing with parimutuel betting at the track in the Prater in Vienna. Tennis matches are held in Vienna and Linz.

Dining

Restaurant food in Austria ranges from fine (and expensive) offerings at elegant gastronomic temples to the simple, inexpensive, and wholesome good meals in small country inns. Wherever you go, you will find traditional restaurants, with all the atmosphere typical of such places—good value included. In this regard, Austria still has much to offer. If you crave a Big Mac you can find it, and you can even get a bad meal in Austria, but it will be the exception; the simplest *Gasthaus* takes pride in its cooking, no matter how standard it may be.

Austrian cuisine is heavily influenced by that of its neighbors, which were once parts of the Austro-Hungarian empire. This accounts for the cross-fertilization of tastes and flavors, with Hungarian, Czechoslovak, Polish, Yugoslav, and Italian cooking all in the mix. The delicious, thick Serbian bean soup came from an area of modern Yugoslavia; the bread dumpling (*Knödel*) that accompanies so many standard dishes has its parentage in Czechoslovakia; the exquisitely rich (more butter than sugar) *Dobostorte* comes straight from Hungary.

Alas, justice is all too often not done to the relatively few Austrian national dishes. You're likely to get a soggy Wiener schnitzel as often as a supreme example, lightly pan-fried in a dry, crisp breading. Now at least it will be honestly presented, as pork or the real thing, veal. Austrian cooking on the whole is more solid than delicate. Try, for example, *Tafelspitz*—boiled beef, if you will, but when well done, it's outstanding in flavor and texture. Reflecting the Italian influence, Austrian cooking also leans heavily on pastas and rice. *Schinkenfleckerl* is a good example: a casserole of confettilike flecks of ham baked with pasta. A standard roast of pork (*Schweinsbraten*) served hot or cold can be exquisite, as the Austrians do not cook it to shoeleather consistency. But since many Austrian dishes are basically simple, they depend on the quality of the ingredients.

Austria's best restaurants—and not just in Vienna—have bounded in recent years into a class and quality earlier unthinkable. A school of inventive chefs has spawned a generation willing to try ideas wholly new to Austria; many of the most successful of these experiments involve imaginative, lighter variations on traditional themes of game and freshwater fish, relying as well on the abundant local produce.

When dining out, you'll get best value for money at the simpler restaurants. Most post menus with prices outside. If you begin with the *Würstelstand* (sausage vendor) on the street, the next category would be the *Imbisstube*, for simple, quick snacks. You'll find many of them at city markets, serving soups and a daily special at noon. Many cafés also are open for lunch, but watch the prices; some can turn out to be more expensive than restaurants. *Gasthäuser* are simple restaurants or country inns with no pretensions. From that basic level of cuisine everything else is upward, ranging from intimate finds to the most elegant. Austrian hotels have some of the best restaurants in the country, and they have hired outstanding chefs to attract the paying customers.

Wine cellars and wine gardens, or *Heuriger* (for new wine), are a special category among Austrian eateries. Mainly in Vienna and Lower Austria, they also can be found throughout the country, serving everything from a limited selection of cold cuts and cheeses to full meals. And some urban wine cellars are known as much for their food as for the wines.

Austrian vintage wines range from good to outstanding. Don't hesitate to ask waiters for their advice, even in the simpler restaurants. The best whites come from the Wachau and Kamptal, Weinviertel (Lower Austria), Styria, and the area around Vienna. Grüner Veltliner, a light, dry to medium-dry that goes well with many foods, is the most popular. The Welschriesling is a slightly heavier, fruitier wine. The favored Austrian reds are those of Burgenland. No single variety dominates. Blauer Portugieser and Zweigelt tend to be lighter. For a slightly heavier red, select a Blaufränkisch, Blauer Burgunder, or St. Laurent. These are all good value, and there is little difference among the years. Most of these wines can be bought by the glass. Look for labels from vintners Beck in Gols; Brundlmayer in Langenlois; Hirtzberger in Spitz/Donau; Jamek in Joching; Sonnhof in Langenlois; Kierlinger in Vienna, and Winzergenossenschaft Wachau in Dürnstein.

For Grüner Veltliner, Blaufränkisch, and St. Laurent, the recommended vintages are '81, '83, '85, '86, and '88. For Rheinriesling and Welschriesling, they are the same years plus '87. In every case '86 was outstanding.

Lunch in Austria is usually served between noon and 2 PM, dinner between 6 and 9 PM, tending toward the later hour. Many restaurant kitchens close in the afternoon, but some post a notice saying *Durchgehend warme Küche*, meaning that hot food is available even between regular mealtimes.

Restaurants in our listings are divided by price into four categories: Very Expensive, Expensive, Moderate, and Inexpensive. *See* Dining in individual chapters for specific prices, which vary from region to region. Prices quoted are for a three-course meal with house wine, including all service and taxes.

Lodging

You can live like a king in a real castle in Austria or get by on a modest budget. Starting at the lower end, you can find a room in a private house or on a farm or dormitory space in a youth hostel. Next up the line come the simpler pensions, many of them identified as *Frühstückspension*, meaning bed-and-breakfast. Then come the *Gasthäuser*, the simpler country inns. The fancier pensions in the cities can often cost as much as hotels; the difference lies in the services they offer. Most pensions, for example, do not man the front desk around the clock. Among the hotels, you can find accommodations ranging from the most modest, with a shower and toilet down the hall, to the most elegant, with every possible amenity.

Among the familiar names you will find in Austria are Hilton, Holiday Inns, InterContinental, Marriott, Novotel, Penta, Ramada, and Sheraton. Most of these chain establishments are in the upper price category, even those you may associate with budget prices at home.

We divide hotels into four price categories: Very Expensive, Expensive, Moderate, and Inexpensive, giving rates for a standard double room with private bath in peak season (where applicable).

All hotel prices include service charges (usually 10% but occasionally higher) and federal and local taxes are added later.

Breakfast is included at virtually all hotels *except* those in the Very Expensive category, where it is extra—and expensive. It may range from rolls, marmalade, and coffee to an expansive buffet with eggs and meat dishes. You can usually get juice or an egg, but, in some cases, you'll be asked to pay extra. Some of the top resort hotels insist on half or full board in season; at other times, you can set your own terms.

Austria has few Very Expensive hotels outside Vienna, Salzburg and the major resorts, but numerous Expensive ones (usually with swimming pools—sometimes indoor and outdoor—saunas, fitness rooms, and other amenities). The Moderate accommodations in country areas or smaller cities and towns are generally more than adequate: food, service, and cleanliness are of high standard. The newer Inexpensive hotels have private showers. *See* Lodging in individual chapters for prices, which vary widely among large cities, resorts, and small country towns, in peak season and in low.

Credit Cards

The following credit card abbreviations are used: AE, American Express; DC, Diner's Club; MC, MasterCard/Access/Barclays; V, Visa.

2 Portraits of Vienna

The Land of the Waltz

by Hans Fantel

A native of Austria and longtime resident of the United States, Hans Fantel is currently a syndicated columnist for the New York Times.

The Viennese traditionally live in two countries. One is on the map. The other is the imaginary region where wine flows, love triumphs, and everything is silk-lined. This is the land of the waltz.

A century ago, during the sunset years of Austria's 1,000-year-old empire, there was no clear demarcation between the real world and that mythical land of the waltz. The two realms merged along the hazy boundary that never quite separates fact from fancy in Vienna.

This region of the Viennese mind is not just a shallow, sybaritic fantasy. Like Viennese music itself, it embodies a substantial premise. If melody could be translated, a Viennese waltz would add up to 100 ways of saying that, all considered, and with due allowance for everything, simply being alive is a cause for celebration.

At its surprising best—in such creations as *The Blue Danube*, the *Emperor Waltz*, or *Tales from the Vienna Woods*—the waltz is perhaps the closest description of happiness ever attained in any art.

Paradoxically, the music is not merry. A haze of wistfulness lies over the sunniest tunes, and their sweetness sometimes touches on melancholy. Though the dance is a swirling embrace, the music countermands sensual abandonment. It insists on grace; it remains pensive in the midst of pleasure. And in this blending of the sensual with the reflective, the Viennese waltz expresses and creates a condition of durable bliss—a measured joy.

For almost 100 years, while the last Habsburg emperors ruled the real Austria, the land of the waltz had its own dynasty—the Waltz Kings. Both were named Johann Strauss.

Johann Strauss I ruled over this mythical realm of music during the first part of the 19th century. A generation later, his son, Johann Strauss II, extended the scope of the waltz to symphonic proportions, writing dance music in the form of orchestral tone poems that transformed the ballroom into a concert stage.

These two men welded their city and their music into a single identity, making Vienna and the waltz almost a single thought. Viennese historians are fond of florid metaphors suggesting that Johann Strauss—father and son—did not so much compose their waltzes as ineffably transmute their city into music. Such notions seem altogether plausible to the romantic Viennese, including the younger Strauss himself. "If it is true that I have talent," he wrote during the latter part of his life, "I owe it, above everything else, to my beloved city of Vienna . . . in whose soil is rooted my whole strength, in whose air float the melodies which my ear has caught, my heart has drunk in, and my hand has written down."

Sentimental, yes. Unrealistic, no. Strauss's own assessment of his creative act is probably accurate. *Zeitgeist* and *genius loci*—the spirits of time and place—have always whispered to the creative imagination, and Strauss, being a musician, surely had a fine ear for such promptings.

I t is impossible to weigh such ephemeral influences, but one can hardly dispute the perceptive comment made by Marcel Brion on Vienna's matchless array of musicians: "They would not have been what they were, what they had to be, if chance had forced them to live anywhere but in Vienna."

Music, like wine, takes its flavor from the soil and the season in which it grows, and the roots of the waltz were nourished by a moment of history in which an aging civilization had reached the peak of mellowness. No other city has ever been so suffused by an art as Vienna was by music. Painting, perhaps, was of similarly intense concern to the Florentines of the Renaissance. But this enthusiasm was confined to a relatively small circle of aristocratic sponsors centering around the Medicis, and it seems unlikely that painting played a major part in the life of the ordinary Florentine.

By contrast, Vienna's involvement with music was shared by its shopkeepers and janitors. The barriers between serious and popular music had not yet become impassable. There was no "music business" in the modern sense, for commercial pressures had not yet debased and polarized public taste. In the crowds who thronged to hear performances of Beethoven symphonies, Haydn oratorios, or Mozart operas, burghers and artisans easily joined princes of the realm. Conversely, in the little rustic inns tucked among the hillsides of the Vienna Woods, members of the nobility mixed quite casually with lesser folk to dance to the sweet and giddy folk tunes of the region. Here lay the tree-shaded courtyards of the *Heurigen*, the vintners' houses where the Viennese sampled the new wine. And if the white wines that grow along the Danube lack the finesse of more famous vintages from the Rhine or the Moselle, they have a tart freshness and a light headiness that make them all the more inviting for casual tippling.

During the long spring and fall seasons, and during the mild summers, these spacious gardens and courtyards were filled daily from about four in the afternoon until the early hours, and their mood of easy conviviality shaped the pattern of Viennese leisure. Drunkenness was not tolerated; the typical Viennese was a thoughtful drinker who made a glass last a long time by puffing, between sips, on a pencil-thin, foot-long cigar that he smoked through a straw. Groups of strolling musicians would pass from one to another of these inns, entertaining the patrons with tunes of the Austrian countryside—the lilting *Ländler*, which was the rural precursor of the not yet invented waltz, and the *Schnadahüpfl*, a jaunty country hop. Here, too, the sound of music created an instant democracy of manners, and class barriers melted in the balmy atmosphere of relaxed hedonism.

This aspect of Vienna's life invariably amazed foreign visitors, particularly those from France, where such casual friendliness between people of widely different social standing was unthinkable either before or after the revolution. "Ancestors and rank seem to be forgotten," reports one traveler, "and aristocratic pride laid aside. Here we see artisans, artists, merchants, councillors, barons, counts and excellencies dancing together with waitresses, women of the middle class, and ladies."

At private concerts, too, there was congenial mingling of persons from different social strata. Tradespeople with sincere musical interests often found access to the musical soirées which were the chief entertainment in the Baroque town houses of the high bourgeoisie.

In an ancient monarchy whose minutely graded class structure might otherwise have calcified into social arthritis, music thus served a vital limbering function. In an order where status—being mostly fixed by birth—could rarely be achieved, music provided the safety valve that kept the pressure of social unrest from building up and enabled absolutism to maintain its sway over Austria long after the American and French revolutions had shaken other thrones.

For centuries, the Habsburg rulers maintained a tradition of fostering the arts. The theater, as long as it confined itself to entertainment and did not become a platform for ideas, received royal encouragement, as did the pictorial arts; sculpture; and, above all, music, architecture, and landscaping.

The implicit tenet was that beauty begets pleasure, and pleasure begets contentment. The great cities of imperial Austria—Vienna, Prague, Salzburg, and Budapest—owe their splendor to the endearing assumption that civic beauty is the key to civic tranquillity.

To accuse the Habsburgs of prostituting art for political aims would be unjust. Its furtherance was no cynically contrived policy. In fact, it was no policy at all, never having been consciously formulated. The state of the arts in Austria sprang quite naturally from a naïvely mystic faith—not uncommon in Catholic countries—that aesthetic grace was akin to divine grace and that to invest a country with outward beauty would somehow bestow civic virtues that would hold it together inwardly. This sort of intuition is legitimate to statecraft. What, after all, is a nation but an agreement on style and a cohesive sharing of myths?

Under these conditions, the whole country seemed pervaded by a certain musicality—an innate, casual feeling for form and harmony. It was evident in the visual charm of the Austrian Baroque that left its mark not alone on the great cities but also on many of the smaller towns and villages.

A feeling for the Baroque and its later, lighter variants, with their graceful, almost melodic lines, was by no means confined to the leading architects employed in the design of palaces and manors. It filtered down to the humblest mason molding garlanded cherubs above the gate of an ordinary house. It shaped the vision of the local builder who quite matter-of-factly bestowed an exquisite harmony of proportions. It guided the hand of the cabinetmaker who filled the house with the playful curves of Rococo and Biedermeier furniture. It influenced the gardener and blacksmith alike, one arranging flowerbeds like calligraphy, the other echoing the scrolls in wrought iron. The tailor and the pastry cook shared a concern for graceful shape, and even the gestures of ordinary citizens reflected a certain elegance as they went about their business.

Industrial manufacture had not yet cast its equalizing pall on the design of objects that fill the household and pass through hands in daily use. Far longer than the more industrialized countries to the west, Austria retained the practice and attitudes of individual craftsmanship. The decorative merit of a product ranked at least as high as its utility. Beauty had market value, and the combination of commercial worth and aesthetic joy bestowed on tradesmen and their customers alike a measure of dignity and satisfaction.

In such an ambience, the ear, too, became attuned to the refinements and delights of form. Music derived from the surroundings. It was inescapable. It lay before the eyes.

Vienna, and much of Austria, thus became a natural breeding ground for musicians. A contemporary chronicler, Eduard Bauernfeld, observes that "every hole is full of musicians who play for the people. Nobody wants to eat his *Bratl* at the inn if he can't have table music to go with it." No feast or celebration was complete without a special overture composed for the occasion. Virtually every bourgeois family could muster a passable string quartet among its members, creating a constant demand for new scores. More than 60 piano factories flourished in the city, which numbered a mere 250,000 inhabitants, and next to good looks and a dowry, musical talent was considered a girl's chief asset.

Every Sunday, the churches resounded with musical settings of the Mass—"operas for the angels," as Mozart called them. Performed by choirs and orchestras of remarkable proficiency, these compositions by Mozart, Haydn, and Schubert were splendidly melodic, and the occasion, despite its ecclesiastical setting, was often more of a public concert than a divine service. The clergy never objected to mixing devotion and enjoyment. In fact, the monasteries owned some of the best vineyards and maintained some of the coziest inns to dispense their wine. Austrian Catholicism had been spared the more Puritan notions of sin that had shaped the restrictive attitudes of northern Europe. It had also escaped much of the cruel virulence of the Counter Reformation. Austria's faith, touchingly expressed in countless sculptures of smiling, childlike Madonnas, never really clashed against that other trinity in Vienna's heaven—wine, women, and song.

Perhaps the most significant aspect of Vienna's musical life was the attitude of the typical listener. In Paris or London, for example, music was regarded as an entertainment. Not so in Vienna. Here it was a personal necessity, an indispensable part of everyday life. In its lighter forms, music was a needed refreshment; in its more demanding forms, an exercise of the spirit in search of illumination.

It is hardly surprising that such a society left considerable room for individuality. The forces of regimentation and efficiency were traditionally resisted, thus preparing the ground for Vienna's famed *gemütlichkeit*, the characteristic attitude of unhurried bonhomie.

No doubt the most benign economic influence on the social climate was the virtual absence of extreme poverty. To be sure, Vienna had its share of improvidents and people suffering ill fortune. But the causes of their plight were personal rather than built into an exploitive system. Hence their number was small and they did not constitute an embittered group endangering the balance of the community. Where in Paris a Jacobin majority marshaled the envy and fear of the deprived into an orgy of class hatred, the Viennese joined all classes in self-indulgent epicureanism.

Even lowly citizens ate well in Vienna. A surviving restaurant menu lists a complete meal for 13 *Kreuzer*—the equivalent of about 25¢. For this modest sum one could regale oneself on soup, smothered liver, roast beef, vegetables, bread, and a quarter-liter of wine. A remarkable document survives in the City Archives showing that during one typical year (1786) some 200,000 Viennese managed to do away with 42,197 oxen, 1,511 cows, 66,353 calves, 43,925 sheep, 164,700 lambs, 96,949 pigs, 12,967 suckling pigs, 454,063 buckets of local wine, 19,276 buckets of Hungarian and Tirolean wine, and 382,478 buckets of beer. No one seems to have made per-capita comparisons, but this document is generally taken as historic proof of an ample appetite.

Such statistics are not irrelevant to music, for they bespeak a love of life and a general greediness for good things, be they products of art or of the kitchen.

With comforts of mind and body abundant and readily available, economic incentive never was honed to an irritant edge. Material possessions alone could not change one's social standing in a fixed-status society, and since the public environment was generally delightful, there was less need for private luxury. Consequently, acquisitive drive, the dominant motivating force in open and industrial societies, rarely inspired the Viennese. Their motivation was not so much material success but satisfaction with the task at hand, or, quite often, simply the leisurely enjoyment of the day. To the Viennese, this was the utmost practicality and realism.

As long as external conditions supported this mode of existence, remarkably little cruelty or vulgarity crept to the surface of Austrian life. The feral substrate at the bottom of any society remained nicely covered. And those who, by dark intuition, knew it was there said nothing of it.

Of course, not even an unfailing surfeit of music and Wiener schnitzel could remove all challenges from life, but in an age of indulgent epicureanism, these challenges could usually be surmounted by not trying too hard. That, too, lies in the music. The cardinal rule for playing a waltz is the same as for mastering other phases of life in Vienna: Don't push it—and keep the tempo loose.

Its cushioned resilience made Vienna relatively crisis-proof—at least until the final, cataclysmic collapse of the empire. Nonchalant self-irony lent Vienna, and all Austria, the buoyancy to clear minor hurdles. For example, during a government scandal involving payoffs at the ministerial level, the noted Viennese journalist Karl Kraus soothed tempers by explaining that the accused civil servant "took such small bribes as to border on incorruptibility."

Scanning 1,000 years of Austrian history, John Gunther observed that the country "in its own inimitable, slippery way wriggled out of any difficulty. Something of the very softness of the Austrian character had been a factor of strength, because the horns of a crisis were apt to disappear through absorption—the crisis lost its point, melted in the prevailing solvent of easygoing compromise."

This is hardly a country to be admired by moralists. Philosophers may not find it much to their liking, either. But poets and musicians have always felt at home there, for the land pulses with the heartbeat of humanity.

Johann Strauss felt that pulse and shaped it into a special music that lifted Vienna from its moorings on the map, wafting the city across that misty line between reality and dream into the land of the waltz.

The Law of the Heuriger

by Alan Levy

Maria Theresa's son, Emperor Joseph II (1741–90), who wanders in and out of the play and movie *Amadeus* muttering, "Well, there you are," uttered far more enduring words on August 17, 1784, when he proclaimed to the Austrian people that "we give every man the freedom to sell or dispense—year-round, in any form, at any time, and at whatever price he wants—food, wine, or fruit juice that he has produced himself."

Handed this entrepreneurial key by royalty, the farmers of the Vienna Woods unlatched the *Heuriger:* a unique wine tavern that proliferates in the capital and eastern Austria. Heuriger is a noun derived from an adjective meaning "this year's," which applies not only to young wines, but also to such crops as cabbage and potatoes. To the thirsty, however, the only real heuriger is the farmhouse facade adorned by a sprig of pine, a branch of fir, or a wreath of holly and a plaque on the door signifying that the new wine is in and has been pressed on the premises. Open that door in summer and you'll feast your eyes upon an inviting courtyard lined with picnic tables and crowded with Austrians making merry (which, often as not, means intense intellectual conversations about trivia), frequently hoisting glasses for toasting or refilling, and occasionally lifting voices, too, in song.

Inside the house you'll usually find a buffet from which you can buy hot or cold food and, in those that stay open year-round, a cozy hearth around which you can also eat, drink, and revel. In the larger heurige (plural) or posher ones that cater to tourists and businesspeople, you'll find live music—usually *schrammelmusik*, named after a 19th-century family who composed, played, sang, and ordained the wistful sound of music still heard in the heuriger.

Rendered by violins, guitar, and clarinet or accordion and sung in an impenetrable Austrian dialect, the songs counterpoint the conversation by treating such earthy themes as a lover's lane in the Vienna Woods that's too small for one person but big enough for two, or lamenting that "the old cog-wheel railway is scrap iron now," or wrestling with the dilemma of a would-be lover who's making headway but watching the clock in the knowledge that the last streetcar leaves soon and he doesn't have money for the taxi ride that would clinch his case. This song is called "The Little Blue Light," and, while the last No. 38 streetcar from the wine suburb of Grinzing no longer wears a blue lamp on its tail, its illuminated destination signs bear equally ominous blue squares of cardboard.

In Grinzing, in particular, one must be wary of places where the Vienna-by-night tour buses draw up every half hour and the schrammel musicians drop everything to play "Deep in the Heart of Texas" or "If I Were a Rich Man." Stick around there and you won't be rich for long. Far better to follow a Viennese drinking song with lyrics that list virtually every wine village within easy reach, starting with "a little Grinzing, a little Sievering, a little Neuwaldegg, Nussdorf, Ottakring and Petersdorf." Or play it safe at the elegantly rustic Grinzinger Hauermandl, where the music, chicken, and wine are consistently first-rate.

Today, within the city limits of Vienna, there are some 800 families growing wine on more than 1,800 acres to produce about 12 million quarter-liter glasses of wine per year. Heuriger wine is mostly white: clear, sparkling, dry, and, thanks to its high acidity, possessed of a fresh bite that can bite back the morning after. It is wise to switch, after a couple of glasses, from new wine to old *(alt)*. The price may be a dime more tonight, but tomorrow's pain will be less.

The Vienna Tourist Board publishes a free brochure in German, English, French, and Italian, "Heurige in Wien," listing 150 of them by neighborhood with helpful maps. There are at least five times that many, and one of the charms of a summer night is to discover your own. Even the farsighted Joseph II, "The People's Emperor" who encouraged Mozart and tried to democratize the Habsburg monarchy, might be astonished at how the cottage industry he envisioned has become a backbone of both Austrian tourism and Viennese life.

"During the warm season, from May to September, people go early, around six o'clock in the evening," says Traudl Lessing, a Viennese chronicler and connoisseur of heuriger living. "They take their children and dogs along, as both provide excellent starting points for conversation and friendly relations. As soon as the benches around the rough wooden tables have filled, people sit down with strangers and begin to confide in each other. They tell their unknown friends about the wife's illness, the cranky boss, and how they avoid the burdens of taxation."

Frau Lessing and her husband, Erich, gave their daughter Hannah's wedding party indoors last January at the spacious and lively Heuriger Schübel-Auer in the Heiligenstadt neighborhood. Beethoven once lived in this district and cursed the church bells he could see tolling but not hear. In fact, just around the corner, a 17th-century house where the peripatetic composer resided for part of 1817 is now one of Vienna's most famous heurige: Mayer am Pfarrplatz.

After Joseph II's 1784 proclamation, known in Vienna as "the law of the heuriger," farmers started selling pork, poultry, and sometimes beef from their own livestock in the front rooms where their customers used to sample their wines. Farmers' daughters found work at home as cooks and waitresses instead of migrating to the city or marrying for survival. Soon, whole families were making cheese and peddling their produce to a market that came to them.

Early in the 20th century, this laissez-faire law of the heuriger was modified for the only time in its 207-year history. Its provisions had spawned too many child alcoholics and adult workaholics—the former souring on not-always-unfermented grape juice; the latter missing church—so certain soft drinks were sanctioned (usually Almdudler Limonade, which tastes like ginger ale), and farmers were forbidden to sell their wines on more than 300 days a year. The amendment also permitted ham and cheese and fowl to be sold by wine farmers who didn't have their own pigs and cows and chickens. Even today, though, a wine tavern peddling beer, coffee, or Coca-Cola isn't an authentic heuriger and shouldn't be displaying the symbolic green bush outside.

During and after two devastating world wars, the heuriger assumed a new social role in Viennese lives. Rather than entertain in cramped, shabby, or bomb-damaged quarters, hosts invited their guests to meet them at "our heuriger," where they would buy drinks and sometimes dinner—though it is still good form in many heurige to bring your own picnic and buy just wine. If the coffeehouse, a tradition a century older than the heuriger, remains the living room of the Viennese—"neither at home nor in the fresh air," they like to say—the heuriger is their summer garden and year-round retreat.

How the heuriger has kept pace with modern times, trends, and thinking can be experienced most happily on a visit to Gumpoldskirchen, a wine village some seven miles outside the city. On the dividing line between the slopes of the *Wienerwald* (Vienna Woods, the northeastern foothills of the Alps) and the *Puszta* (the flat Hungarian plain that begins in Austria), Gumpoldskirchen is a more early-to-sing, early-to-bed place than Grinzing—and the prices are better. If you arrive around 3 or 4 PM, there is ample light to explore some of the 100 charming courtyards behind welcoming green laurels and tarry perhaps in the Renaissance sobriety of the Benedictine monks' heuriger or the cozy nook carved out of a wine barrel in Schabl's Pressehaus (both on the main street) before bearing left at the onion-domed church around which the town was built several centuries ago.

This will put you on a *weinwanderweg* through the vineyards: a 30- to 45-minute circle walk designed and decorated in 1975 by the vintners of Gumpoldskirchen. An ancient wine press looms up on a hillside like a gallows. A modern metal sculpture of an insect magnifies and gentrifies the *reblaus* (phylloxera), a plant pest that came over from California in the 1870s and destroyed most of Europe's wines; the vines were restored only when reblaus-resistant strains were also imported from California.

Along its way, the weinwanderweg relates the history of Austrian wines from the third century, when the Roman Emperor Probus first allowed grapes to be grown outside Italy, up through Joseph II to the present day, when Gumpoldskirchen leads all of Austria in the production of Zierfandler, another white wine deceptively called Rotgipfler, and Blau Portugiese, which is red and Austrian.

Somehow, one develops a thirst along the weinwanderweg, and in gathering darkness, dozens of pine bushes of Gumpoldskirchen are already illuminated and beckoning below. Safely down, you should head for one of the twin heurige of the Bruckberger family at Wienerstrasse 1 and Kirchenplatz 1, where the music has already started and the partying has been going on for hours.

The Bruckbergers have been in the wine business for more than three centuries. They slaughter their homefed livestock once a week. Apple-cheeked young Hans Bruckberger presides over the noisy, happy, 800-seat heuriger that bears the family name on the main street. A couple of blocks away, right where the weinwanderweg begins and ends, his sister Elisabeth runs a more intimate cellar heuriger for romantic dining by candlelight and softer music. The wine, music, and strudel in both places are just right—and so are the duck at Elisabeth's and the crisp bread and spicy Liptauer cheese, roast chicken, and steamy pigs' knuckles at Hans's.

Hans's and Elisabeth's sister, Hansi, runs a *heuriger-proviant*, a food-supply store adjacent to the larger heuriger. Here you can buy cold cuts and bread for snacking along the weinwanderweg or on a wienerwald hike or if you just don't feel like hacking the buffet in the heuriger. At the end of an evening, when a Bruckberger patron expresses the need for a cup of coffee before heading back to the real world, particularly by car, the dirndled wine waitress will respond demurely with: "That would be against the law of the heuriger. But we can send out. Give me the money and I'll go next door and buy you one."

Taking your schillings and accepting a small tip, she strides through Hans's kitchen into Hansi's store. As a shopkeeper, Hansi is allowed to brew and sell coffee. The law of the heuriger has been circumvented, but if it helps a drinker to arrive home safely, well, as Joseph II might say, there you are.

3 Vienna

Introduction

by George H. Sullivan

Vienna is a city that deeply loves its past. For many centuries it was one of the great capitals of Europe, home to the Habsburg rulers of the Austro-Hungarian Empire. Today the Empire is long gone, but many reminders of the city's Imperial heyday remain, carefully preserved by the tradition-loving Viennese. Most of Vienna's renowned 18th- and 19th-century buildings have been preserved as well, attesting to a brilliant architectural past that few cities can match.

From the late 18th century until World War I, Vienna's culture—particularly its musical culture—was famous throughout Europe. Haydn, Mozart, Beethoven, Schubert, Brahms, Strauss, Mahler, and Bruckner all lived in the city, producing music that is still played in concert halls all over the world. And at the tail end of the 19th century the city's artists and architects—Gustav Klimt, Egon Schiele, Oskar Kokoschka, Josef Hoffmann, Otto Wagner, and Adolf Loos among them—brought about an unprecedented artistic revolution, a revolution that swept away the past and set the stage for the radically experimental art of the 20th century.

At the close of World War I the Austro-Hungarian Empire was dismembered, and Vienna lost its cherished status as the seat of Imperial power. Its influence was much reduced, and (unlike most of Europe's other great cities) its population began to decline, from around 2 million to the current 1.5 million. Today, however, the city's future looks bright, for with the collapse of the Iron Curtain, Vienna may at long last regain its traditional status as the hub of central Europe.

For many first-time visitors, the city's one major disappointment is the Danube River. The inner city, it turns out, lies not on the river's main stream but on one of its narrow offshoots, known as the Danube Canal. As a result, the sweeping river views expected by most newcomers fail to materialize.

The Romans are to blame, for when Vienna was founded as a Roman military encampment around AD 100, the walled garrison was built not on the Danube's main stream but rather on the largest of the river's eastern branches, where it could be bordered by water on three sides. (To this day the outline of the Roman walls, a lopsided square, can be seen in the street plan of the inner city: Naglergasse and the Graben to the southwest, Kramergasse and Rotgasse to the southeast, Salzgasse to the northeast, and Tiefer Graben to the northwest.) The wide present-day Danube did not take shape until the late 19th century, when its various branches were rerouted and merged to prevent flooding.

The Romans maintained their camp for some 300 years (the emperor Marcus Aurelius is thought to have died there in AD 180) and finally abandoned it around AD 400. The settlement survived, however, and by the 13th century growth was sufficient to require new city walls to the south. According to legend, the walls were financed by the English: In 1192 the local duke kidnapped King Richard I, who was on his way home from the Third Crusade, and held him prisoner for two years until he was expensively ransomed.

Vienna's third set of walls dates from 1544, when the existing walls were improved and extended. The new fortifications were built by the Habsburg dynasty, who ruled the Austro-Hungarian Empire for an astonishing 640 years, beginning with Rudolf I in 1273 and ending with Karl I in 1918. The walls stood until 1857, when Emperor Franz Josef finally decreed that they be demolished and replaced by the famous Ringstrasse ("Ring Street").

During medieval times the city's growth was relatively slow, and its heyday as a European capital did not begin until 1683, after a huge force of invading Turks laid siege to the city for two months and were finally routed by an army of Habsburg allies. Among the supplies left behind by the fleeing Turks were sacks filled with coffee beans. It was these beans, so the story goes, that gave a local entrepreneur the idea of opening the first public coffeehouse. Cafés remain a Viennese institution to this day.

The passing of the Turkish threat produced a Viennese building boom, and the Baroque style was the architectural order of the day. The style had originated in Italy around 1600, when a group of brilliantly inventive Italian architects began to embroider and transform the classical motifs that the High Renaissance had copied from ancient Rome. Architects in other countries throughout Europe followed suit, and during the 17th century England, France, and Austria all developed Baroque styles that were very much their own. Austrian Baroque possessed a special grace, described in detail in the walking tours to follow, and it is this grace that gives Vienna the distinctive architectural character that sets the city so memorably apart from its great rivals London, Paris, and Rome.

Essential Information

Important Addresses and Numbers

by George W. Hamilton

We show the Vienna telephone area code (0222) with all numbers; if you are calling within the city or to or from the airport, dial only the other numbers in the series.

Tourist Information

The main point for information is the **Vienna City Tourist Office** *(Fremdenverkehrsstelle der Stadt Wien)*, around the corner from the Hotel Sacher, at Kärntner Strasse 38 (tel. 0222/513–8892). From 9 to 7 daily, the extremely helpful and knowledgeable staff will assist you with everything from museum and transportation information to room reservations. The **Österreichisches Verkehrsbüro** (in Opernpassage, underground in front of the Opera, tel. 0222/586–2352) offers similar services and can provide theater tickets, Monday–Saturday 9–6, Sunday 9–2. Good, detailed city maps and public transport maps are available at all these offices (look for the *i* sign).

If you need a room, go to **Information-Zimmernachweis** in the Westbahnhof (tel. 0222/835185, open daily 6:15 AM–11 PM) and in the Südbahnhof (tel. 0222/505–3132, open daily 6:15 AM–10 PM). At the airport, the information and room-reservation office (tel. 0222/71110–2617) is open daily 9 AM to 10:30 PM. The information office at the DDSG dock on the Danube (tel. 0222/218–0114 or 218–1954) is open when ships are docking and embarking. But none of these offices can arrange room bookings by telephone.

If you're driving into Vienna, get information or book rooms at **Information-Zimmernachweis** at the end of the Westautobahn at Wientalstrasse/Auhof (tel. 0222/971271) or at the end of the Südautobahn at Triesterstrasse 149 (tel. 0222/674151 or 0222/677100).

Embassies The **U.S. embassy** is at Boltzmanngasse 16, tel. 0222/315511; the **consulate** is at Gartenbaupromenade, Parkring 12a, in the Marriott building, tel. 0222/51451. The **Canadian embassy** is at Dr. Karl Lueger–Ring 10, tel. 0222/533–3691. The **U.K. embassy and consulate** are at Jauresgasse 10; embassy tel. 0222/713–1575, consulate tel. 0222/713–6117.

Emergencies The emergency numbers are 133 for the **police,** 144 for an **ambulance,** 122 for the **fire department.** If you need a doctor and speak no German, try calling the **American Medical Society of Vienna** (Lazarettgasse 13, tel. 0222/424568).

English-language Bookstores **Big Ben Bookstore** (Porzellangasse 24, tel. 0222/316412), **British Bookstore** (Weihburggasse 8, tel. 0222/512–1945), **English Bookshop Heidrich** (Plankengasse 7, tel. 0222/512–3701), **Pickwick's** (Marc-Aurel-Str. 10–12, tel. 0222/630182), **Shakespeare & Co.** (Sterngasse 2, tel. 0222/535–5053).

English-language Radio "Blue Danube Radio" on FM at 103.8 MHz carries news, music, and information in English (and some in French) from 7 AM to 1 PM and again from 6 to 8 PM.

Late-night Pharmacies In each area of the city one pharmacy stays open 24 hours; if a pharmacy is closed, a sign on the door will tell you the address of the nearest one that is open. Call 0222/1550 for names and addresses (in German) of the 24-hour pharmacies open that night.

Lost and Found Check with the police at the **Fundamt** (Wasagasse 22, tel. 0222/313440). If your loss occurred on a train, check the *Bundesbahn Fundamt* (railway lost property office, Westbahnhof, tel. 0222/5650–2996).

Travel Agencies **American Express** (Kärntner Str. 21–23, tel. 0222/51540, and at Parkring 10, actually around the corner in Liebenberggasse, tel. 0222/515–1180), **Thomas Cook/Wagon-Lits** (Kärntner Ring 2, tel. 0222/50160), **Cosmos** (Kärntner Ring 15, tel. 0222/515330), **Ruefa Reisen** (Fleischmarkt 1, tel. 0222/53404), **Österreichisches Verkehrsbüro** (Friedrichstr. 7, opposite Sezession, tel. 0222/588000).

Arriving and Departing by Plane

Vienna's airport is at Schwechat, about 19 km (12 mi) southeast of the city. For flight information, call 0222/71110–2231. **American Airlines, Pan American, Air Canada, Singapore Airlines,** and **Tarom/Romanian Airlines** fly into Schwechat from North America.

Between the Airport and City Center *By Bus* A bus leaves the airport every 20 minutes for the city air terminal beside the Hilton Hotel. The trip takes about 25 minutes and costs AS50; you buy your ticket on the bus, so be sure to have Austrian money handy. A bus also runs every half hour to the Westbahnhof (West rail station) via the Südbahnhof (South station); this bus might land you closer to your hotel, and taxis are available at the station.

By Taxi Taxis will take about 30 minutes to most downtown locations, longer when traffic is heavy (7–8:30 AM and 4:30–6:30 PM on weekdays). Taxis from Vienna are not allowed to pick up passengers at the airport unless they've been ordered; only those from Lower Austria (where the airport is located, beyond the city limits) can take passengers into town. This means that taxi travel one way empty, so the meter fare is doubled; you'll end up with a bill of about AS350. You can cut the charge in half by phoning one of the Vienna cab companies from the airport (tel. 0222/31300, 0222/60160, 0222/40100, or 0222/91011) and asking for a taxi to take you into town. They'll give you the last couple of digits of the taxi license, and you wait until it arrives. Be sure to arrange where the taxi will meet you. The same scheme applies when you leave: not all Vienna cabs have permits for airport service, so call in advance to get one that can take you out for about AS220–AS270.

By Limousine *Mazur* limos provide door-to-door transportation cheaper than a taxi. Look for the *Mazur* stand at the airport, or call 0222/604–9191 or 0222/604–2233.

By Train Fast trains run from the airport to the **Wien Mitte** station across the street from the Hilton Hotel and to the **Wien Nord** station, Praterstern, but the rail service is less frequent than the bus (about one train an hour), and both land you in virtually the same spot. Fare: AS30, or a Vienna streetcar ticket plus AS15. Both the frequency and the fare may increase by 1992.

Arriving and Departing by Car, Train, Boat, and Bus

By Car On the road from the airport and on highways from points south or west, *Zentrum* signs clearly mark the route to the center of Vienna. From there, however, finding your way to your hotel can be no mean trick, for traffic planners have installed a devious scheme prohibiting cars in the city core (the First District) and scooting them out again via a network of exasperating one-way streets. In the city itself a car is a burden, though very useful for trips outside town.

By Train Trains from Germany, Switzerland, and western Austria arrive at the **Westbahnhof** (West Station), on Europaplatz, where the Mariahilfer Strasse crosses the Gürtel. If you're coming from Italy or Hungary, you'll generally arrive at the **Südbahnhof** (South station, Wiedner Gürtel 1). The current stations for trains to and from Prague and Warsaw are **Wien Nord** (North Station, Praterstern) and **Franz-Josef Bahnhof** (Julius-Tandler-Platz). Central train information will have details (tel. 0222/1717 or tel. 0222/1552 for taped schedule information).

By Boat If you arrive in Vienna via the Danube, the DDSG ship will leave you at **Praterlände** near Mexikoplatz (Handelskai 265, tel. 0222/217100), although some downstream ships also make a stop at **Nussdorf** (Heiligenstädter Str. 180, tel. 0222/371257). The Praterlände stop is a short taxi ride from the Vorgartenstrasse subway station, or you can take a taxi directly into town.

By Bus There is virtually no long-distance bus service into Vienna, but the postal and railroad buses arrive at the **Wien Mitte** central bus station (Landstrasser Haupstr. 1b, tel. 0222/711070 or 0222/71101), across from the Hilton Hotel.

Getting Around

Vienna is divided into 23 numbered districts. Taxi drivers may need to know which district you seek, as well as the street address. The district number is coded into the postal code with the second and third digits; thus A–1010 (the "01") is the First District, A–1030 is the Third, A–1110 is the 11th, and so on. Some sources and some maps still give the district numbers, either in roman or arabic numerals, as Vienna X or Vienna 10.

Vienna is a city to tackle on foot. With the exception of the Schönbrunn and Belvedere palaces and the Prater amusement park, most sights are concentrated in the center, the First District (A–1010), much of which is a pedestrian zone anyway.

Get public-transport maps at a tourist office or at the transport-information offices (*Wiener Verkehrsbetriebe*), underground at Karlsplatz, Stephansplatz, and Praterstern. Vienna's public transportation system is fast, clean, safe, and easy to use. You can transfer on the same ticket between subway, streetcar, bus, and long stretches of the fast suburban railway, *Schnellbahn (S–Bahn)*. You can buy single tickets valid for the subway, streetcars, and buses for AS20 from dispensers on the streetcar or bus or at one of the subway stations. You'll need exact change. At *Tabak-Trafik* (cigarette shops/ newsstands) or the underground *Wiener Verkehrsbetriebe* offices you can get a block of five tickets for AS75, each ticket good for one uninterrupted trip in more or less the same general direction with unlimited transfers. Or you can get a three-day ticket for AS115, good on all lines for 72 hours from the time you validate the ticket; there's also a 24-hour ticket for AS45. If you're staying longer, get an eight-day (AS235) ticket, which can be used on eight separate days or by any number of persons (up to eight) at any one time.

You validate any ticket by inserting it into the small blue canceling maching (*Entwerter*) found on all buses and streetcars and at the entrance to subway stations. The multiple-ride tickets have to be folded back so the indicated strip can be stamped.

By Rental Car **Avis** (at airport, tel. 0222/71110–2700), *Opernring 1, tel. 0222/ 587–6241.*
Budget (at airport, tel. 0222/71110–2711), *Hilton Hotel, Am Stadtpark, tel. 0222/756–565.*
Hertz (at airport, tel. 0222/71110–2661), *Kärntner Ring 17, tel. 0222/512–8677; international reservations, tel. 0222/713– 1596.*
National (Europcar/interRent at airport, tel. 0222/71110– 3316), *Denzel Autovermietung, Kärntner Ring 14, tel. 0222/ 505–4166.*

By Subway Five subway lines (*U-bahn*), whose stations are prominently marked with blue *U* signs, crisscross the city. Karlsplatz and Stephansplatz are the main transfer points between lines. The last subway (U4) runs at about 12:20 AM.

By Streetcar and Bus The first streetcars run about 5:15 AM, for those Viennese who start work at 8. From then on, service (barring gridlock on the streets) is regular and reliable, and most lines operate until about midnight. Where streetcars don't run, buses do; route maps and schedules are posted at each bus or subway stop.

Vienna Subways

Should you miss the last streetcar or bus, special night buses with an *N* designation operate at half-hour intervals on weekends over several key routes; the starting (and transfer) point is Schwedenplatz. The night-owl buses take a special fare of AS25, tickets available on the bus; normal tickets are not valid.

Within the heart of the city, bus lines 1A, 2A and 3A are useful crosstown routes. These carry a reduced fare of AS7.50 per trip if you have bought the *Kurzstrecke* ticket (AS30), good for four trips or up to four people on one trip (with no transfer). The *Kurzstrecke* tickets are also valid for two stops on the subway or shorter distances on the streetcar lines.

By Taxi Taxis in Vienna are relatively inexpensive. The initial charge is AS22 for as many as four people. AS10 is added for each piece of luggage that must go into the trunk, and a charge is added for waiting beyond a reasonable limit. A night and weekend surcharge of AS10 is also added to the meter reading. It's customary to round up the fare to cover the tip. Taxis can be flagged on the street (when the roof light is on), taken from regular stands, or ordered by phone. To get a radio cab, call 0222/31300, 0222/40100, 0222/60160, or 0222/91011. Service is usually prompt, but at rush hour, when weather is bad, or if you need to keep to an exact schedule, call ahead and order a taxi for a specific time. If your destination is the airport, say so, and ask for a reduced-rate taxi.

By Limousine For a chauffeured limousine call **Avis-Adler** (tel. 0222/216–0990), **Göth** (tel. 0222/713–7196), **Mazur** (tel. 0222/604–2233),

Mietwagen Sidlo (tel. 0222/312514), or **Peter Urban** (tel. 0222/713–5255 or 713–3781).

Guided Tours

Orientation When you're pressed for time, a good way to see the highlights of Vienna is via a sightseeing-bus tour, which gives you a once-over-lightly of the heart of the city and allows a closer look at Schönbrunn and Belvedere palaces. **Vienna Sightseeing Tours** (Stelzhammergasse 4/11, tel. 0222/712–4683; a booking office is downstairs in the Opernpassage) runs a 1¼-hour "get acquainted" tour daily, leaving from in front of the Opera at 10:30 and 11:45 AM and 3 PM (Adults AS170, children AS60). You can cover almost the same territory on your own by taking either the No. 1 or No. 2 streetcar around the Ring, and then walking through the heart of the city. Vienna Sightseeing and **Cityrama/Gray Line** (Börsegasse 1, tel. 0222/534–130) both have tours of about three hours (Adults AS340, children AS120), including visits to Schönbrunn and Belvedere palaces (check to be certain you will go *inside* both; some tours just drive past). Both depart at 9:30 AM and 2:30 PM; Vienna Sightseeing also has one at 10:30 AM. Both firms offer a number of other tours as well (your hotel will have detailed programs), and both provide hotel pickup for most tours. For other than the "get acquainted" tours, the Vienna Sightseeing buses leave the central loading point in front of the Opera 10 minutes before scheduled tour departures to make the hotel pickups. Cityrama tours start from Johannesgasse at the Stadtpark station on the U4 subway line, across from the InterContinental hotel.

Streetcar Tours From early May through mid-October, a 1929 vintage streetcar leaves each Saturday at 2:30 PM and Sundays and holidays at 10 AM from the Otto Wagner Pavilion at Karlsplatz for a guided tour. For AS150 (children AS50), you'll go around the Ring, out past the big Ferris wheel in the Prater and past Schönbrunn and Belvedere palaces in the course of the two-hour trip. Get tickets in advance at the transport-information office underground at Karlsplatz, weekdays 7–6, weekends and holidays 8:30–4 (tel. 0222/587–3186).

Boat Tours The **Donau-Dampfschiffahrts-Gesellschaft** (DDSG; tel. 0222/217100) runs a three-hour boat tour up the Danube Canal and down the Danube, from Schwedenbrücke, by Schwedenplatz, May through September, daily at 1 and 4:30 PM. There are occasional moonlight cruises and weekly on-board evening *Heuriger* (new wine) parties, "golden oldies" dancing cruises, and Saturday night disco trips as well, with departures at 8:30 PM.

Personal Guides Guided tours (in English) on foot are a great way to see the city highlights. Tour topics range from "Unknown Underground Vienna" through "1,000 Years of Jewish Tradition" to "Vienna Around Sigmund Freud." Tours take about 1½ hours, are held in any weather provided at least three persons turn up, and cost AS100 (ages 15–18, AS50; plus any entry fees. No reservations are needed. Get a list of the guided-tour possibilities at the city information office at Kärntner Strasse 38 (tel. 0222/513–8892), or phone 0222/512–9735, 0222/468–5322, 0222/216–0466, 0222/220–6620, 0222/365–7033, or 0222/513–1261 for details. You can also arrange to have your own privately guided tour for AS900.

Self-guided   Get a copy of *Vienna: Downtown Walking Tours* by Henriette Mandl (Ueberreuter, 1987), from any bookshop. The six tours take you through the highlights of central Vienna with excellent commentary and some entertaining anecdotes, which most of your Viennese acquaintances won't know. The booklet "Vienna from A to Z" (in English; available at bookshops) explains the numbered plaques attached to all major buildings.

Horse Cab   A *Fiaker*, or horse cab, will trot you around to whatever destination you specify, but today this is an expensive way to have a look at the city. A short basic tour (just under ½ hour) costs AS400, and a longer one (about an hour) costs AS800, for the whole Fiaker. The carriages accommodate four (five if someone sits next to the coachman). Starting points are Heldenplatz in front of the Hofburg, Stephansplatz beside the cathedral, and across from the Albertina, all in the First District. For longer trips, or any variation of the regular route, agree on the price first.

Exploring Vienna

Orientation

by George H. Sullivan

To the Viennese, the most prestigious address of Vienna's 23 *Berzirke*, or districts, is the First District (the inner city, bounded by the Ringstrasse and the Danube Canal). The Second through the Ninth Districts surround the inner city (starting with the Second District across the Danube Canal and running clockwise); the 10th through the 23rd Districts form a second concentric ring of suburbs. The vast majority of sightseeing attractions are to be found in the First District. For hard-core sightseers who wish to supplement the walking tours that follow, the Tourist Office (*see* Important Addresses and Numbers in Essential Information, above) has a booklet "Vienna A to Z" (AS30) that gives short descriptions of some 250 sights around the city, all numbered and keyed to a fold-out map at the back, as well as to wall plaques on the buildings themselves. The more important churches possess coin-operated (AS10) tape machines that give an excellent commentary in English on the history and architecture of the church.

The description of the city on the following pages is divided into seven tours: six walks that explore the architectural riches of central Vienna, and a seventh tour that describes Schönbrunn Palace and its gardens. If you arrive in the city in the early afternoon and do not want to plunge into inner-city sightseeing, a visit to Schönbrunn is highly recommended.

Before beginning the walking tours, a word about Viennese palaces is perhaps in order. In most cases, the term "palace" is a misnomer, for by English-language standards only the Hofburg, Schönbrunn, and Belvedere palaces are large enough to be described as palatial. The remainder of the Viennese palaces are in fact very large town houses that originally served as the inner-city residences of the aristocracy. Many of them have been restored in recent years, and the facades have been repainted in beautiful old pastel colors that somehow manage to look refreshingly cool in summer and comfortably warm in winter. Many more facades remain unpainted, however; try to envision them as they were meant to be, dressed up in softly contrasting colors like their more fortunate peers. It will be well worth the effort.

Highlights for First-time Visitors

St. Stephen's Cathedral (*see* Tour 1: The City's Ancient Core)

The Hofburg (*see* Tour 4: The Hofburg and the Ringstrasse)

Schönbrunn Palace (*see* Tour 7: Schönbrunn Palace)

Belvedere Palace (*see* Tour 6: South of the Ring to the Belvedere)

Museum of Art History (*see* Tour 4: The Hofburg and the Ringstrasse)

Museum of Viennese History (*see* Tour 6: South of the Ring to the Belvedere)

Tour 1: The City's Ancient Core

Numbers in the margin correspond with points of interest on the Vienna map.

The citizens of Vienna, it has often been said, waltz only from the waist down, whirling around the crowded dance floor while holding their upper bodies motionless and ramrod straight. The sight can be breathtaking in its sweep and splendor, and its elegant coupling of freewheeling exuberance and rigid formality—of license and constraint—is quintessentially Viennese.

Architecture is frozen music, said the German poet Goethe, and the closest that European architecture ever came to embodying the Viennese waltz, appropriately enough, is the Viennese town palace. Built mostly during the 18th century, these Baroque mansions can be found all over the inner city, and they present in stone and stucco the same artful synthesis of license and constraint as the dance that was so often performed inside them. They make Vienna a Baroque city that is, at its best, an architectural waltz.

The inner city is by no means exclusively Baroque, however. Occasional survivors from medieval times as well as many additions from the 19th and 20th centuries dot the cityscape, and sometimes they present startling alternatives to the city's prevailing architectural style. These anomalies are of inestimable value to the city, however, for they supply surprise, variety, and the spice of argument, keeping the urban architectural dialogue alive and vital. Without them Vienna would be a much duller place.

① Tour 1 begins with the most prominent of these anomalies: **St. Stephen's Cathedral,** at the heart of the inner city. Consecrated in 1147, St. Stephen's is the hub of the city's wheel; for more than eight centuries its enormous bulk has served as the nucleus around which the city has grown. The top of its tall south tower is the city's preeminent lookout point, offering fine views in all directions. Be warned, however, that the 345-step ascent is long and arduous; you may want to postpone it until the last day of your visit, when the city's landmarks will be familiar and the views will serve to fix them in your memory. *Admission: AS20. Tower ascent open daily 9–4:30; closed Jan. 8–31.*

Vienna

As architecture, St. Stephen's possesses a fierce presence that is blatantly un-Viennese. Hunkering down rather than soaring up, its hulking frame bristles with prickly Gothic outgrowths, and the overall effect is far from refined. This is an architecture of encrustation, of bits and pieces—towers and pinnacles and gables—added here and there over hundreds of years. The result is a stylistic jumble, ranging from 13th-century Romanesque (the primitive and sometimes ill-matched arrangement of windows and decoration on the front facade) to 15th-century Gothic (the sophisticated stone tracery of the gables along the base of the roof on the sides). Such a hodgepodge ought to be indigestible, but the cathedral's magnificent steeply pitched roof comes to the rescue; with its forceful zigzag tiles (the design derives from Oriental carpeting) it locks the bits and pieces together with tremendous authority and gives the main body of the church the power to stand up to the massive southside Gothic tower.

Like the exterior, St. Stephen's barnlike interior lacks the soaring unity of Europe's greatest Gothic cathedrals, with much of its decoration dating from the later Baroque era. The change in style from Gothic to Renaissance to Baroque is best illustrated at the southwest corner of the crossing (where the nave and transept meet). The small 15th-century choir gallery, with its fancifully carved balcony above and spindly columns below, is typically Gothic, but the 17th-century doorway immediately to the right is framed in an entirely different style. Classical elements (plain columns with Corinthian capitals supporting a triangular pediment) have taken over—a sure sign of the Renaissance, with its passionate rediscovery of the architecture of ancient Rome. Baroque architects, in their turn, continued to use this classical vocabulary, but they molded and twisted and broke the ancient motifs into forms that had never been seen before. The ornate altars that dot the nave and side aisles (at the bases of the freestanding piers and against the side-aisle walls) beautifully illustrate this later change in taste. The altars were added in the early 18th century, and although most of them still use plain columns to frame their altarpiece paintings, the pediments on top have erupted into full-blown Baroque.

The wealth of decorative sculpture in St. Stephen's can be demoralizing to the nonspecialist, so if you wish to explore the cathedral in detail, you may want to buy the admirably complete English-language description sold in the small room marked *Schriften und Opferkerzen* (Pamphlets and Votive Candles). One particularly masterly work, however, should be seen by everyone: the stone pulpit attached to the second freestanding pier on the left of the central nave, carved by Anton Pilgram around 1510. The spun-sugar delicacy of its decoration would in itself set the pulpit apart, but even more intriguing are its five sculpted figures. Carved around the outside of the pulpit proper are the four Latin Fathers of the Church (from left to right: Saint Augustine, Saint Gregory, Saint Jerome, and Saint Ambrose), and each is given an individual personality so sharply carved as to suggest satire, perhaps of living models. (The four figures may also have been meant to represent the Four Temperaments of ancient lore: melancholic, phlegmatic, choleric, and sanguine.) There is no satire suggested by the fifth figure, however; below the pulpit's stairs Pilgram sculpted a fine self-portrait, showing himself peering out a half-open window.

St. Stephen's was devastated by bombing during World War II, and the extent of the damage may be seen by leaving the cathedral through the south porch, where a set of prereconstruction photographs commemorates the disaster. Restoration was protracted and difficult, but today the cathedral once again dominates the center of the city. The final effect is of crude power rather than polished sophistication, but in a city that sometimes suffers from a surfeit of refined architectural manners, St. Stephen's serves as a bracing and enlivening centerpiece.

Works of art associated with the long history of the cathedral can be found in the **Dom und Diözesanmuseum** (the Cathedral and Diocese Museum), located in a passageway at the northeast corner of the cathedral square. Despite the wide range of styles represented (Gothic carving to Baroque printing) the collection is not overly large; its exclusively religious focus, however, does make it somewhat specialized in its appeal. *Stephansplatz 6, tel. 0222/51552–429. Admission: AS30. Open Tues.–Wed., Fri.–Sat. 10–4, Thurs. 10–6, Sun. 10–1.*

On the north side of Dr.-Ignaz-Seipel-Platz (named for the theology professor who was chancellor of Austria during the 1920s) is the **Jesuitenkirche,** built around 1630. Its flamboyant Baroque interior contains a fine trompe l'oeil ceiling fresco by that master of visual trickery, Andrea Pozzo, who was imported from Rome in 1702 for the job. Pozzo's painted dome is worth examining twice, first from the entrance end of the nave and then from the altar.

The exterior of the church provides an illuminating contrast to the **Academy of Science** on the west side of the square. While the church's facade exhibits a rudimentary classicism—the decorative pediments above the windows and the double-story pilasters are plain and rather awkwardly arranged—there is nothing awkward about the Academy of Science, built more than a century later, in 1753. Here the Baroque style is in full flower. The classical elements no longer look pasted on; instead, the columns and pediments act both to frame the building's windows and to organize the facade into a carefully balanced composition of considerable complexity.

The architect, J. N. Jadot de Ville-Issey, was French, and the influence of French architecture is strong; indeed, the plain ground floor, the recessed windows separated by paired columns on the floor above, and the pilastered end pavilions are all facade features of that most famous of French buildings, the Louvre. Here, however, Jadot de Ville-Issey added extra touches, which, though far from lavish—mostly limited to decorative carving above the windows—nevertheless transform the facade, adding insouciant grace notes to what might otherwise be sober plainsong. The result is impeccably elegant: a proud classical facade decked out in high-style special-occasion Baroque finery. Like so many of Vienna's great Baroque buildings, the Academy of Science looks as if it is about to set out for the Opera Ball.

In contrast to the academy, more modest buildings of the period tended to be less concerned with classical dignity. The house at No. 3 Sonnenfelsgasse (the street on the north side of the academy) is a case in point. Known as **Hildebrandthaus** (it was designed in 1721 by an unknown follower of the architect Johann Lukas von Hildebrandt), the facade is a purist's nightmare. Not only are the pilasters between the lower windows elaborately carved, they are then merged with (and visually made to support) far weightier uncarved pilasters above, thus breaking one of the cardinal rules of traditional classical facade design: weightier elements on the bottom, lighter elements on top. Renaissance propriety has here given way to Baroque license, and anything goes. But with carving like this, who could complain? The Academy of Science may present a more balanced architectural meal, but this is pure Viennese pastry.

In their own small way, the Academy of Science and Hildebrandthaus mark the extremes of Viennese Baroque architecture—the one urbane and patrician, the other frivolous and frothy. Most of the famous Viennese Baroque facades fall somewhere in between these extremes, but the fundamental architectural dialogue—the interplay between classical dignity and decorative vivacity—remains a constant, and it can be found all over the inner city.

Turn north from Sonnenfelsgasse on Köllnerhofgasse, then immediately right onto the short Grashofgasse. The door at the far end leads into **Heiligenkreuzerhof** (Holy Cross Court), one of the city's most peaceful backwaters. This complex of buildings, owned by the Holy Cross Abbey, 32 km (20 mi) south of the city, dates from the 17th century (but with an 18th century face-lift). Appropriately, the restraint of the architecture—with only here and there a small outburst of Baroque spirit—gives the courtyard a distinct feeling of retreat. The reigning tranquillity is a welcome respite from the bustle of the narrow streets outside.

Through the far gate of Heiligenkreuzerhof is Schönlaterngasse (Beautiful Lantern Street), named for the wall lantern at No. 6. No. 7, the house known as the **Basiliskenhaus,** was according to legend first built for a baker; on June 26, 1212, a foul-smelling basilisk (half rooster, half toad, with a glance that could kill) took up residence in the courtyard well, poisoning the water. An enterprising apprentice dealt with the problem by climbing down the well armed with a mirror; when the basilisk saw its own reflection it turned to stone. The petrified creature can still be seen in a niche on the building's facade. Today, modern science accounts for the contamination with a more prosaic explanation: natural-gas seepage.

To the east of Schönlaterngasse, on Postgasse, is an unexpected visitor from Rome: the **Dominikanerkirche.** Built in the 1630s, some 50 years before the Viennese Baroque building boom, its facade is modeled after any number of Roman churches of the 16th century. The interior, too, is Italian in design and detail; only the extensive use of plain white paint fails to suggest Rome (the Italians would have gilded the carved stucco and painted any flat surfaces to look like colored marble). The interior illustrates why the Baroque style came to be considered the height of bad taste during the 19th century and still has many detractors today. "Sculpt 'til you drop" seems to have been the motto here, and the viewer's eye is given no respite. Happily, this sort of Roman architectural orgy never really gained a foothold in Vienna, and when the great Viennese architects did pull out all the decorative stops—Hildebrandt's interior at the Belvedere Palace, for instance (*see* Tour 6, below)—they did it in a very different style and with far greater success.

Two blocks northeast of the Dominikanerkirche is the **Georg-Coch-Platz,** a small square bounded on the east by the **former War Ministry** and on the west by the **Post Office Savings Bank.** The War Ministry was constructed in 1909 at the tail end of the 19th-century Viennese building boom. Its Baroque Revival facade derives from the Academy of Science, but here the small scale of the academy is blown up to ponderous proportions, and the earlier building's delicate decoration has been transformed into bellicose piles of carved weaponry meant to symbolize Imperial might.

The Post Office Savings Bank is one of Modern architecture's greatest curiosities. It was designed in 1904 by Otto Wagner, whom many consider the father of 20th-century architecture. In his famous manifesto, *Modern Architecture,* Wagner condemned 19th-century revivalist architecture and pleaded for a modern style that honestly expressed modern building methods. Accordingly, the exterior walls of the Post Office Savings Bank are mostly flat and undecorated; visual interest is supplied merely by varying the pattern of the bolts that were used to hold the marble slabs in place on the wall surface during construction. Later architects were to embrace Wagner's beliefs wholeheartedly, although they used different, truly modern building materials: glass and concrete rather than marble. As a result the oddly metallic look Wagner created here has today the air of a failed futuristic fantasy, akin to the clunky spaceships in an old Buck Rogers movie serial. The Post Office Savings Bank was indeed a bold leap into the future, but unfortunately the future took a different path.

Next go to Fleischmarkt, where between Nos. 9 and 11 the picturesque Griechengasse forks off to the right, just beyond the glittering 19th-century Greek Orthodox church. This corner of the inner city has a medieval feel that is quite genuine; there has been a tavern at **No. 11 Fleischmarkt** for some 500 years. The wooden carving on the facade of the current Griechenbeisl restaurant commemorates Max Augustin—known best today from the song "Ach du lieber Augustin"—an itinerant musician who sang here during the plague of 1679. Augustin survived being thrown alive into a pit filled with dead plague victims; he had been thought dead by the body collectors, when in fact he had only been dead drunk.

Time Out Take a break for coffee at the corner of Fleischmarkt and Wolfengasse, at the **Café Vienne,** famous for baking the biggest cakes in the city. Or for a snack on the run, pick out one of the mouth-watering pastries at **Elias Bäckerei,** a few doors along Fleischmarkt (opposite No. 9).

No. 14 Fleischmarkt is an oddity for Vienna but an instructive one: a bad example of Jugendstil, the crisper, more geometric, Austrian version of French Art Nouveau that enjoyed its heyday around the turn of the century. Jugendstil motifs, when successfully applied to building facades, sometimes look poured, sometimes look hung, and sometimes look draped; they sometimes look as if they are climbing up the wall, and sometimes look as if they're creeping down. But they never, as here, look merely stuck on; they are never mere space fillers; and they are never randomly and aimlessly gilded.

From Fleischmarkt, a turn south onto Rotenturmstrasse and a right turn onto Lichtensteg leads into **Hoher Markt.** The square was badly damaged during World War II, but the famous Anker Clock at the east end survived the bombing. The huge mechanical timepiece took six years to build (1911–17) and still attracts crowds at noon when the full panoply of mechanical figures representing Austrian historical personages parades by. The graceless buildings erected around the square since 1945 are not aging well and do little to show off the square's lovely Baroque centerpiece, the St. Joseph Fountain, designed in 1729 by Joseph Emanuel Fischer von Erlach, son of the great Johann Bernhard Fischer von Erlach. The Hoher Markt does harbor one wholly unexpected attraction, however: ❼ **underground Roman ruins.** This is what was once the main east–west axis of the Roman encampment of Vindobona, and the foundations of several officers' houses built in the 2nd century have been uncovered. The excavations are entered through the snack bar in the passageway at No. 3; a short descriptive pamphlet in English is available at the ticket-table. *Hoher Markt 3, tel. 0222/535–5606. Admission: AS 15. Open Tues.–Sun. 9–12:15 and 1–4:30.*

Beginning beneath the Anker Clock, follow Bauernmarkt back to Fleischmarkt. To the left, next to the steps leading up to Ruprechtsplatz, is one of the city's most eccentric buildings: the **Kornhäusel Tower,** built around 1825. Joseph Kornhäusel was the most puritanical of Vienna's great architects; his restrained classicism rejected all but the plainest decoration and ran distinctly counter to the Viennese love of architectural finery. Apparently he had a misanthropic personality to match, for the starkly unornamented tower here, which was attached to his home, was reportedly built so he could get away from his wife (the studio at the top could be reached only by climbing up a ladder and through a trap door). Whatever the truth may be, the Kornhäusel Tower remains a profoundly antisocial building.

Several of Kornhäusel's more conventional buildings can be seen up the steps and around the corner to the right, at Seitenstettengasse at **Nos. 2–4** and at **No. 5.** The building at Nos. 2-4 houses the only synagogue in Vienna to survive the Nazi holocaust; its lack of an appropriate facade results from the 19th-century Viennese law that required all synagogues to be hidden from street view.

To the north of the Kornhäusel Tower lies Ruprechtsplatz, another of Vienna's time-warp backwaters. The church in the ❽ middle, **Ruprechtskirche** (St. Rupert's), is the city's oldest. According to legend it was founded in 740; the oldest part of the present structure (the lower half of the tower) dates from the 11th century. Set on the ancient ramparts overlooking the Danube Canal, it is serene and unpretentious, and its modest church-on-the-village-green feel lends to the tiny square a welcome breath of rural fresh air.

To the west of the Ruprechtsplatz entrance, steps on Sterngasse lead down to Marc-Aurel-Strasse. The lump of stone set into a wall niche at Sterngasse 3, at the top of the stairs, is a cannonball fired into the city during the unsuccessful Turkish siege of 1683; the larger lump of stone near the bottom of the stairs is a section of wall from the ancient Roman baths.

Continue west; at the end of Sterngasse a left turn and a short flight of steps lead to Salvatorgasse, with a timeworn Renaissance doorway at No. 5 (circa 1525). As you walk west, Salvatorgasse curves slightly, skirting the edge of the Gothic church of **Maria am Gestade** (St. Mary on the Banks). Built around 1400 (but much restored in the 17th and 19th centuries), the church incorporated part of the Roman city walls into its foundation; the north wall, as a result, takes a slight but noticeable dogleg to the right halfway down the nave. Like St. Stephen's, Maria am Gestade is rough-hewn Gothic, with a simple but forceful facade. The church is especially beloved, however, because of its unusual details—the pinnacled and saint-bedecked gable that tops the front facade, the stone canopy that hovers protectively over the front door, and (most appealing of all) the intricate openwork lantern atop the south-side bell tower. Appropriately enough in a city famous for its pastry, the lantern lends to its tower an engaging suggestion of sugar caster.

The small square in front of Maria am Gestade overlooks Tiefer Graben, which until the 15th century was a tributary of the Danube that served as a moat just outside the city walls. The view is worth noting, for on clear days the famed Vienna Woods can be seen to the west, down the line of Börsegasse.

Tour 2: Baroque Gems

From Maria am Gestade, walk south on Schwertgasse and turn left onto Wipplingerstrasse. At No. 7 is the former **Bohemian Court Chancery,** built between 1708 and 1714 by Johann Bernhard Fischer von Erlach. Fischer von Erlach and his contemporary Johann Lukas von Hildebrandt were the reigning architectural geniuses of Baroque Vienna; they designed their churches and palaces during the building boom that followed the defeat of the Turks in 1683. Both had studied architecture in Rome, and both were deeply impressed by the work of the great Italian architect Francesco Borromini, who had brought to his designs a wealth and freedom of invention that was looked upon with horror by most contemporary Romans. But for Fischer von Erlach and Hildebrandt, Borromini's ideas were a source of triumphant architectural inspiration, and when they returned to Vienna they between them produced many of the city's most beautiful buildings.

Like Jadot de Ville-Issey's Academy of Science (*see* Tour 1), the Chancery facade displays a beautifully calculated balance between plain and fancy. The central and end sections of the building are quite staid, but their simplicity serves an obvious purpose: It frames and contrasts with the entryway portals, where Fischer von Erlach gives his Baroque ingenuity free reign. The use of atalantes—muscular figures growing out of the tapered pilasters on the ground floor—is typically Baroque in its denial of the earlier Renaissance convention by which facade compositions were supposed to be carefully graduated, from heavier bottoms to lighter tops. Fischer von Erlach flouts this dogma with breathtaking assurance: His pilasters taper away to nothing at the bottom and grow heavier as they move upward, leaving the atalantes to struggle mightily with the weight of the massive protruding cornice. Likewise, the ornate window treatments on the upper floor would have shocked the Renaissance—such swoops and swirls and sinuous curves would have been viewed as an insult to the dignity and straightforward nobility of ancient Greek and Roman architecture. But like all the great Baroque architects, Fischer von Erlach wanted to eat his cake and have it, too: He wanted dignity *and* panache, nobility *and* grace. And so he softened and melted and molded the plain geometric window pediments of old, and he embellished them with sumptuous carved decoration. The facade that resulted is Baroque Vienna at its best.

Across the street from the Bohemian Chancery is the **Altes Rathaus** (Old City Hall), dating from the 14th century but sporting 18th-century Baroque motifs on its facade. The interior passageways and courtyards, which are open during the day, house a Gothic chapel (open at odd hours), a much-loved Baroque wall fountain (Georg Raphael Donner's **Andromeda Fountain** of 1741), and display cases exhibiting maps and photos illustrating the city's history.

From Wipplingerstrasse, follow the short Fütterergasse south to **Judenplatz,** from the 13th century onward the center of Vienna's ghetto. An old carved plaque at No. 2 recounts the events of 1421, when more than 200 Jews—the plaque calls them "Hebrew dogs"—were burned alive and the rest of the Jewish community was banished en masse to Hungary. Today the square's centerpiece is a statue of the 18th-century Jewish playwright Gotthold Ephraim Lessing, erected after World War II; disconcertingly, the statue suggests the work of the American artist R. Crumb, famous during the 1960s for his underground comics.

Kurrentgasse leads south from the square's east end; the beautifully restored 18th-century houses on its east side make this one of the most unpretentiously appealing streets in the city. And at the far end of the street is one of Vienna's most unpretentiously appealing museums: the **Uhrenmuseum,** or Clock Museum (entrance around the corner to the right on the Schulhof side of the building). The museum's three floors display a splendid array of clocks and watches—more than 3,000 timepieces—dating from the 15th century to the present. *Schulhof 2, tel. 0222/533–2265. Admission: AS 30. Open Tues.–Sun. 9–4:30.*

Time Out A number of restaurants in the Kurrentgasse area serve good traditional Viennese food at moderate prices, among them **Ofenloch** (Kurrentgasse 8), **Gösser Bierklinik** (Sterndlgasse 4), and **Stadtbeisl** (Naglergasse 21). All three will supply English menus on request.

From the Clock Museum, Schulhof leads into Am Hof, one of the city's oldest squares. In the Middle Ages, the ruling Babenberg family built their castle on the site of No. 2; hence the name of the square, which means simply "at court." The Baroque **Column of Our Lady** in the center dates from 1667; the **Civic Armory** at the northwest corner has been used as a fire station since 1685 (the high-spirited facade, with its Habsburg eagle, dates from 1731) and today houses the headquarters of Vienna's fire department.

 The **Kirche Am Hof,** on the east side of the square, can lay fair claim to being the least successful piece of important architecture in the city. The flaccid, sprawling Baroque facade (1662) is thoroughly mediocre; there is no special Viennese grace here, only a hapless overall plastering-on of conventional Baroque motifs. Inside, though the ceiling remains Gothic, the rest is later decoration at war with itself. The nave piers have been given clumsy classical capitals, the side chapels are entered through fussy Baroque triumphal arches, and the choir carries a heavy mock-Roman coffered ceiling that is visually (and insufficiently) supported by spindly, hideously painted pilasters. Only the tall altars on either side of the choir entrance manage to muster up a bit of real Baroque conviction, but the surrounding muddle destroys their impact almost completely.

Bognergasse leaves the square to the right of the church. At No. 9 is the **Engel Pharmacy,** with a Jugendstil mosaic depicting winged women collecting the elixir of life in outstretched chalices. At the turn of the century the inner city was dotted with storefronts decorated in a similar manner; today this is the sole survivor.

From Bognergasse, the tiny Irisgasse—only a few yards long— leads to Naglergasse, another of Vienna's beautifully restored Baroque streets. The curve at the street's west end is due to the much earlier curve of the Roman city wall, which turned north here to run along Tiefer Graben to the Danube.

Naglergasse leads, at its curved end, into Heidenschuss, which in turn leads down a slight incline to Freyung, meaning "freeing." The square was so named because for many centuries the monks at the adjacent Schottenkirche (Scottish Church, though in fact the original monks were probably Irish) possessed the privilege of offering sanctuary. In the center of the square stands the allegorical **Austria Fountain** (1845), notable because its Bavarian designer, one Ludwig Schwanthaler, had the statues cast in Munich and then supposedly filled them with cigars to be smuggled into Vienna for black-market sale.

12 At Freyung 2 stands the recently restored **Palais Ferstel,** which is not a palace at all but a commercial shop-and-office complex designed in 1856 and named for its architect, Heinrich Ferstel. The facade is Italianate in style, harking back, in its 19th-century way, to the Florentine palazzi of the early Renaissance. The interior is unashamedly eclectic: vaguely Romanesque in feel and Gothic in decoration, with here and there a bit of Renaissance or Baroque sculpted detail thrown in for good measure. Such eclecticism is sometimes dismissed as mindlessly derivative, but here the architectural details (recently restored) are so respectfully and inventively combined that the interior becomes a pleasure to explore. Pastiche the building may be, but it is pastiche brought alive by a manifestly genuine love of architectural history.

Returning to Freyung, proceed to its west end, dominated by the hulking and haphazardly decorated Schottenkirche. The square's best-known palace, one of the most sophisticated pieces of Baroque architecture in the city, is across the street at **13** No. 4: the **Kinsky Palace,** built between 1713 and 1716 by Hildebrandt. As at Fischer von Erlach's Bohemian Chancery, the facade is a happy marriage of plain and fancy: The two pairs of outer double-story pilasters are left undecorated, while the four central pilasters are fancifully carved; the middle row of windows is given simple window-surrounds, while the upper row is decorated in full-blown Baroque style (these are the beloved Viennese "eyebrows" that are a recurring motif all over the city). The entire composition thus becomes an essay in carefully controlled vertical and horizontal contrasts, with the contrasts arranged so that the simple and the complex are inextricably interlocked.

Compared to the Kinsky Palace, the buildings on either side fall distinctly short: The 16th-century facade on the left looks like a plain-jane wallflower, while the 19th-century facade on the right looks like an overdressed fussbudget. The Kinsky Palace's only real competition comes a few yards farther on: the Greek temple facade of **Schottenhof,** attached at right angles to the church. Designed by Joseph Kornhäusel in a very different style from his antisocial tower seen earlier, the Schottenhof facade typifies the change that came over Viennese architecture during the Biedermeier Era (1815–48). The Viennese, according to the traditional view, were at the time so relieved to be rid of the upheavals of the Napoleonic Wars that they accepted without protest the iron-handed repression of Prince Metternich, chancellor of Austria, and retreated into a cozy and complacent domesticity. The era's passion for conventional rectitude was later satirized in a famous series of poems, published in 1855–57 and ostensibly written by Gottfried Biedermeier, an upright (but fictitious) German schoolteacher whose name soon became synonymous with mindless bourgeois respectability.

During the Biedermeier Era restraint also ruled in architecture, with Baroque license rejected in favor of a new and historically "correct" style that was far more controlled and reserved. Kornhäusel led the way in Vienna; his Schottenhof facade is all sober organization and frank repetition. But in its marriage of strong and delicate forces it still pulls off the great Viennese-waltz trick of successfully merging seemingly antithetical characteristics.

Follow Teinfaltstrasse (just opposite the Schottenkirche facade) one block west to Schreyvogelgasse on the right. The doorway at No. 8 (up the incline) was made famous in 1949 by the film *The Third Man;* it was here that Orson Welles, as the malevolently knowing Harry Lime, stood hiding in the dark, only to have his smiling face illuminated by a sudden light from the upper-story windows of the house across the alley.

⑭ Around the corner at No. 8 Mölker Bastei is the **Pasqualatihaus,** where Beethoven lived while he was composing his only opera, *Fidelio,* as well as his Seventh Symphony and Fourth Piano Concerto. Today his apartment houses a small commemorative museum. *Tel. 0222/637-0665. Admission: AS15. Open Tues.–Sun. 9–12:15 and 1–4:30.*

Four blocks south of Schreyvogelgasse is the Minoritenplatz, **⑮** named after its centerpiece, the **Minoritenkirche** (Church of the Minorite Order), a Gothic stump of a church built mostly in the 14th century. The front is brutally ugly, but the back is a wonderful (if predominantly 19th-century) surprise. The interior contains the city's most imposing piece of kitsch: a large mosaic reproduction of Leonardo da Vinci's *Last Supper,* commissioned by Napoleon in 1806 and later purchased by the Emperor Franz I.

From the east end of Minoritenplatz, follow Landhausgasse one block east to Herrengasse. Across the street to the left is the entrance to the **Café Central,** part of the Ferstel Palace complex and one of Vienna's most famous cafés, recently restored. No matter how crowded the café may become, you can linger as long as you like over a single cup of coffee and a newspaper from the huge international selection the café keeps on hand.

In its prime (before World War I), the Café Central was home to some of the most famous literary figures of the day—home in the literal as well as the figurative sense. In those days, housing was one of the city's most intractable problems. The large apartment houses that had gone up to accommodate the surge in Vienna's population were often (despite their imposing facades) no better than tenements, and overcrowding was so extreme that many apartment dwellers sublet space by the square foot—just enough room for a spare bed. As a result, many of Vienna's artists and writers spent as little time as possible in their "homes" and instead ensconced themselves at a favorite café, where they ate, socialized, worked, and even received mail. The denizens of the Central favored political argument; indeed, their heated and sometimes violent discussions became so well known that in October 1917, when Austria's foreign secretary was informed of the outbreak of the Russian Revolution, he dismissed the report with a facetious reference to a well-known local Marxist, the chess-loving (and presumably harmless) "Herr Bronstein from the Café Central." The remark was to become famous all over Austria, for Herr Bronstein had disappeared and was about to resurface in Russia bearing a new name: Leon Trotsky.

Herrengasse is lined with Baroque town houses and is also home to the inner city's first "skyscraper," on the corner of Herrengasse and Fahnengasse. This 20th-century addition to the cityscape (called *Hochhaus*, or high house) is much decried by the Viennese, although it will seem innocuous enough to visitors from New York or London. At No. 13 is the Palace of the Lower Austrian Diet, more familiarly known as the **Landhaus**. In front of this building on March 13, 1848, Imperial troops fired into a crowd of demonstrators, killing four men and one woman and signaling the beginning of the abortive Revolution of 1848.

Tour 3: From Michaelerplatz to the Graben

At the south end of Herrengasse, in **Michaelerplatz,** one of Vienna's most evocative squares, the feel of the medieval city remains very strong; the buildings seem to crowd in toward the center of the small plaza as if the city were bursting at its seams, desperate to break out of its protective walls. The buildings around the perimeter present a synopsis of the city's entire architectural history: medieval church spire, Renaissance church facade, Baroque palace facade, 19th-century apartment house, and 20th-century bank (originally a clothing store). In the center, recent excavations have turned up extensive traces of the old Roman city and relics of the 18th and 19th centuries. **Michaelerkirche** (the Church of St. Michael's), with its unpretentious spire, dates from the 13th and 14th centuries, although the ground-floor entrance porch and upper-story decoration were not added until several hundred years later. The result is awkward, to say the least.

The curved, domed **entrance to the Imperial Palace** (part of the Hofburg, which we'll explore at length in Tour 4) is far from awkward, but unfortunately it is also far from inspired. It was designed by Joseph Emanuel Fischer von Erlach in the first half of the 18th century, although the design was not executed until the 1890s, and then in a somewhat modified form. It is a competent, conventional, French-influenced work that possesses very little decorative exuberance and therefore ends up looking more Parisian than Viennese.

The **Palais Herberstein,** across Herrengasse, echoes some of the motifs of the palace entrance, but it is not afraid of showing off. It was built in 1903, and its recognizably Viennese decoration is typical of the neo-Baroque style of the day. Eight years later Adolf Loos, one of the founding fathers of 20th-century Modern architecture, built the **Looshaus** next door, facing the palace entrance. It was anything but typical—it was more like an architectural declaration of war. After two hundred years of Baroque and neo-Baroque exuberance, the first generation of 20th-century architects had had enough. Loos led the revolt against architectural tradition; *Ornament and Crime* was the title of his famous manifesto in which he inveighed against the conventional architectural wisdom of the 19th century— against the style of the Palais Herberstein—and denounced Vienna's decorative vivacity. Instead, he advocated buildings that were plain, honest, and functional. When he built the Looshaus for Goldman and Salatsch (men's clothiers) in 1911 the city was scandalized. "The house without eyebrows," hooted his critics. Archduke Franz Ferdinand, heir to the throne, was so offended that he vowed never again to use the Michaelerplatz entrance to the Imperial Palace. Everyone in the city took sides, and the debate over the merits of Modern architecture began. Nowadays the Looshaus has lost its power to shock, and the facade seems quite innocuous. The recently restored interior, however, remains a breathtaking suprise. Loos's plain surfaces allow his carefully selected materials, particularly the richly grained wood he so loved, to shine with a luster that positively dazzles. This is plainness, to be sure, but it is a plainness that is downright voluptuous. Here, for once, less really *is* more.

The passageway just to the right of St. Michael's, with its large 15th-century relief depicting Christ on the Mount of Olives, leads into the Stallburggasse, named after the Imperial Stables on the right. The area is dotted with antiques stores, attracted by the presence of the **Dorotheum,** the famous Viennese auction house that began as a state-controlled pawnshop in 1707 (known as "Aunt Dorothy" to its patrons). Merchandise coming up for auction is on display at Dorotheergasse 11, at the far end of Stallburggasse to the left.

At No. 6 Dorotheergasse, hidden behind an unprepossessing doorway, the **Café Hawelka** is one of the few famous inner-city cafés that has survived without major restoration. The Hawelka's air of romantic shabbiness—the product of Viennese *fortwursteln*, or "muddling through"—is especially evocative; long may it muddle along, exactly as it is.

The Dorotheergasse leads out into the Graben, a pedestrian mall lined with luxury shops and open-air cafés. Turn right into Stock-im-Eisenplatz, where opposite the southwest corner of St. Stephen's, set into the corner of the building on the west side of Kärntner Strasse, is one of the city's most revered relics: the **Stock-im-Eisen,** or iron tree stump. Chronicles first mention the Stock-im-Eisen in 1533, but it is probably far older, and for hundreds of years any apprentice metalsmith who came to Vienna to learn his trade hammered a nail into the tree trunk for good luck. During World War II, when there was talk of moving the relic to a museum in Munich, it mysteriously disappeared; it reappeared, perfectly preserved, after the threat of removal had passed.

Across the street from Stock-im-Eisen is Vienna's newest and (for the moment, at least) most controversial piece of architecture: **Neues Haas Haus.** It was designed by Hans Hollein, Austria's best-known living architect; *The Architectural Review* described it as "a collagist collision of heavy concrete and masonry with suave metal and glass cladding." Detractors consider its aggressively contemporary style out of place opposite St. Stephen's, while advocates consider the contrast enlivening; whatever the verdict, it should be noted that the banal postwar building it replaced was no great loss.

The **Graben,** leading west from Stock-im-Eisenplatz, is a street whose unusual width gives it the presence and weight of a city square. Its shape is due to the Romans, who dug the city's southwestern moat here, adjacent to the original city walls. The Graben's centerpiece is the **Pestsäule,** or Plague Column, erected by Emperor Leopold I between 1687 and 1693, in thanks to God for delivering the city from a particularly virulent plague. The style (High Baroque) is immediately clear from the frenzied feel of the piece, but the subject matter (the Trinity supported by an angel-covered cloud) may not be so apparent. Still, the monument proved extremely popular, and imitations of it can be found all over Austria.

The real glory of the Graben, however, is not the Plague Column but the architecture that surrounds it, creating the city's finest ensemble of buildings. Most of the buildings date from the late 19th century, but a few of them are earlier or later, and the contrast is illuminating.

The oldest building is **No. 11,** near the square's southeast corner. It was probably designed around 1720 by the great Johann Lukas von Hildebrandt, architect of the Kinsky Palace (*see* Tour 2) and the Belvedere Palace (*see* Tour 6); the top story is a later addition. This was a modest building, and Hildebrandt's facade is quite simple. But his love of decoration still comes through above the windows, where the traditional classical pediments, usually plain triangles, are reshaped and embroidered to become the famous Viennese "eyebrows" (in this case, raised eyebrows).

By the first half of the 19th century a reaction against Baroque decoration had set in, as can be seen at **No. 21,** at the northwest corner. Designed by Alois Pichl in 1835, the building's middlestory window pediments are impeccably traditional, and in its sober organization Pichl's facade clearly shows the influence of the leading architect of the day, Joseph Kornhäusel. Still, the overall effect is surprisingly fragile. Viennese exuberance has (for the moment) been banished, but Viennese delicacy remains.

There is nothing delicate about the **Graben-Hof,** built in 1873 (Nos. 14–15, on the south side). The overall organization of the facade is similar to the Academy of Science (*see* Tour 1), but the general effect is quite different, for the classical elements are used to give the building a weighty and imposing presence—to make it stand proud. The result here is more than a little ponderous, and if Otto Wagner, the building's codesigner, had continued to build in this style, he would today be as forgotten as his collaborator, Otto Thienemann. But Wagner was an experimenter, and he later came to reject the classical vocabulary entirely, as can be seen in his 1895 design at **No. 10** (southeast corner), which employs an entirely new free-form style of decoration. The building was structurally unconventional as well, using iron and glass in new ways on the ground floor and roof. Wagner was to continue his experiments (*see* the Post Office Savings Bank, Tour 1) to become a pioneer of 20th-century architecture.

Wagner's influence can be seen clearly at **No. 16,** one of the Graben's youngest buildings (1911). Again, iron and glass are used in a novel way at the top and bottom. But a special feel to the decoration, and a suggestion of sleekness to the building's curved corner, proclaims the arrival of Jugendstil, the Austrian version of Art Nouveau (and a forerunner of Art Deco). The upper-story stucco-work motifs in particular stand out; hanging from the corner windows like jewelry, they give the facade an air of glamour that, in its day, must have seemed as modern as the automobile and the flapper.

⑲ Just north of the Graben is Petersplatz, site of **Peterskirche** (St. Peter's Church), constructed between 1702 and 1708 by Hildebrandt, using an earlier plan by the Italian Gabriele Montani. The facade possesses angled towers, graceful towertops (said to have been inspired by the tents of the Turks during the siege of 1683), and an unusually fine entrance porch. All this is dignified enough, but somehow the overall effect is perversely (if appealingly) humorous. This is a building with a serious weight problem. It looks as if it's trying to waddle its way into the Graben but has been eating too much strudel and has gotten too fat to squeeze through. Inside the church, the Baroque decoration is elaborate, with some fine touches (particularly the glass-crowned galleries high on the walls to either side of the altar), but the lack of light and years of accumulated dirt create a prevailing gloom, and the much praised ceiling frescoes by J. M. Rottmayr are impossible to make out.

Proceed west on Milchgasse and turn left onto Tuchlauben. The lusciously painted building at **No. 5** was constructed in 1984, but it retains the 1719 facade of its predecessor; it wears its miscellany of Baroque window pediments like so many party hats, classical dignity be damned.

⑳ Tuchlauben leads back to the west end of the Graben and then continues on as **Kohlmarkt.** None of the buildings here are remarkable, although they do include an entertainingly ironic odd-couple pairing: **No. 11** (early 18th century) and **No. 9** (early 20th century). The mixture of architectural styles is similar to the Graben, but the general feel is low-key, as if the street were consciously deferring to its splendid view stopper, the dome over the Michaelerplatz entrance to the Imperial Palace (*see* Tour 4). Still, Kohlmarkt lingers in the memory when flashier streets have faded. In its conjunction with imperial pomp, it is self-assured without being self-conscious—exactly the right approach.

Time Out
㉑
Demel's (Kohlmarkt 14), Vienna's best-known (and priciest) pastry shop, offers a dizzying selection, and if you possess a sweet tooth, a visit will be worth every penny of the extra cost. Chocolate lovers will want to participate in the famous Viennese Sachertorte debate by sampling Demel's version and then comparing it with its rival at the Hotel Sacher (*see* Tour 5).

Tour 4: The Hofburg and the Ringstrasse

㉒ The Imperial Palace, known as the **Hofburg,** faces Kohlmarkt on the opposite side of Michaelerplatz. Until 1918 the Hofburg was the home of the Habsburgs, rulers of the Austro-Hungarian Empire; today it is a vast smorgasbord of sightseeing attractions: the Imperial Apartments, two Imperial treasuries, *six* museums, the National Library, and the famous Winter Riding School all vie for attention. The entire complex takes a minimum of a full day to explore in detail; if your time is limited (or if you want to save most of the interior sightseeing for a rainy day), you should omit the Imperial Apartments, the Court Silver and Tableware Treasury (now closed for renovation), and all the museums mentioned below except the Kunsthistorisches (the Museum of Art History). An excellent multilingual full-color booklet describing the palace in detail is on sale at most ticket counters within the complex; it gives a complete list of attractions and maps out the palace's complicated ground plan and building history wing by wing.

Architecturally, the Hofburg is (like St. Stephen's) far from refined. It grew up over a period of 700 years (its earliest mention in court documents is 1279, at the very beginning of Habsburg rule), and its spasmodic, haphazard growth kept it from attaining any sort of unified identity. But many of the bits and pieces are fine, and one interior (the National Library) is a tour de force.

The entrance on the Michaelerplatz leads to a domed rotunda; the **Silberkammer** (the Court Silver and Tableware Treasury) is to the right, while the **Imperial Apartments** are to the left. The former is much as might be expected, an extremely well stocked royal pantry turned royal museum, now closed for renovation. The latter, however, may come as a shock. The long, repetitive suite of conventionally luxurious rooms has a sad and poignant feel. The decoration (19th-century imitation of 18th-century Rococo) tries to look regal, but much like the Empire itself in its latter days, it is only going through the motions and ends up looking merely official. Among the few signs of genuine life are Emperor Franz Joseph's Spartan iron field bed, on which he slept every night, and the Empress Elizabeth's wooden gymnastics equipment, on which she exercised every morning. Amid all the tired splendor they look decidedly forlorn. *Silberkammer, tel. 0222/93424–099. Closed for renovation. Imperial Apartments, tel. 0222/587–5554–515. Admission: AS25; Open Mon.–Sat. 8:30–noon, 12:30–4; Sun. 8:30–12:30.*

The Hofburg (Imperial Palace)

0 150 yards
0 150 meters

Kärntner Strasse
Albertinaplatz
Hanuschgasse
Operngasse
Nibelungengasse
Elisabethstrasse
Opernring
Goethegasse
Burggarten
Augustinerstrasse
Albertina
Reitschulgasse
Michaelerplatz
Schauflergasse
Minoritenplatz
Bankgasse
Teinfaltstr.
Dr. Karl Lueger-Ring
Burgtheater
Löwelstrasse
Ballhausplatz
Volksgarten
Parliament
Dr. Karl Renner-Ring
Josefsplatz
Heldenplatz
Burgring
Fürichgasse

Augustinerkirche, 11
Burgtor, 22
Collection of Musical
Instruments, 19
Collection of
Weapons, 20
Emperor Joseph II
monument, 9

Ephesus Museum, 18
Ethnological
Museum, 21
Heldenplatz, 16
Hofbibliotek
Prunksaal, 12
Hofburgkapelle, 6

Imperial
Apartments, 2
In der Burg, 3
Josefsplatz, 8
Leopold Wing, 15
Neue Burg, 17
Schatzkammer, 7
Schweizertor, 4

Schweizer Hof, 5
Silberkammer, 1
Spanish (winter)
Riding School, 10
Stallburg, 13
Stallburghof
(courtyard), 14

On the far side of the rotunda is a large courtyard (known as In der Burg); set into the far left-hand wall is the **Schweizertor,** or Swiss Gate (dating from 1552 and decorated with some of the earliest classical motifs in the city), which leads through to the oldest section of the palace, a small courtyard known as the **Schweizer Hof.** In the southeast corner (at the top of the steps) is the entrance to the **Hofburgkapelle,** or Imperial Chapel, where the Vienna Boys' Choir sings Mass on Sundays and holidays from September to June (*see* Music in the Arts and Nightlife, below). At ground level is the entrance to the **Schatzkammer,** or Imperial Treasury, with its 1,000 years' of treasures. The display here is a welcome antidote to the monotony of the Imperial Apartments, for the entire Treasury was completely renovated in 1983–87, and the crowns and relics and vestments fairly glow in their new surroundings. *Schweizer Hof, tel. 0222/533–7931. Admission: AS60. Open Apr.–Oct., Mon. and Wed.–Fri. 10–6.*

A covered passageway leads from the Schweizer Hof into **Josefsplatz,** the most imposing of the Hofburg courtyards, with an equestrian monument (1807) to Emperor Joseph II in the center. To the left is the entrance to the **Spanische Reitschule,** the famous Spanish Riding School. Tickets to performances must be ordered in writing many weeks in advance, but daily practice is usually open to the public. The line starts forming at 9:30 for the opening at 10, but most sightseers are unaware that visitors may come and go as they please between 10 and noon, so it is often possible to walk right in between 11 and noon. The interior, the work of Fischer von Erlach the younger, is itself an attraction—surely Europe's most elegant sports arena— and if the prancing horses begin to pall, move up to the top balcony and examine the ceiling. *Josefsplatz 6, tel. 0222/533–9031. Admission: AS60 adults, AS15 children. Open mid-Feb.–June and Sept.–mid-Dec. (tour weeks excluded), Tues.–Sat. 10– noon.*

Across the square from the Riding School is the entrance to the **Augustinerkirche** (Church of the Augustinian Order), built during the 14th century and possessing the most unified Gothic interior in the city. But the church is something of a fraud; the interior, it turns out, dates from the late 18th century, not the early 14th. During the 1600s the old Gothic interior was completely remodeled in the Baroque style; then, at the beginning of the Gothic Revival in 1784, it was gutted and "restored" by the architect Ferdinand von Hohenberg.

A historical fraud the church may be, but a spiritual fraud it is not. The view from the entrance doorway is a stunner: a soaring harmony of vertical piers, ribbed vaults, and hanging chandeliers that makes Vienna's other Gothic interiors look earthbound by comparison. Farther inside, however, the effect is marred by a sculptural set piece against the right-hand wall: the memorial to the Archduchess Maria Christina (daughter of the Empress Maria Theresa), designed by Antonio Canova in 1798.

Back out on the square, a left turn from the Augustinerkirche exit leads to the entrance to the **Hofbibliothek Prunksaal** (the Gala Hall of the National Library), and a greater contrast between two interiors would be hard to imagine. The Augustinerkirche is one of the city's most restrained compositions; the

National Library is one of its most ornate. Designed by Fischer von Erlach the elder just before his death in 1723 and completed by his son, the Gala Hall is full-blown High Baroque, with trompe l'oeil ceiling frescoes by Daniel Gran taking over where the architecture flags. As usual, the frescoes are elaborately allegorical, the side ceilings are devoted to personifications of the sciences of peace and war, and the dome is devoted to a complicated symbolic glorification of the Emperor Charles VI, pictured in a medallion as supported by Apollo and Hercules.

The library may not be to everyone's taste. Certainly it is open to the charge of bombast, for only the central-oval balcony (with its elegantly squared and tapered supporting piers) suggests the special lightness and grace that serves, elsewhere in the city, as a counterbalance to conventional Baroque rhetoric. In the end it is the books themselves that come to the rescue. They are as lovingly displayed as the gilding and the frescoes, and they give the hall a warmth and humanity that the rest of the palace decidedly lacks. *Josefsplatz 1 (at the top of the stairs inside), tel. 0222/53410–397. Admission: AS15. Open May–Oct., Mon.–Sat. 10–4, Sun. 10–1; Nov.–Apr., Mon.–Sat. 10:30–noon.*

Walking back through the Schweizertor, turn left and walk under the Leopold Wing and out into the vast Heldenplatz. The long wing on the left is the youngest section of the palace, called the **Neue Burg.** It houses no less than four specialty museums: the **Ephesus Museum,** containing Roman antiquities unearthed by Austrian archaeologists in Turkey at the turn of the century; the **Collection of Musical Instruments,** including pianos that belonged to Beethoven, Brahms, Schumann, and Mahler; the **Collection of Weapons,** one of the most extensive arms-and-armor collections in the world; and the **Ethnological Museum,** devoted to anthropology (Montezuma's feathered headdress is a highlight of its collection). The first three museums are entered at the triumphal arch set into the middle of the curved portion of the facade; the Ethnological Museum is entered farther along, at the end pavilion. *Heldenplatz, tel. 0222/934541. Admission to Ephesus, Musical Instrument, and Weapons Museums on one ticket: AS30. Open Wed.–Mon. 10–4. Admission to Ethnological Museum: AS30. Open Mon. and Thurs.–Sat. 10–1, Wed. 10–5, Sun. 9–1.*

The Neue Burg stands today as a symbol of architectural overconfidence. Designed for Emperor Franz Joseph in 1869, it was part of a much larger scheme that was meant to make the Hofburg rival the Louvre, if not Versailles. The German architect Gottfried Semper planned a twin of the present Neue Burg on the opposite side of the Heldenplatz, with arches connecting the Neue Burg and its twin with the other pair of twins on the Ringstrasse, the Kunsthistorisches Museum (Museum of Art History) and the Naturhistorisches Museum (Museum of Natural History). But World War I intervened, and with the Empire's collapse the Neue Burg became merely the last in a long series of failed attempts to bring architectural order to the Hofburg.

The failure to complete the Hofburg building program left the Heldenplatz without a discernible shape, and today it's an amorphous sea of parked cars, with the Burgtor (the old main palace gate) stranded in the middle. On the other side of the Burgtor, across the Ringstrasse, is a much more successfully organized space, the **Maria-Theresien-Platz,** laid out in the 1870s around a matronly centerpiece monument to the matronly Empress Maria Theresa. To the west is the **Naturhistorisches Museum,** or Natural History Museum, home of, among other artifacts, the famous Venus of Willendorf, a tiny statuette thought to be some 20,000 years old. *Maria-Theresien-Platz tel. 0222/934541. Admission: AS30. Open Wed.–Mon. 9–6; in winter, ground floor only, 9–3.*

㉓ To the east is the **Kunsthistorisches Museum,** or Museum of Art History, housing one of the finest art collections in Europe. The collection was assembled by the ruling Habsburgs over several hundred years, and even a cursory description would run on for pages. Most of the great European old masters are represented, although many of the masterpieces are disgracefully dirty. Even the shortest list of highlights must include Rogier van der Weyden's *Crucifixion Triptych,* Raphael's *Madonna in the Meadow,* Holbein's *Portrait of Jane Seymour, Queen of England,* Titian's *Portrait of the Elector Johann Friedrich of Saxony,* the world-famous roomful of masterworks by Brueghel, Caravaggio's *Madonna of the Rosary,* a fine selection of Rembrandt portraits, and Vermeer's peerless *Allegory of the Art of Painting.* Benvenuto Cellini's famous gold saltcellar—certainly one of the most sumptuous pieces of tableware ever created—is on display amid the treasures of the applied-arts wing. *Maria-Theresien-Platz, tel. 0222/934541. Admission: AS45. Open Tues.–Sun. 10–6; Egyptian, antiques, and coin collections open Nov.–Mar., Tues.–Sun. 10–4; Apr.–Oct., Tues.–Sun. 10–6. Picture gallery open Tues. and Fri. evenings 7–9 (Mar.–Oct., 6–9).*

One block northwest of Maria-Theresien-Platz, walk west on Burggasse. The engaging 18th-century survivors at **Nos. 11 and 13** are adorned with religious and secular decorative sculpture, the latter with a niche statue of St. Joseph, the former with cherubic work-and-play bas reliefs. For several blocks around—walk down Gutenberggasse and back up Spittelberggasse—the 18th-century houses in the area have been beautifully restored (the entire area was scheduled for demolition in the 1970s but was saved by student protest). The sequence from **No. 5 to No. 19 Spittelberggasse** is an especially fine array of Viennese plain and fancy.

The huge, ominous concrete tower beyond the wall at the far end of Gutenberggasse is a grim reminder of World War II. It is **㉔** one of six **Flaktürme** (flak-towers) built in pairs around the city: concrete bunkers designed to withstand direct bombing hits and meant to serve as the Nazis' bastion of last resort against Allied attack. The towers remain standing because the only cost-effective means of demolishing them is dynamite, but any explosion powerful enough to do the job would damage the surrounding buildings.

Time Out Stop for a typical Viennese lunch at **Witwe Bolte** (Gutenberggasse 13), where in 1778, as noted on the arch just inside the entrance, the management unknowingly ejected Emperor Joseph II (apparently he was out for an incognito night on the town and was acting a bit strange). Good unpretentious Viennese food can also be found at **Boheme** (Spittelberggasse 19) and downstairs at **Zu ebener Erde und im ersten Stock** (Burggasse 13).

After continuing north from Spittelberggasse, take a right on Neustiftgasse and then cross Museumstrasse to Volksgartenstrasse; Volksgartenstrasse leads to the **Volksgarten,** on the east side of Dr.-Karl-Renner-Ring. The beautifully planted garden contains a little 19th-century Greek temple that offers an appropriate spot to sit for a few minutes and consider Vienna's most ambitious piece of 19th-century city planning: the famous **Ringstrasse.**

On December 20, 1857, Emperor Franz Josef issued a decree announcing the most ambitious piece of urban redevelopment Vienna had ever seen. The inner city's centuries-old walls were to be torn down, and the glacis—the wide expanse of open field that acted as a protective buffer between inner city and outer suburbs—was to be filled in. In their place was to rise a wide, tree-lined boulevard, upon which would stand an imposing collection of new buildings that would reflect Vienna's special status as the political, economic, and cultural heart of the Austro-Hungarian Empire.

During the 50 years of building that followed, many factors combined to produce the Ringstrasse as it now stands, but the most important was the gradual rise of liberalism after the failed Revolution of 1848. By the latter half of the Ringstrasse era, support for constitutional government, democracy, and equality—for all the concepts that liberalism traditionally equates with progress—was steadily increasing. As the turn of the century approached, the emperor's subjects were slowly but surely doing away with the Empire's long-standing tradition of absolute imperial power, and it looked as if the transition from absolute to constitutional monarchy would be peaceful and unchallenged. Liberal Viennese voters could point with pride to a number of important civic improvements: The Danube was controlled and canalized, a comprehensive municipal water-supply system was constructed, a public-health system was established, and the countryside bordering the city (including the Vienna Woods) was protected by new zoning laws. As it went up, the Ringstrasse stood as the definitive symbol of this liberal progress; as Carl E. Schorske put it in his *Fin-de-Siècle Vienna*, it celebrated "the triumph of constitutional *Recht* right over Imperial *Macht* might, of secular culture over religious faith. Not palaces, garrisons, and churches, but centers of constitutional government and higher culture dominated the Ring."

But what should these centers of culture look like? The answer was the result of a new passion among the intelligentsia: architectural Historicism. Greek temples, it was argued, reminded the viewer of the cradle of democracy; what could be more appropriate than a Parliament building designed in Greek Revival style? Gothic architecture, on the other hand, betokened the rule of the church and the rise of the great medieval city-states; the new Votive Church and the new City Hall would therefore be Gothic Revival. And the Renaissance Era, which produced the unprecedented flowering of learning and creativity that put an end to the Middle Ages, was most admired of all; therefore, the new centers of high culture—the museums, the theaters, and the university—would be Renaissance Revival.

In building after building, architectural style was dictated by historical association, and gradually the Ringstrasse of today took shape.

The highest concentration of public building occurred in the area around the Volksgarten, where are clustered (moving from south to north, from Burgring to Schottenring) the **Museum of Art History,** the **Museum of Natural History,** the **(26) (27)** **Justizpalast** (Palace of Justice), the **Parlament** (Parliament), **(28) (29)** the **Rathaus** (City Hall), the **Burgtheater** (National Theater), **(30) (31)** the **Universität** (University of Vienna), and the **Votivkirche.** As an ensemble, the collection is astonishing in its architectural presumption: It is nothing less than an attempt to assimilate and summarize the entire architectural history of Europe. As critics were quick to notice, however, the complex suffers from a serious organizational flaw: Most of the buildings lack effective context. Rather than being the focal points of an organized overall plan, they are plunked haphazardly down on an avenue that is itself too wide to possess a unified, visually comprehensible character. In such surroundings, the buildings' monumental size works against them, and they end up looking like so many beached whales washed up on the inner-city shore.

The individual buildings, too, came in for immediate criticism. The Gothic Revival design of the City Hall, for instance, produced an interior so dark that large parts of it had to be fully lit all day long; the National Theater auditorium was so incompetently designed (bad sight lines and worse acoustics) that it had to be thoroughly reworked a few years later. And the Greek Revival Parliament building emerged looking monolithic and ponderous—traits more characteristic of bad bureaucracy than good government. The City Hall and the National Theater present the best face; they, at least, are sensibly placed, nodding soberly to each other across the Rathausplatz. But it is hard, when exploring the avenue, not to be oppressed by the overbearing monumentality of it all.

Exploring the Ringstrasse complex requires a considerable amount of time, but two attractions beyond the Votive Church at the Schottenring end deserve mention: Sigmund Freud's apartment (now a museum) and the Museum of Modern Art.

(32) **Freud's Apartment** at Berggasse 19 (Apt. 6, one flight up; ring the bell and push the door simultaneously) was his residence from 1891 to 1938. The three-room collection of memorabilia is mostly a photographic record of Freud's life, with some documents, publications, and a portion of his collection of antiquities also on display. The waiting-room furniture is authentic, but the consulting-room and study furniture (including the famous couch) can be seen only in photographs. *Berggasse 19, tel. 0222/311596. Admission: AS30. Open daily 9–3.*

(33) The **Museum Moderner Kunst** (Museum of Modern Art) is at Fürstengasse 1, three blocks north of Freud's apartment. The large 18th-century mansion was originally the Liechtenstein Summer Palace; today it houses the national collection of 20th-century art. Artists from Gustav Klimt to Robert Rauschenberg and Nam June Paik are represented, and a more inappropriate environment for modern art would be hard to imagine. Twentieth-century art and 18th-century architecture here declare war on each other and fight to an uneasy draw. Still, if you can shut out the architecture (or the art, depending on your taste), the museum is well worth a visit. *Fürsten-gasse 1, tel. 0222/341259. Admission: AS30. Open Wed.–Mon. 10–6.*

Tour 5: From St. Stephen's to the Opera

From the tall south tower of St. Stephen's Cathedral, the short Churhausgasse leads south to Singerstrasse. Two 18th-cent-ury palaces on this street are worth noting: the **Neupauer-Breuner Palace,** at No. 16 (1715, architect unknown), with its monumental entranceway and inventively delicate windows, and the **Rottal Palace,** at No. 17 (1750, attributed to Hilde-brandt), with its wealth of classical wall-motifs. For a contrast, turn up the narrow Blutgasse, with its simple 18th-century fa-cades. The little building at No. 3 is especially appealing, for it looks as if it's being bullied by the buildings on either side and has buckled under the pressure.

Blutgasse ends at Domgasse; at No. 5 is the **Figarohaus,** one of Mozart's 11 rented Viennese residences. It was here that he wrote *The Marriage of Figaro* and the six quartets dedicated to Joseph Haydn; the apartment he occupied now contains a small commemorative museum. *Domgasse 5, tel. 0222/513–6294. Ad-mission: AS15. Open Tues.–Sun. 10–12:15 and 1–4:30.*

At the east end of Singerstrasse the 19th century takes over and the 18th-century interplay between strength and delicacy disappears. Monumentality has won out, as can be seen at the **Coburg Palace** (1843) on Seilerstätte. The Coburg facade lacks all sense of play compared to the Neupauer-Breuner and Rottal palaces. Its garden side, however, boasts a fine historical curi-osity: a section of the ancient Viennese city walls, one of the few that managed to escape demolition during the construction of the Ringstrasse.

Two blocks south of the Coburg Palace, turn west on Himmel-pfortgasse. The modest house at **No. 15** possesses a curlicued gable that derives from the facade of the Dominikanerkirche (*see* Tour 1); the interior passageway remains much as it was 150 years ago—woodpile, communal water basin, Biedermeier carriage, and all. Next door, at No. 13, the **Erdödy-Fürstenberg Palace** (1724) has design motifs mostly lifted from the Neupauer-Breuner Palace. The beautiful yellow-and-cream paint job gives the facade a finish that the architecturally more sophisticated Neupauer-Breuner lacks.

Also sporting a fine painted (and in places gilded) exterior is the **Ministry of Finance** at No. 8. Designed by Fischer von Erlach in 1697 and later expanded by Hildebrandt, the building was originally the town palace of Prince Eugene of Savoy, who, as commander-in-chief of the Imperial Army in the War of the Spanish Succession, led Austrian forces (alongside the English under the Duke of Marlborough) to victory over the French at the Battle of Blenheim in 1704. The Baroque details here are among the most inventively conceived and beautifully executed in the city. The large windows carry elegantly crafted pedi-ments that are more like top hats than eyebrows, and all the decorative motifs are so softly carved that they appear to have been freshly squeezed from a pastry tube. The Viennese are lovers of the baroque in both their architecture and their pas-try, and here the two passions seem visibly merged.

From Himmelpfortgasse, turn right onto Rauhensteingasse and then immediately right on Ballgasse, which winds to the left and then dwindles down to a short arched passageway leading into Franziskanerplatz. The **Moses Fountain** in the center of the square dates from 1798; the small **Franziskanerkirche** on the east side is an international hybrid, with a facade (1603) that imitates German churches of the early Renaissance and a later interior that imitates Italian churches of the Baroque. The small shopping arcade at the garishly painted No. 6 is worth exploring for its disturbingly surreal decoration.

From Franziskanerplatz, Weihburggasse leads west to **Kärntner Strasse,** Vienna's premier shopping street. These days Kärntner Strasse is much maligned. Too commercial, too crowded, too many tasteless signs, too much gaudy neon—the complaints go on and on. Nevertheless, the Viennese continue to arrive regularly for their evening promenade, and it is easy to see why. Vulgar the street may be, but it is also alive and vital, possessing an energy that the more tasteful Graben and the impeccable Kohlmarkt lack. For the sightseer beginning to suffer from art-history overdose, a Kärntner Strasse window-shopping break will be welcome.

The short Donnergasse (across Kärntner Strasse from Himmelpfortgasse) leads into Neuer Markt. The square's centerpiece, Georg Raphael Donner's **Providence Fountain,** has not had a happy life. Put up in 1739, it was at the time the very latest word in civic improvements, with elegantly mannered nude statuary meant to personify the Danube and four of its tributaries. The Empress Maria Theresa, however, was offended; despite having had 16 children, she disapproved of nudity in art. The figures were removed and stored away and later nearly melted down for munitions. They were finally restored in 1801, but were once again moved away (to be replaced by the present copies) in 1873. The original figures can be studied in quiet at the Lower Belvedere Palace (*see* Tour 6).

38 The church at the southwest corner of the Neuer Markt is the Kapuzinerkirche; in its basement (entrance to the left of the church) is the **Kaisergruft,** or Imperial Burial Vault. The crypts contain the partial remains of some 140 Habsburgs (the hearts are in the Augustinerkirche and the entrails in St. Stephen's) plus one non-Habsburg governess ("She was always with us in life," said Maria Theresa, "why not in death?"). The sarcophagi are often elaborate and occasionally bizarre: Maria Theresa is shown in bed with her husband awaking to the Last Judgment as if it were just another weekday morning, while the remains of her son (the ascetic Joseph II) lie in a simple casket at the foot of the bed as if he were the family dog. *Neuer Markt, tel. 0222/ 512–6853–12. Admission: AS30. Open daily 9:30–4.*

39 From the southwest corner of Neuer Markt, walk south on Tegetthofstrasse to Albertinaplatz. On the square's west side the **Albertina Museum** houses a vast collection of drawings and prints dating to the 15th century. Because of their fragility, only a very small selection of the more than 200,000 pieces of art is on view at any one time, and most of the famous works (for example, Albrecht Durer's *Praying Hands*) must usually be viewed in reproduction. *Augustinerstr. 1, tel. 0222/53483. Admission: AS30. Open Mon., Tues., Thurs. 10–4; Wed. 10–6; Fri. 10–2; Sat. and Sun. 10–1; closed Sun. July and Aug.*

Time Out   Take a coffee break at one of three nearby cafés. The **Café Sacher,** in the Hotel Sacher on Philharmonikerstrasse—the street leading east from the south end of Albertinaplatz—is the most formal of the three (no shorts allowed inside during the summer); its famous Sachertorte can also be purchased at a small Kärntner Strasse shop on the hotel's east side. The **Café Mozart,** on the hotel's west side, opposite the Albertina, is almost as elegant as the Sacher, while the **Café Tirolerhof,** on the north side of Albertinaplatz, is a less upscale (but more typically Viennese) alternative.

From the north end of Albertinaplatz, Führichgasse leads east across Kärntner Strasse to Annagasse. The small neighborhood church at No. 2, the **Annakirche,** possesses a fine bulbous dome atop its tower and an unusually consistent Baroque decorative scheme inside, but the main attraction is the curved street itself, with its fine collection of unpretentious facades. The high point, undoubtedly, is **No. 14,** with its carved frieze of impish, gossiping cherubs. The poses here are conventional, but the execution is not, for the frieze achieves with ease the spontaneity that Baroque sculpture always sought but too often failed to find.

Return to Kärntner Strasse, and follow it south to the Ringstrasse. The building on the right, facing Opernring, is the famous Vienna **Opera House.** The first of the Ringstrasse projects to be completed (in 1869), it suffered severe bomb damage during World War II (only the front facade and the main staircase area behind it survived). Though it was rebuilt, it remains something of a shell, for the cost of fully restoring the 19th-century interior decor was prohibitive. Tours of the Opera are given regularly, but starting times vary according to opera rehearsals; the current schedule is usually posted at the west side entrance, where the tours begin.

The construction of the Opera is the stuff of legend. When the foundation was laid, the plans for Opernring were not yet complete, and in the end the avenue turned out to be several feet higher than originally planned. As a result, the Opera lacked the commanding prospect that its architects, Eduard van der Nüll and August Sicard von Sicardsburg, had intended, and even Emperor Franz Josef pronounced the building a bit low to the ground. For the sensitive van der Nüll (and here the story becomes a bit suspect), failing his beloved emperor was the last straw. In disgrace and despair, he committed suicide. Sicardsburg died of grief shortly thereafter. And the emperor, horrified at the deaths his innocuous remark had caused, limited all his future artistic pronouncements to a single immutable formula: *Es war sehr schön, es hat mich sehr gefreut* ("It was very nice, it pleased me very much").

Tour 6: South of the Ring to the Belvedere

Two blocks southwest of the Opera, facing the Schillerplatz, the **Academy of Fine Arts** was built in the later 19th century to house an institution founded in 1692. The academy's Renaissance Revival architecture was meant to instill in its students an appreciation of the past; traditional standards were staunchly maintained here in the face of the artistic rebellions of the early 20th century. In 1907 and again in 1908, an aspiring artist named Adolf Hitler was refused admission on the grounds of insufficient talent. Today the academy contains an old-master art collection that will be of interest mostly to specialists, the one exception being Hieronymus Bosch's famous *Last Judgment* triptych, which more than makes up in horrific imagination what it lacks in painterly sophistication. *Schillerplatz 3, tel. 0222/58816. Admission: AS15. Open Tues., Thurs., Fri. 10–2; Wed. 10–1, 3–6; weekends 9–1.*

If the Academy of Fine Arts represents the conservative attitude of the arts in the late 1800s, then its antithesis can be **42** found immediately behind it to the southeast: the **Secession Building.** Restored in the mid-1980s after years of neglect, the Secession Building is one of Vienna's preeminent symbols of artistic rebellion; rather than look to the architecture of the past like the revivalist Ringstrasse, it looked to a new anti-Historicist future. It was, in its day, a riveting trumpetblast of a building, today considered by many to be Europe's first piece of full-blown 20th-century architecture.

The Secession movement began in 1897 when 20 dissatisfied Viennese artists headed by Gustav Klimt "seceded" from the Künstlerhausgenossenschaft, the conservative artists' society associated with the Academy of Fine Arts. The movement promoted the radically new kind of art known as Jugendstil, which found its inspiration in both the organic, fluid designs of Art Nouveau and the related but more geometric designs of the English Arts and Crafts movement. (The Secessionists founded an arts-and-crafts workshop of their own, the famous Wiener Werkstätte, in an effort to embrace the applied arts.) The Secession Building was the movement's exhibition hall, designed by the architect Joseph Olbrich and completed in 1898. The lower story, crowned by the entrance motto *Der Zeit Ihre Kunst, Der Kunst Ihre Freiheit* (To Every Age Its Art, To Art Its Freedom), is classic Jugendstil: The restrained but assured decoration (by Koloman Moser) beautifully complements the facade's pristine flat expanses of cream-colored wall. Above the entrance motto sits the building's most famous feature, the gilded openwork dome that the Viennese were quick to christen "the golden cabbage" (Olbrich wanted it to be seen as a dome of laurel, a subtle classical reference meant to celebrate the triumph of art). The plain white interior—"shining and chaste," in Olbrich's words—was also revolutionary; its most unusual feature was movable walls, allowing the galleries to be reshaped and redesigned for every show. One early show, in 1902, was an exhibition devoted to art celebrating the genius of Beethoven; Gustav Klimt's *Beethoven Frieze*, painted for the occasion, has now been restored and is permanently installed in the building's basement. *Friedrichstr. 12, tel. 0222/587–5307. Admission: AS40, Beethoven Frieze only: AS15. Open Tues.– Fri. 10–6, weekends 10–4.*

To the south of the Secession Building run two parallel streets, the Linke (left) and Rechte (right) Wienzeile. Farther to the south, the River Wien, a tributary of the Danube, runs between them, but here the river was covered over at the turn of the century. The site is now home to the Naschmarkt, Vienna's main outdoor produce market.

Time Out Explore the **Naschmarkt** and pick up a meal as you go. The stands marked *Imbisse* (Snack) will sell you a *Hühnerschnitzel-Semmel* (chicken schnitzel inside a Viennese roll), the **Meeres-**

Buffet offers a vast array of seafood, **Heindl & Co. Palat-
schinkenkuch'l** (pancake kitchen) sells a wide variety of meat
and dessert crepes, and the **Naschmarkt Bäckerei** can supply
the necessary pastry. If you want a more leisurely sit-down
meal, try **Sopherl,** a favorite hangout of Naschmarkt vendors,
on Linke Wienzeile on the market's west side.

The Ringstrasse-style apartment houses that line Linke
Wienzeile are mostly an undistinguished lot, but four blocks
south of the Secession Building, two unexpectedly stand out:
Nos. 38 and 40, designed (1898–99) by the grand old man of
Viennese fin-de-siècle architecture, Otto Wagner, during his
Secessionist phase.

A good example of what Wagner was rebelling against can be
seen next door, at **No. 42,** where Baroque decorative enthusiasm has degenerated into Baroque Revival decorative hysteria,
and the overwrought facade seems to drown in a jumble of classical motifs. Wagner had come to believe that this sort of display was nothing but empty pretense and sham; modern
apartment houses, he wrote in his pioneering text *Modern
Architecture,* are entirely different from 18th-century town
palaces, and architects should not pretend otherwise. Accordingly, Wagner banished classical decoration and introduced a
new architectural simplicity, with flat exterior walls and plain,
regular window treatments meant to reflect the orderly layout
of the apartments behind them. For decoration, he turned to
his younger Secessionist cohorts Joseph Olbrich and Koloman
Moser, who designed the ornate Jugendstil patterns of red ma-
jolica-tile roses and gold stucco medallions that brighten the facades of Nos. 38 and 40. The crisp facades that resulted make
the huffing-and-puffing classicism next door look tired and
dowdy.

More of Wagner's secessionist work can be seen two blocks east
of the Secession Building on the northern edge of Karlsplatz. In
1893 Wagner was appointed architectural supervisor of the
new Vienna City Railway, and the matched **pair of small pavilions** he designed for the Karlsplatz station in 1898 are among
the city's most ingratiating buildings. Their structural frame-
work is frankly exposed (in keeping with Wagner's belief in architectural honesty), but they are also lovingly decorated (in
keeping with the Viennese love of architectural finery). And
Wagner's chronic failing—a pretentious desire to impress—is
entirely absent. The result is Jugendstil at its very best, meld-
ing plain and fancy with grace and insouciance.

Like the space now occupied by the Naschmarkt, the Karlsplatz was formed when the River Wien was covered over at the
turn of the century. At the time Wagner expressed his frustra-
tion with the result—too large a space for a formal square and
too small a space for an informal park—and the awkwardness
persists to this day. The buildings surrounding the Karlsplatz,
on the other hand, are quite sure of themselves: on the south
side the **Technical University** (1816–18) and on the north side
the **Kunstlerhaus** (the exhibition hall in which the Secessionists
refused to exhibit, built in 1881 and still in use) and the
Musikverein (finished in 1869, now home to the Vienna Philharmonic). Much the most important building, however, is the oldest: the Church of Saint Charles Borromeo, familiarly known as
43 the **Karlskirche,** built in the early 18th century on what was

then the bank of the River Wien and is now the Karlsplatz's southeast corner.

The church had its beginnings in a disaster. In 1713, Vienna was hit by a brutal plague outbreak, and Emperor Charles VI made a vow: If the plague abated, he would build a church dedicated to his namesake Saint Charles Borromeo, the 16th-century Italian bishop who was famous for his ministrations to Milanese plague victims. In 1715 construction began, using an the ambitious design by Johann Bernhard Fischer von Erlach that combined architectural elements from ancient Greece (the columned entrance porch), ancient Rome (the freestanding columns, modeled after Trajan's Column), contemporary Rome (the Baroque dome), and contemporary Vienna (the Baroque towers at either end). When it was finished, the church received (and continues to receive) a decidedly mixed press. Some critics view the facade as an unqualified success, a masterpiece that fuses its disparate elements into a triumphantly unified whole. Others think it a failure, contending that the visual weight of the Baroque dome seems to crush the Greek-temple porch below, and that the freestanding columns cut off the end towers, setting them uncomfortably adrift. History, incidentally, delivered a negative verdict: In its day the Karlskirche spawned no imitations, and it went on to become one of European architecture's most famous curiosities.

The main interior of the church utilizes only the area under the dome, and is surprisingly conventional given the unorthodox facade. The space and architectural detailing are typical High Baroque; the fine vault frescoes, by J. M. Rottmayr (1725-1730), depict Saint Charles Borromeo imploring the Holy Trinity to end the plague.

44 Finally, one last Karlsplatz building remains: the **Historisches Museum der Stadt Wien** (Museum of Viennese History), hidden away at the east end of the square next to the Karlskirche. The museum possesses a dazzling array of Viennese historical artifacts and treasures, all beautifully organized and displayed: models, maps, documents, photographs, antiquities, stained glass, paintings, sculpture, crafts, mementos, reconstructed rooms. For once, urban history is lovingly and comprehensively served. This is, it turns out, one of the finest museums in Europe, and the most woefully undervisited attraction in all Vienna. *Karlsplatz, tel. 0222/505–8747. Admission: AS30. Open Tues.–Sun. 9–4:30.*

Beyond the Karlsplatz to the east is the **French Embassy,** built in 1909 in an Art Nouveau style that offers a clear contrast to the more geometric Austrian Jugendstil. Beyond the embassy lies **Schwarzenbergplatz.** The militant monument occupying the south end of the square is the **Russian War Memorial,** set up at the end of World War II by the Soviets; the Viennese, remembering the Soviet occupation, call its unknown soldier "the unknown plunderer." South of the memorial is the formidable **Schwarzenberg Palace,** designed by Johann Lukas von Hildebrandt in 1697 and now (in part) a luxury hotel.

45 Hildebrandt's most important Viennese work is farther along, at Rennweg 6A: the **Belvedere Palace.** In fact the Belvedere is two palaces with extensive gardens between. Built just outside the city fortifications between 1714 and 1722, the complex originally served as the summer palace of Prince Eugene of Savoy;

much later it became the home of Archduke Franz Ferdinand, whose assassination in 1914 precipitated World War I. Though the lower palace is impressive in its own right (it served as Prince Eugene's living quarters), it is the much larger upper palace, used for state receptions, banquets, and balls, that is Hildebrandt's acknowledged masterpiece.

Best approached through the gardens, the upper palace displays a remarkable wealth of architectural invention in its facade. The main design problem—common to all palaces because of their excessive size—is to avoid monotony on the one hand and pomposity on the other. Hildebrandt's solution is inspired. To ward off monotony, he has varied the building's upper story and roof line so as to create seven separate compositions, all variations on the same central theme and all arranged in a gradual *diminuendo* from the center outward, with accented ends to supply the coda. To ward off pomposity, he has created an overall decorative scheme that possesses both variety and balance: Each section of the facade is given its own set of decorative motifs, but in all cases the decoration grows more complex with each story, with the upper story given less height so that its decorative complexity does not overwhelm the simpler stories below.

Hildebrandt's decoration here approaches the Rococo, that final style of the Baroque era when traditional classical motifs all but disappeared in a whirlwind of seductive asymmetric fancy. The main interiors of the palace go even further: Columns are transformed into muscle-bound giants, pilasters grow torsos, capitals sprout great piles of symbolic Imperial paraphernalia, and the ceilings are set aswirl with molded stucco. The result is the finest Rococo interior in the city.

One other architectural detail is especially worthy of notice, on the facade of the south side of the palace (actually the front, facing away from the center city). Hildebrandt here added an extra fillip: an exuberantly decorated entrance porch topped with a luscious dollop-of-whipped-cream pediment. It was a motif he clearly loved, for he used it repeatedly, and today it is considered his architectural signature.

Today both the upper and lower palaces are museums devoted to Austrian painting. **The Austrian Museum of Baroque Art,** in the lower palace, displays Austrian art of the 18th century (including the original figures from Georg Raphael Donner's *Providence Fountain* in the Neuer Markt). Next to the Baroque Museum (outside the west end) is the converted Orangerie, devoted to works of the medieval period. The main attraction, however, is the upper palace's collection of **19th- and 20th-century Austrian paintings,** centering on the work of Vienna's three preeminent early 20th-century artists: Gustav Klimt, Egon Schiele, and Oskar Kokoschka. Klimt was the oldest, and by the time he helped found the Secession movement, he had forged a highly idiosyncratic painting style that combined realistic and decorative elements in a way that was completely revolutionary. Schiele and Kokoschka went even further; rejecting the decorative appeal of Klimt's glittering abstract designs and producing works that completely ignored conventional ideas of beauty. Today they are considered the fathers of modern art in Vienna. (The Kokoschka collection has recently been moved to the Lower Belvedere Stables, reached through the Baroque Museum; one hopes that this quarantine is only temporary.) *Tel. 0222/784158. Admission: AS30. Open Tues.–Sun. 10–5.*

Tour 7: Schönbrunn Palace

Schönbrunn Palace, the huge Habsburg summer palace laid out by Johann Bernhard Fischer von Erlach in 1696, lies well within the city limits, just a few subway stops west of Karlsplatz on line U4. The vast and elegantly planted gardens are open daily from dawn till dusk, and multilingual guided tours of the palace interior take place daily. The **Wagenburg** (Imperial Coach Collection) can be seen in the west wing, entered at the far end of the small courtyard off the southwest corner of the main courtyard, and the **Tiergarten** (the Imperial Menagerie, now the Vienna Zoo), founded in 1752 during the reign of Maria Theresa, is on the west side of the gardens.

The best approach to the palace and its gardens is through the front gate, located on Schönbrunner Schloss-Strasse halfway between the Schönbrunn and Hietzing subway stations. The vast main courtyard is ruled by a formal design of impeccable order and rigorous symmetry: Wing nods at wing, facade mirrors facade, and every part stylistically complements every other. The courtyard, however, turns out to be merely appetizer; the feast lies beyond. The breathtaking view that unfolds on the other side of the palace is one of the finest set pieces in all Europe and one of the supreme achievements of Baroque planning. Formal *allées* (garden promenades) shoot off diagonally, the one on the right toward the Zoo, the one on the left toward a rock-mounted obelisk and a fine false Roman ruin. But these, and the woods beyond, are merely a frame for the astonishing composition in the center: the sculpted fountain, the carefully planted screen of trees behind, the sudden almost vertical rise of the grass-covered hill beyond. And at the crest of the hill, topping it all off, sits a Baroque masterstroke: Johann Ferdinand von Hohenberg's incomparable **Gloriette.** Perfectly scaled for its setting, the Gloriette holds the whole vast garden composition together, and at the same time crowns the ensemble with a brilliant architectural tiara.

The 18th century was the Age of Reason, and its obsession with order produced elaborately formal gardens all over Europe. But Schönbrunn is exceptional, for here architecture combines with nature—man puts his stamp on God's design—with an assurance and an elegance that the 18th century rarely, if ever, surpassed.

After the superb gardens, the palace interior comes as something of an anticlimax. Of the 1,400 rooms, 45 are open to the public, and two are of special note: the Hall of Mirrors, where the six-year-old Mozart performed for the Empress Maria Theresa in 1762, and the Grand Gallery, where the Congress of Vienna (1815) danced at night after carving up Napoleon's collapsed empire during the day. The most unusual interior at Schönbrunn, however, is not within the palace at all. It is the newly restored Imperial subway station, known as the **Hofpavillon,** located just outside the palace grounds (at the northwest corner, a few yards east of the Hietzing subway station). Designed by Otto Wagner in conjunction with Joseph Olbrich and Leopold Bauer, the Hofpavillon was built in 1899 for the exclusive use of the Emperor Franz Josef and his entourage. The exterior, with its proud architectural crown, is Wagner at his best, and the lustrous interior is one of the finest examples of Jugendstil decoration in the city. The building is little more than a single enclosed room, but it is a true gem. *Schönbrunner Schloss-Str., subway stop Schönbrunn, tel. 0222/81113–238. Guided tours of palace interior AS50. Open Apr.–June and Oct., daily 8:30–5; July–Sept., daily 8:30–5:30; Nov.–Mar., daily 9–4. Gloriette roof admission: AS10. Open May–Oct., daily 8–6. Wagenburg, tel. 0222/823244. Admission: AS30. Open Tues.–Sun., Oct.–Apr., 10–4; May–Sept. 10–5. Tiergarten subway stop Hietzing, tel. 0222/837–1206. Admission: AS35, children AS10. Open daily 9–dusk, 6 PM the latest. Hofpavillon, Schönbrunner Schloss-Str. 13, tel. 0222/877–1571. Admission: AS15. Open Tues.–Sun. 9–12:15, 1–4:30.*

The vast **Technical Museum,** located close by though not within the Schönbrunn grounds, houses the world's first sewing machine, the first typewriter (and later models), the first gasoline-powered car, early airplanes, an outstanding collection of steam locomotives and railroad cars, a coal mine you can go through, and many other technical exhibits that include aluminum smelting and a collection of musical instruments. History and circumstances intervened in 1918, just as the museum opened to showcase Austrian industry, so that in some industries—papermaking, for example—models that were up to date then are now fascinating relics of the past. Changing shows supplement the fixed exhibits. *Mariahilfer Str. 212, tel. 0222/891010. Admission: AS30 adults, AS15 children. Open Sun.–Fri. 9–4:30. Subway stop Schönbrunn, or No. 52 or 58 streetcar to Technisches Museum.*

Vienna for Free

Vienna is not famous for its sightseeing generosity—there is even an admission charge when the Vienna Boys' Choir sings Mass at the Hofburgkapelle (in fairness, however, it should be noted that the musical masses at the nearby Augustinerkirche are free). The city's many public parks are the main no-cost attraction, notably the **Schönbrunn Gardens** (*see* Tour 7), the **Volksgarten** (*see* Tour 4), and the **Belvedere Gardens** (*see* Tour 6). In addition, the **Stadtpark** (on the Ringstrasse near its east end) offers early-evening band concerts in the summer; it also contains some fine turn-of-the-century architecture and a frothy monument to Johann Strauss. The beautifully planted **Burggarten** (on the east side of the Neue Burg) is flanked at its north end by the Imperial greenhouses, built in 1905. The famed **Wienerwald** (Vienna Woods) is not a park but a series of low wooded hills west of the city, actually the easternmost foothills of the Alps. Exploring the woods in fine weather is a time-honored Viennese pastime; the view of the city and the Danube from the Leopoldsberg Hill is especially beloved.

What to See and Do with Children

Vienna's main attraction for children is the famous **Wurstelprater** (or Volksprater), Vienna's foremost amusement park (at the Prater's north end; take the U1 subway line to Praterstern). It has all the traditional modern amusementpark rides plus a number of less innocent indoor, sex-oriented attractions and a museum devoted to the Wurstelprater's long history. The best-known attraction is the giant Ferris wheel that figured so prominently in the 1949 film *The Third Man*. One of three built in Europe at the end of the last century (the others were in England and France but have long since been dismantled), the wheel was badly damaged during World War II and restored shortly thereafter. Its progress is slow and stately, the views from its cars magnificent.

The **Vienna Zoo** will also appeal and possesses the added advantage of being located in the Schönbrunn Gardens (*see* Tour 7). In the basement of the **Theater Museum** is a children's museum that is reached by a slide (Lobkowitzpl., tel. 0222/512–3705). Also see the specialty museums, below. Lesser attractions include the **Museum of Natural History** (*see* Tour 4) and a notably bizarre **aquarium,** grotesquely housed in a World War II flak-tower in the middle of the tiny Esterhazy Park between Mariahilfer Strasse and Gumpendorferstrasse (tel. 0222/587–1417; admission: AS15; open daily 9–6). Finally, the climb to the top of the **south tower of St. Stephen's Cathedral** (*see* Tour 1) should work up an appetite for a visit, if the pocketbook allows, to **Demel's** (Kohlmarkt 14), Vienna's most famous pastry shop, where all children should at least once in their lives be allowed to eat themselves sick.

Off the Beaten Track

Vienna's most exalted piece of Jugendstil architecture is not in the inner city but in the suburbs to the west: the **Am Steinhof Church,** designed by Otto Wagner in 1904 during his Secessionist phase. Built on the grounds of the Lower Austrian State Asylum (now the Vienna City Psychiatric Hospital), Wagner's design united mundane functional details (rounded edges on the pews to prevent injury to the patients and a slightly sloped tile floor to facilitate cleaning) with a soaring, airy dome and glittering Jugendstil decoration (mosaics by Remigius Geyling and stained glass by Koloman Moser). The church is open once a week for guided tours (in German). *Baumgartner Höhe 1, tel. 0222/949060–2391. Admission free. Open Sat. 3–4. Subway stop: Unter-St.-Veit, then No. 47A bus to Psychiatrisches Krankenhaus.*

Music lovers will want to make a pilgrimage to the **Zentralfriedhof** (Central Cemetery, in the 11th District on Simmeringer Hauptstrasse), which contains the graves of most of Vienna's great composers, some moved here from other cemeteries: Ludwig van Beethoven, Franz Schubert, Johannes Brahms, the Johann Strausses (father and son), and Arnold Schönberg, among others. The monument to Wolfgang Amadeus Mozart is a memorial only; the approximate location of his actual burial, in an unmarked grave, can be seen at the now deconsecrated St. Marx-Friedhof at Leberstrasse 6–8; *streetcar 71.*

Musical residences abound as well. Schubert—a native to the city, unlike most of Vienna's other famous composers—was born at Nussdorferstrasse 54 (tel 0222/345–9924), in the Ninth District, and died in the Fourth District at Kettenbrückengasse 6 (tel. 0222/573–9072). Joseph Haydn's house is at Haydngasse 19 (tel. 0222/596–1307) in the Sixth District; Beethoven's Heiligenstadt residence, where at age 32 he wrote the "Heiligenstadt Testament," an anguished cry of pain and protest against his ever-increasing deafness, is at Probusgasse 6 in the 19th District (tel. 0222/375–408). Finally, the home of the most popular composer of all, waltz king Johann Strauss the younger, can be visited at Praterstrasse 54 (tel. 0222/240–121), in the Second District; he lived here when he composed "The Blue Danube Waltz" in 1867. All the above houses contain commemorative museums (Admission: AS15. Open Tues.–Sun. 9–12:15 and 1–4:30).

Two museums not covered on the walking tours are of special note: the **Museum of Applied Arts** (on the Ring at Stubenring 5; tel. 0222/71136; admission AS30; open Wed.–Mon. 11–6) contains a large collection of Austrian furniture and art objects; the Jugendstil display devoted to Josef Hoffman and his followers at the Wiener Werkstätte is particularly fine. And the **Museum of Military History** (south of the Belvedere on Ghegastr.; tel. 0222/782303; admission AS30: open Sat.–Thurs. 10–4) contains a vast array of Austro-Hungarian military relics and mementos, including the car in which Archduke Franz Ferdinand was riding when he was assassinated in 1914 at Sarajevo.

Sightseeing Checklists

This list includes both attractions that were covered in the preceding tours and additional ones that are described here for the first time.

Historic Buildings and Sights

Beethoven Heiligenstadt residence (*see* Off the Beaten Track). *Subway stop: Heiligenstadt, then No. 38A bus to Armbrustergasse.*
Café Central (*see* Tour 2). *Subway stop: Stephansplatz.*
Café Hawelka (*see* Tour 3). *Subway stop: Stephansplatz.*
City Hall (*see* Tour 4). *Subway stop: Rathaus.*
Dorotheum (Auction House; *see* Tour 3). *Subway stop: Stephansplatz.*
Figarohaus (Mozart Residence; *see* Tour 5). *Subway stop: Stephansplatz.*
Freud's Apartment (*see* Tour 4). *Subway stop: Schottentor.*
Haydn Residence (*see* Off the Beaten Track). *Subway stop: Pilgramgasse.*
Hofburg (Habsburg Imperial Palace; *see* Tour 4). *Subway stop: Herrengasse.*
Hofpavillon (*see* Tour 7). *Subway stop: Hietzing.*
Hundertwasserhaus. A 50-apartment public-housing complex, designed by Friedrich Hundertwasser, Austria's best-known living painter. Looking as if it was painted by a crew of mischievous circus clowns wielding giant crayons, the building caused a sensation when it went up in 1985. It remains a tourist attraction not to be missed. *Corner of Kegelgasse and Löwengasse. Subway stop: Schwedenplatz, then streetcar N to Hetzgasse.*
Imperial Burial Vault (*see* Tour 5). *Subway stop: Stephansplatz.*
Looshaus (House Without Eyebrows; *see* Tour 3). *Subway stop: Herrengasse.*
National Library (in the Hofburg; see Tour 4). *Subway stop: Herrengasse.*
National Theater (*see* Tour 4). *Subway stop: Rathaus.*

Opera House (*see* Tour 5). *Subway stop: Karlsplatz.*
Palace of Justice (*see* Tour 4). *Subway stop: Volkstheater.*
Parliament (*see* Tour 4). *Subway stop: Lerchenfelder Strasse.*
Pasqualatihaus (Beethoven's residence; *see* Tour 2). *Subway stop: Schottentor.*
Schönbrunn Palace (*see* Tour 7). *Subway stop: Schönbrunn.*
Schubert's Birthplace. (*see* Off the Beaten Track). *Subway stop: Schottentor, then No. 37 or No. 38 tram to Nussdorfer Strasse/Canisiusgasse.* **The house where he died.** *Subway stop: Kettenbrückengasse.*
Strauss Residence (*see* Off the Beaten Track). *Subway stop: Nestroyplatz.*
University of Vienna (*see* Tour 4). *Subway stop: Schottentor.*
Virgilkapelle. An old and mysterious chapel, uncovered during excavations for the subway system in the 1970s. It was probably constructed in the 13th century by hollowing out the ground underneath the charnel house next to St. Stephen's; no trace of an entrance door was found, its only possible means of access apparently being a trap door in the ceiling. Visible from the first underground level of the Stephansplatz subway station. *Subway stop: Stephansplatz.*
Winter Riding School (Hofburg; *see* Tour 4). *Subway stop: Herrengasse.*

Museums and Galleries

Academy of Fine Arts (*see* Tour 6). *Subway stop: Karlsplatz.*
Albertina Museum (*see* Tour 5). *Subway stop: Stephansplatz.*
Belvedere Palace (*see* Tour 6). *Subway stop: Karlsplatz.*
Cathedral and Diocese Museum (*see* Tour 1). *Subway stop: Stephansplatz.*
Clock Museum (*see* Tour 2). *Subway stop: Stephansplatz.*
Collection of Musical Instruments (Hofburg; *see* Tour 4). *Subway stop: Mariahilfer Strasse.*
Collection of Weapons (Hofburg; *see* Tour 4). *Subway stop: Mariahilfer Strasse.*
Court Silver and Tableware Treasury (Hofburg; *see* Tour 4). *Subway stop: Herrengasse.*
Ephesus Museum (Hofburg; *see* Tour 4). *Subway stop: Mariahilfer Strasse.*
Ethnological Museum (Hofburg; *see* Tour 4). *Subway stop: Mariahilfer Strasse.*
Imperial Apartments (Hofburg; *see* Tour 4). *Subway stop: Herrengasse.*
Imperial Coach Collection (Schönbrunn; *see* Tour 7). *Subway stop: Schönbrunn.*
Imperial Treasuries (Hofburg; *see* Tour 4). *Subway stop: Herrengasse.*
Museum of Applied Arts (*see* Off the Beaten Track) *Subway stop: Stubentor.*
Museum of Art History (*see* Tour 4). *Subway stop: Mariahilfer Strasse.*
Museum of Military History (*see* Off the Beaten Track). *Subway stop: Süd-Tiroler-Platz.*
Museum of Modern Art (*see* Tour 4). *Subway stop: Rossauer-Lände.*
Museum of Natural History (*see* Tour 4). *Subway stop: Volkstheater.*
Museum of Viennese History (*see* Tour 6). *Subway stop: Karlsplatz.*

Secession Building (*see* Tour 6). *Subway stop: Karlsplatz.*

In addition to the above, which are mentioned in the walking tours, Vienna possesses an astonishing array of little specialty museums, some of which are free, most of which have small admission fees.

Bell Museum. Troststr. 38, tel. 0222/604–3460. Open Wed. 2–5. *Subway stop: Reumannplatz.*

Circus and Clown Museum. Karmelitergasse 9, tel. 0222/21106–229. Open Wed. 5:30–7 PM, Sat. 2:30–5 PM, Sun. 10–noon. *Subway stop: Schwedenplatz.*

Doll and Toy Museum. Schulhof 4, tel. 0222/535–6860. Admission: AS60 adults, AS30 children. Open Tues.–Sun. 10–6. *Subway stop: Stephansplatz.*

Esperanto Museum. Hofburg (Michaelerplatz entrance), tel. 0222/535–5145. Open Mon., Wed., Fri. 9–3:30. *Subway stop: Herrengasse.*

Film Museum. Augustinerstr. 1, tel. 0222/533–7054. Film showings Oct.–May, Mon.–Sat. 6 and 8 PM. *Subway stop: Karlsplatz.*

Firefighting Museum. Am Hof 10, tel. 0222/53199. Open Sat. 10–noon, Sun. 9–noon. *Subway stop: Herrengasse.*

Folk Art Museum. Laudongasse 15–19, tel. 0222/438905. Closed for renovation. *Subway stop: Rathaus.*

Folk Art Museum (Religious). Johannesgasse 8, tel. 0222/512–1337. Open Wed. 9–4, Sun. 9–1. *Subway stop: Stephansplatz.*

Football (Soccer) Museum. Meiereistr. (in the Praterstadium), tel. 0222/21718. Open Mon., Fri. 10–1, Tues., Thurs. 2–6. Closed July–mid-Aug. *Subway stop: Praterstern, then streetcar 21.*

Glass Museum. Kärntner Str. 26 (Lobmeyr Store), tel. 0222/512–0508. Open weekdays 10–6, Sat. 10–1. *Subway stop: Stephansplatz.*

Globe Museum. Josefsplatz (National Library, 3rd floor), tel. 0222/53410–297. Open Mon.–Wed., Fri. 11–noon; Thurs. 2–3 PM. *Subway stop: Herrengasse.*

Heating Technology Museum. Längenfeldgasse 13–15 (Berufschule), tel. 0222/4000–93231 or 0222/4000–93319. Open Tues. 1–6 PM. *Subway stop: Längenfeldgasse.*

Horsedrawn Cab Museum. Veronikagasse 12, tel. 0222/432607. Open first Wed. of every month 10–noon. *Subway stop: Josefstädter Strasse.*

Horseshoeing, Harnessing and Saddling Museum. Linke Bahngasse 11, tel. 0222/71155–372. Open Mon.–Thurs. 1:30–3:30 PM by arrangement. *Subway stop: Rochusgasse.*

Medical History Museum. Währinger Str. 25/1 (in the Josephinum), tel. 0222/432154. Open weekdays 9–3. *Subway stop: Schottentor.*

Pathological Anatomy Museum. Spitalgasse 2 (in the Allgemeines Krankenhaus), tel. 0222/438672. Open Thurs. 8–11 AM, first Sat. each month 11–2; closed Aug. *Subway stop: Schottentor.*

Period Furniture Museum. Mariahilfer Str. 88, tel. 0222/934240. Open Tues.–Fri. 9–4, Sat. 9–noon. *Subway stop: Mariahilfer Strasse.*

Postal and Telegraph Services Museum. Mariahilfer Str. 212, tel. 0222/89101. Open Sun.–Fri. 9–4:30. *Subway stop: Schönbrunn.*

Railway Museum. Mariahilfer Str. 212, tel. 0222/89101. Open Sun.–Fri. 9–4:30. *Subway stop: Schönbrunn.*

Streetcar Museum. Erdbergstr. 109, tel. 0222/587–3186. Open May 7–Oct. 7, weekends and holidays 9–4. *Subway stop: Schlachthausgasse.*

Technology Museum. Mariahilfer Str. 212, tel. 0222/89101. Open Sun.–Fri. 9–4:30. *Subway stop: Schönbrunn.*

Theater Museum. Lobkowitzplatz 2, tel. 0222/512–3705. *Subway stop: Stephansplatz.*

Tobacco Museum (smoking allowed). Mariahilfer Str. 2 (Messepalast), tel. 0222/961716. Open Tues. 10–7; Wed.–Fri. 10–3; weekends 9–1. *Subway stop: Mariahilfer Strasse.*

Treasury of the Order of Teutonic Knights. Singerstr. 7, tel. 0222/512–1065–6. Open Mon., Thurs., Sat., Sun. 10–noon, Wed., Fri., Sat. 3–5; Closed Sun. Nov.–Apr. *Subway stop: Stephansplatz.*

Undertaker's Museum. Goldeggasse 19, tel. 0222/50195–227. Open weekdays noon–3 by prior arrangement only. *Subway stop: Südtiroler-Platz.*

Viticultural Museum. Döblinger Hauptstr. 96, tel. 0222/361–0042. Open Sat. 3:30–6 PM, Sun. 10–noon. *Subway stop: Heiligenstadt.*

Churches and Temples

Am Steinhof Kirche (*see* Off the Beaten Track). *Subway stop: Unter St. Veit, then No. 47A bus to Psychiatrisches Krankenhaus.*

Annakirche (*see* Tour 5). *Subway stop: Stephansplatz.*

Augustinerkirche (Hofburg; *see* Tour 4). *Subway stop: Herrengasse.*

Dominikanerkirche (*see* Tour 1). *Subway stop: Stephansplatz.*

Franziskanerkirche (*see* Tour 5). *Subway stop: Stephansplatz.*

Jesuitenkirche (*see* Tour 1). *Subway stop: Stephansplatz.*

Karlskirche (*see* Tour 6). *Subway stop: Karlsplatz.*

Kirche Am Hof (*see* Tour 2). *Subway stop: Stephansplatz.*

Maria am Gestade (*see* Tour 1). *Subway stop: Stephansplatz.*

Michaelerkirche (*see* Tour 3). *Subway stop: Herrengasse.*

Minoritenkirche (*see* Tour 2). *Subway stop: Herrengasse.*

Peterskirche (*see* Tour 3). *Subway stop: Stephansplatz.*

Ruprechtskirche (*see* Tour 1). *Subway stop: Schwedenplatz.*

Schottenhof (*see* Tour 2). *Subway stop: Schottentor.*

St. Stephen's Cathedral (*see* Tour 1). *Subway stop: Stephansplatz.*

Synagogue (*see* Tour 1). *Subway stop: Schwedenplatz.*

Votivkirche (*see* Tour 4). *Subway stop: Schottentor.*

Parks and Gardens

Burggarten (*see* Vienna for Free). *Subway stop: Mariahilfer Strasse.*

Prater In 1766, to the dismay of the aristocracy, the emperor Joseph II decreed that the vast expanse of imperial parklands known as the Prater would henceforth be open to the public. East of the inner city between the Danube Canal and the Danube proper, the Prater is a public park to this day, notable for its long promenade (the Hauptallee, over 3 miles in length), its sports facilities (a golf course, a stadium, a race track, and a swimming pool, for starters), and the Wurstelprater. *Subway stop: Praterstern.*

Schönbrunn Gardens (*see* Tour 7). *Subway stop: Schönbrunn.*

Stadtpark (*see* Vienna for Free). *Subway stop: Stadtpark.*

Volksgarten (*see* Tour 4). *Subway stop: Lerchenfelder Strasse.*
Wurstelprater (*see* What to See and Do with Children). *Subway stop: Praterstern.*

Other Places of Interest

Aquarium (*see* What to See and Do with Children). *Subway stop: Kettenbrückengasse.*
Central Cemetery (*see* Off the Beaten Track). *Subway stop: Karlsplatz.*
Danube Tower: In the middle of the Danube Park (a reclaimed garbage dump), 827 feet high with two revolving restaurants and fine views. Tel. 0222/235368. *Subway stop: Kaisermühlen.*
Flea Market: Held on Saturday (except public holidays), just south of the Naschmarkt on Linke Wienzeile. *Subway stop: Kettenbrückengasse.*
Naschmarkt (*see* Tour 6). *Subway stop: Karlsplatz.*
Roman ruins (Hoher Markt, Tour 1). *Subway stop: Stephansplatz.*
Vienna Zoo (Schönbrunn gardens; *see* Tour 7). *Subway stop: Hietzing.*

Shopping

Shopping Districts The **Kärntner Strasse, Graben,** and **Kohlmarkt** pedestrian areas claim to have the best shops in Vienna, and for some items, such as jewelry, some of the best anywhere, although you must expect high prices. The side streets within this area have developed their own character, with shops offering antiques, art, clocks, jewelry, and period furniture. Outside the center, concentrations of stores are on the **Mariahilfer Strasse** straddling the Sixth and Seventh districts; the **Landstrasser Hauptstrasse** in the Third District; and, still farther out, the **Favoritenstrasse** in the 10th District.

A collection of attractive small boutiques has sprung up in the **Sonnhof** passage between Landstrasser Hauptstrasse 28 and Ungargasse 13 in the Third District. The **Spittelberg** market, on the Spittelberggasse between Burggasse and Siebensterngasse in the Seventh District, has drawn small galleries and handicrafts shops and is particularly popular in the weeks before Christmas. That is the time also for the tinselly **Christkindlmarkt** on Rathausplatz in front of city hall; in protest over its commercialization, smaller markets specializing in handicrafts have sprung up on such traditional spots as Am Hof (First District).

Vienna's **Naschmarkt** (between Linke and Rechte Wienzeile, starting at Getreidemarkt) is one of Europe's great and most colorful food and produce markets. Stalls open at 5 or 6 AM, and the pace is lively until 1 or 2 PM. Saturday is the big day, when farmers come into the city to sell at the back end of the market. It's closed Sunday.

Department Stores The department stores are concentrated in the Mariahilfer Strasse. By far the best is **Herzmansky** (Mariahilfer Str. 26–30, tel. 0222/931–6360), definitely upmarket; outstanding gourmet shops and restaurants are in the basement. Farther up the street you will find slightly cheaper goods at **Gerngross** (Mariahilfer Str. and Kirchengasse, tel. 0222/932–5250) and **Stafa** (Mariahilfer Str. 120, tel. 0222/938621).

Flea Markets Every Saturday (except holidays) rain or shine, from about 7:30 AM to 5 or 6, the **Flohmarkt** in back of the Naschmarkt, stretching along the Linke Wienzeile from the Kettenbrücken subway station, offers a staggering collection of stuff ranging from serious antiques to plain junk. Haggle over prices.

Saturday and Sunday in summer from 2 to about 7:30 PM an outdoor **Art and Antiques** market takes place along the Danube Canal, stretching from the Schwedenbrücke to beyond the Salztorbrücke. Lots of books are sold, some in English, plus generally better goods than at the Saturday flea market. Bargain over prices all the same.

Auctions The **Dorotheum** (Dorotheergasse 17, tel. 0222/515600) is a state institution dating to 1707, when Emperor Josef I determined that he didn't want his people being taken advantage of by pawnbrokers. The place is intriguing, with goods ranging from furs to furniture auctioned almost daily. The special sections for fine art and postage stamps (at Dorotheergasse 11) are worth a visit just to look. Information on how to bid is available in English.

Specialty Stores You will find the best antiques shops located in the First District, many clustered close to the Dorotheum auction house, in the **Dorotheergasse, Stallburggasse, Plankengasse,** and **Spiegelgasse.** And you'll also find interesting shops in the **Josefstadt** (Eighth) district, with prices considerably lower than those in the center of town. Wander up Florianigasse and back down the Josefstädter Strasse, not overlooking the narrow side streets.

Antiques

D & S (Plankengasse 6, tel. 0222/512–2972) specializes in old Viennese clocks. Look in at **Galerie Kovacek** (Stallburg 2, tel. 0222/512–9954) to see a remarkable collection of glass paperweights and other glass objects; you'll also find paintings and furniture here. **Peter Feldbacher** (Annagasse 6, tel. 0222/512–2408) has items ranging from glass to ceramics to furniture. For art deco, look to **Galerie Metropol** (Dortheergasse 12, tel. 0222/513–2208) or **Galerie bei der Albertina** (Lobkowitzplatz 1, tel. 0222/513–1416).

Books Several good stores with books in English as well are on the Graben and Kärntner Strasse in the First District. For bookstores specializing in English-language books, *see* Important Addresses and Numbers, above.

Men's Clothing Clothing in Vienna is far from cheap but usually of better quality for the money than in the United States. The best shops are in the First District.

Sir Anthony (Kärntner Str. 21–23, tel. 0222/512–6835).
E. Braun (Graben 8, tel. 0222/512–5505).
House of Gentlemen (Kohlmarkt 12, tel. 0222/533–3258).
ITA (Graben 18, tel. 0222/533–6004).
Malowan (Opernring 23, tel. 0222/587–6296).
Silbernagel (Kärntner Str. 15, tel. 0222/512–5312).
Teller (Landstrasser Hauptstr. 88–90, tel. 0222/712–6397) for particularly good value.
Venturini (Spiegelgasse 9, tel. 0222/512–8845) for custom-made shirts.

For men's *Trachten,* or typical Austrian clothing, including lederhosen, try **Loden-Plankl** (Michaelerplatz 6, tel. 0222/533–8032), and go to **Collins Hüte** (Opernpassage, tel. 0222/587–1305) to get the appropriate hat.

A. E. Köchert, **36**
A. Heldwein, **12**
Albin Denk, **13**
Adlmüller, **49**
Arcadia, **56**
Art and Antiques
Market, **3**
Augarten, **17**
Bakalowits, **18**
Berger, **33**
Berta Smejkal, **61**
Burgenland, **60**
Carius & Binder, **37**
Carola, **58**
da Caruso, **53**
Collins Hüte, **62**
Columbia, **48**
D & S, **32**
Dorotheum, **41**
E. Braun, **15**
Elfi Müller, **59**
Flohmarkt/
Naschmarkt, **66**
Flamm, **31**
Galerie bei der
Albertina, **46**
Galerie Kovacek, **26**
Galerie Metropol, **23**
Gerngross, **64**
Haban, **19**
Havlicek, **11**
Hemerle, **51**
Herzmansky, **63**
House of
Gentlemen, **10**
Humanic, **57**
ITA, **6**
Kunz, **39**
Lanz, **30**
Liska, **5, 25**
Lobmeyr, **47**
Loden-Plankl, **14**
Maldone, **4, 21, 44**
Malowan, **55**
Niederösterreichisches
Heimatwerk, **7**
Nigst, **43**
Österreichische
Werkstätten, **24**
Pawlata, **38**
Peter Feldbacher, **50**
Plessgott, **29**
Popp &
Kretschmer, **54**
Rasper & Söhne, **9**
Resi Hammerer, **45**
Rosenthal, **40**
Schullin, **8**
Silbernagel, **34**
Sir Anthony, **42**

Vienna Shopping

Women's Clothing The couturier to Vienna is **Adlmüller** (Kärntner Str. 41, tel. 0222/512–6661). Check also **Flamm** (Neuer Markt 12, tel. 0222/512–2889, **Braun, ITA,** or **Malowan** (*see* Men's Clothing, above). You'll find modern young styling at **Maldone** (Kärntner Str. 4, tel. 0222/512–2761; Kärntner Str. 12, tel. 0222/512–2234; Graben 29, tel. 0222/533–6091; and Hoher Markt 8, tel. 0222/533–2555).

Check out the selection of dirndls and women's *Trachten*, the typical Austrian costume with white blouse, print skirt, and apron, at **Lanz** (Kärntner Str. 10, tel. 0222/512–2456), **Niederösterreichisches Heimatwerk** (Herrengasse 6–8, tel. 0222/533–3495), **Resi Hammerer** (Kärntner Str. 29–31, tel. 0222/512–6952), and **Tostmann** (Schottengasse 3a, tel. 0222/533–5331). (*See* also **Loden-Plankl** under Men's Clothing, above.)

The best shop for furs is **Liska** (Kärntner Str. 8, tel. 0222/512–4120; Hoher Markt 8, tel. 0222/533–2211). Be sure to arrange to get the value-added tax (VAT) returned on your purchase.

Ceramics and Ceramics are anything but dull at **Berger** (Weihburggasse 17,
Porcelain tel. 0222/512–1434); the more standard patterns of Gmunden ceramics are at **Pawlata** (Kärntner Str. 14, tel. 0222/512–1764) and around the corner at **Plessgott** (Kärntnerdurchgang, tel. 0222/512–5824). Check out Viennese porcelain patterns at **Augarten** (Graben/Stock-im-Eisen-Platz 3, tel. 0222/512–1494) and **Albin Denk** (Graben 13, tel. 0222/512–4439), **Rosenthal** (Kärntner Str. 16, tel. 0222/512–3994), and **Wahliss** (Kärntner Str. 17, tel. 0222/512–3856).

Crystal and Glass Select famous Vienna glassware at **Bakalowits** (Spiegelgasse 3, tel. 0222/512–6351) and **Lobmeyr** (Kärntner Str. 26, tel. 0222/512–0508), which also has a small museum of its creations upstairs; the firm supplied the crystal chandeliers for the Metropolitan Opera in New York City, a gift from Austria. **Tabletop** (Passage, Freyung 2, tel. 0222/535–4256) has the exquisite Riedl glass (though readers have reported that goods were never received), as does **Rasper & Söhne** (Graben 15, tel. 0222/534330).

Gift Items **Österreichische Werkstätten** (Kärntner Str. 6, tel. 0222/512–2418) offers handmade handicrafts, gifts, and souvenirs ranging from jewelry to textiles.
Souvenir in der Hofburg (Hofburgpassage 1 and 7, tel. 0222/533–5053) is another source of gifts.
Niederösterreichisches Heimatwerk (*see* Women's Clothing, above) has handmade folk objects and textiles.
Elfi Müller (Kärntner Str. 53, tel. 0222/512–6996) has a nice selection, but problems have been reported when goods were shipped.

Jewelry **Carius & Binder** (Kärntner Str. 17, tel. 0222/512–6750) is good for watches.
Haban (Kärntner Str. 2, tel. 0222/512–6730; Graben 12, tel. 0222/512–1220), has a fine selection of watches and jewelry.
A. Heldwein (Graben 13, tel. 0222/512–5781) sells elegant jewelry, silverware, and watches.
A. E. Köchert (Neuer Markt 15, tel. 0222/512–5828) has original creations.
Kunz (Neuer Markt 13, tel. 0222/512–7112) sells stunning modern pieces for men and women.

Schullin (Kohlmarkt 7, tel. 0222/533–9007) is known for some of the most original work to be found anywhere.

Jade Discover interesting pieces of Austrian jade at **Burgenland** (Opernpassage, tel. 0222/587–6266).

Needlework For Vienna's famous petit-point, head for **Berta Smejkal** (in the Opernpassage, tel. 0222/587–2102) or **Stransky** (Hofburg-passage 2, tel. 0222/533–6098).

Records Look for records and tapes at **Arcadia** (Kärntner Str. 40, in the Staatsoper Passage, tel. 0222/513–9568), which also features books and music-related souvenirs.

Carola is best for pop LPs and CDs (Albertinapassage, by the Opera, tel. 0222/564114).
Columbia (Kärntner Str. 30, tel. 0222/512–3675) and **da Caruso** (Operngasse 4, tel. 0222/513–1326) specialize in classics, with an emphasis on opera.
Havlicek (Herrengasse 5, tel. 0222/533–1964) features classics and is particularly knowledgeable and helpful.

Shoes and Try **Humanic** (Kärntner Str. 51, tel. 0222/512–5892 or
Leather Goods Singerstr. 2, tel. 0222/512–9101). For exclusive styles, go to **Zak** (Kärntner Str. 36, tel. 0222/512–7257), **Popp & Kretschmer** (Kärntner Str. 51, tel. 0222/512–7801), and **Nigst** (Neuer Markt 4, tel. 0222/512–4303).

Wrought Iron *Weinhebers* (wine dispensers with pear-shape glass containers) and other iron items can be found at **Hemerle** (Annagasse 7, tel. 0222/512–4746) or **Zach** (Bräunerstr. 8, tel. 0222/533–9939).

Sports and Fitness

Participant Sports

Bicycling Vienna has more than 300 km (nearly 190 mi) of cycling paths, including specially marked routes through the center of the city; look for the special pathways either in red brick or marked with a stylized cyclist in yellow. Note and observe the special traffic signals at some intersections. Excellent paved cycling trails run along the Danube, the Danube Canal, and through the *Donauinsel*, the artificial island on the north bank of the Danube. You can take a bike on the subway (except during rush hours) for half fare, but only in cars with a blue shield on the door, and only on stairs or elevators with the "bike" shield, not the escalators. At most bookstores you can purchase a cycling map of Vienna put out by ARGUS (Frankenberggasse 11, tel. 0222/505–8435). You can rent a bike for about AS30 per hour, leaving your passport or other identification as a deposit. Pick up a bike at **Cooperative Fahrrad** from April to mid-October (Franz-Josefskai at Salztorbrücke, by the canal, tel. 0222/460–6072); at **Radverleih Hochschaubahn,** mid-March through October (in the Prater amusement park, by the Hochschaubahn, bear slightly right after you pass the Big Wheel, tel. 0222/260165); at **Radverleih Praterstern,** April–October (on the street level under Praterstern North rail station, tel. 0222/268557); or at **Fahrradstadl Semmering,** March–November (Ravelinstr., under the railroad bridge, tel. 0222/748859).

Boating Both the **Alte Donau** (Old Danube), a series of lakes to the north of the main stream, and the **Neue Donau,** on the north side of the Donauinsel (the artificial island in the river), offer good waters for paddleboats, rowboats, kayaks, sailboats, and windsurfing. The Danube itself is somewhat fast-moving for anything but kayaks. Rent boats from **Auzinger Boote** (Laberlweg 22, tel. 0222/235788), **Karl Hofbauer** (Obere Alte Donau 186, tel. 0222/236733), **Eppel** (Wagramer Str. 48, tel. 0222/235168), **Irzl** (Florian Berndl-Gasse 33 and 34, tel. 0222/236743), and **Newrkla** (An der Obere Alte Donau, tel. 0222/366105). For details about sailing and sailing events, check with **Haus des Sports** (Prinz-Eugen-Str. 12, tel. 0222/505–3742).

Golf   The one in-town golf course is at **Freudenau** in the Prater (tel. 0222/218–9564). But the 18-hole par-70 course is so popular from April to November, even with the AS450 fee, that you'll probably need to be invited or have an introduction from a member to play. The alternative is **Föhrenwald,** an 18-hole par-72 course about 43 km (27 mi) away, at Wiener Neustadt (tel. 02622/27438 or 02622/29171), but this, too, is generally overbooked. Weekdays, of course, will be best for either course.

Health and   Try **Gym and Art** (in Kursalon, Johannesgasse 33, tel. 0222/
Fitness Clubs   757775), **Fitness Center Harris** (Niebelungengasse 7, tel. 0222/ 587–3710, and in the Plaza Hotel, Schottenring 11, tel. 0222/ 31390–640), or **Zimmermann Fitness** (Linke Bahngasse 9, tel. 0222/753212; Kaiserstr. 43, tel. 0222/528–2000; and Kreuzgasse 18, tel. 0222/434625, women only).

Hiking   The city has eight *Stadt-Wander-Wege*, marked routes whose starting points are reachable from a streetcar stop. Get route maps and information at the information office in City Hall (Friedrich Schmidt-Platz, tel. 0222/4000–2938). You can easily strike out on your own, city map in hand, taking a route through the vineyards up and around Kahlenberg/Leopoldsberg, starting either from the end station of the No. 38 streetcar (Grinzing) or from the Kahlenberg stop of the No. 38A bus and heading back down to Nussdorf (streetcar D). Another possibility is to wander the Lainzer Tiergarten, an enormous nature preserve with deer, wild boar, and other fauna within the city; reach it via the No. 60 streetcar from Kennedybrücke/ Hietzing on the U4 subway, then the No. 60B bus.

Ice Skating   The **Wiener Eislaufverein** (Lothringer Str. 22, behind the InterContinental Hotel, tel. 0222/713–6353) has public outdoor skating with skate rentals, October through March. Weekends are crowded. For indoor skating, check the **Donaupark-Eishalle** (Wagramerstr. 1; U1 subway to Kaisermühlen, tel. 0222/ 234596).

Jogging   Jogging paths run alongside the Danube Canal, and runners also frequent the Stadtpark and the tree-lined route along the Ring, particularly the Parkring stretch. Farther afield, in the Second District, the Prater Hauptallee, from Praterstern to the Lusthaus, is a favorite.

Riding   Splendid bridle paths crisscross the Prater park. To hire a mount, contact the **Reitclub Donauhof** (Hafenzufahrtstr. 63, tel. 0222/218–3646 or 0222/218–9716).

Skiing   Nearby slopes such as **Hohe Wand** (take No. 49B bus from the Hütteldorf stop of the U4 subway), west of the city in the 14th District offer limited skiing, with a ski lift and man-made snow when the heavens refuse, but serious Viennese skiers (that includes nearly everybody) will head out to nearby Niederösterreich (Lower Austria), with the area around the **Semmering** (about an hour from the city) one of the favorite locations for a quick outing. You can take a train or bus to get there.

Swimming Vienna has at least one pool for every one of the 23 districts; most are indoor pools, but some locations have an outdoor pool as well. If you prefer a less formal environment, head for the swimming areas of the **Alte Donau** or the **Donauinsel.** The pools and the Alte Donau (paid admission) will be filled on hot summer weekends, so the informal Donauinsel can be a surer bet. Some beach areas are shallow and suitable for children, but the Donauinsel has no lifeguards, though there are rescue stations for emergencies. Changing areas are few, lockers nonexistent, so don't take valuables. And don't be tempted to jump into the Danube Canal; the water is definitely not for swimming, nor is the Danube itself, because of heavy undertows and a powerful current.

The city has information on all places to swim; contact City Hall (Rathaus, Friedrich Schmidt-Platz, tel. 0222/40005). Ask for directions on reaching the following:

Donauinsel Nord: a huge recreation area with a children's section and nude bathing.

Donauinsel Süd: good swimming and boating and a nude bathing area. Harder to get to and less crowded than other areas, but food facilities are limited.

Gänsehäufel: a bathing island in the Alte Donau (tel. 0222/ 235392), with lockers, changing rooms, children's wading pools, topless and nude areas, and restaurants; likely to be full by 11 AM or earlier.

Krapfenwaldbad: an outdoor pool tucked among the trees on the edge of the Vienna Woods (tel. 0222/321501). Full of Vienna's beautiful people, topless females, and singles. But get there early on sunny Sundays or you won't get in.

Stadionbad: a huge sports complex, popular with the younger crowd; go early. There is no direct transportation; take the No. 80B bus from Stadionbrücke in the Third District to the "Hauptallee" stop, or for the fun of it as well, ride the miniature railway (*Liliputbahn*) from behind the big wheel in the Prater amusement park to the "Stadion" station and walk the rest of the way (Prater, Marathonweg, tel. 0222/262102).

Tennis Though Vienna has plenty of courts close to wherever you'll be, they'll be booked solid. Try anyway; your hotel may have good connections, but you'll have to book at least a few days in advance. **Sportservice Wien-Sport** (Bacherplatz 14, tel. 0222/ 543131) operates a central court-booking service (100 courts in summer, four halls in winter) and **Vereinigte Tennisanlagen** (Prater Hauptallee, tel. 0222/218–1811) has courts in other locations as well. Or you can try **Tennisplätze Arsenal** (58 sand courts; Arsenalstr. 1, by the Südbahnhof, tel. 0222/782132; Faradaygasse 4, tel. 0222/787265; Gudrunstr. 31, tel. 0222/ 621521), **Tennisplätze Stadionbad** (Prater Hauptallee, tel. 0222/ 248261), or **Wiener Eislaufverein** (Lothringer Str. 22, behind the InterContinental Hotel, tel. 0222/713–6353).

Spectator Sports

Football (Soccer)   Matches are played mainly in the **Vienna Stadium** in the Prater
(Meiereistr., tel. 0222/218–0854) and the **West Stadium** (Keiss-
lergasse 6, tel. 0222/945519). Indoor soccer takes place in the
Stadthalle (Vogelweidplatz 14, tel. 0222/95490). **Cosmos**
(Karntner Ring 15, A-1010, tel. 0222/51533). **Vienna Ticket
Service** (Postfach 160, A-1060, tel. 0222/587–9843), tickets
must be ordered a month in advance. **Kartenbüro Flamm**
(Kärntner Ring 3, A-1010, tel 0222/512–4225). Tickets can usu-
ally be bought at the gate, but the better seats are available
through ticket agencies.

Horse Racing   The race track (both flat and sulky racing) is in the Prater
(Trabbrennplatz, tel. 0222/218–9535), and the season runs Ap-
ril–November. The highlight is the Derby, which takes place
the third Sunday in June.

Tennis   Professional matches are played either in the Prater or in the
Stadthalle (*see* above). Ticket agencies will have details.

Dining

In recent years Vienna, once a culinary backwater, has produced a new generation of chefs willing to slaughter sacred
cows and create a New Vienna Cuisine. The movement is well
past the "less is more" stage that nouvelle cuisine traditionally
demands (and to which most Viennese vociferously objected),
relying now on lighter versions of the old standbys and clever
combinations of such traditional ingredients as liver pâtés and
sour cream.

In a first-class restaurant you will pay as much as in most other
Western European capitals. But you can still find good food at
refreshingly low prices in the simpler restaurants, particularly
at neighborhood *Gasthäuser* in the suburbs. If you eat your
main meal at noon (as the Viennese do), you can take advantage
of the luncheon specials.

Many restaurants are closed one or two days a week (often Saturday and Sunday), and most serve meals only 11:30–2:30 and
6–10. An increasing number now serve after-theater dinners,
but reserve in advance. *Wien wie es isst* (in German; from almost any bookstore) gives up-to-date information on the restaurant, café, and bar scene.

Vienna's restaurant fare ranges from Arabic to Yugoslav, but
assuming you've come for what makes Vienna unique, our listings focus not on the exotic but on places where you'll meet the
Viennese and experience Vienna. Highly recommended restaurants are indicated by a star ★ .

Category	Cost*
Very Expensive	over AS500
Expensive	AS300–AS500
Moderate	AS150–AS300
Inexpensive	under AS150

**per person, excluding drinks but including service (usually
10%) and sales tax (10%)*

Very Expensive

★ **Korso.** Vienna's top restaurant, in the Bristol Hotel, surrounds you with subdued dark-paneled and gold elegance; tables are set with fine linen, glassware, and silver. The food matches the setting; chef Reinhard Gerer is one of Austria's great creative cooks. Try such specialties as scallops in white tomato butter or *Rehnüsschen*, tiny venison fillets. Ask sommelier Leopold Doppler to recommend an appropriate wine. *Mahlerstr. 2, tel. 0222/515-16-546. Reservations required. Jacket and tie required. AE, DC, MC, V. Closed Sat. lunch.*

★ **Palais Schwarzenberg.** This restaurant, in a former private palace, has one of the most impressive settings in Vienna, but be sure to book a table on the glassed-in terrace. You'll be surrounded inside by greenery, with a view out over the formal gardens. The food is a notch or two below Korso's (above), but still extremely good. The service may lag if the restaurant is full, so be prepared to relax and enjoy the setting. You can't go wrong with the fillet of beef in red wine sauce or the delicate pike. The wine list is excellent but the prices exaggerated; the house wines are a fully acceptable substitute. *Schwarzenbergplatz 9, tel. 0222/784515. Reservations required. Jacket and tie required. AE, DC, MC, V.*

★ **Rotisserie Prinz Eugen.** The setting, in the Hilton Hotel, is resplendent with dark woods, crystal and silver place-settings, and fresh flower arrangements on the tables. Chef Eduard Mitsche, who produces some of the finest food in town, is a master of the delicate touch, even with such dishes as *Kaninchenragout* (rabbit stew). Sample the roast young lamb with thyme or the exquisite scallops in orange sauce. The wine list is extensive, with excellent Austrian varieties as well as imports. *Am Stadtpark, tel. 0222/717-000-355. Reservations required. Jacket and tie required. AE, DC, MC, V. Closed Sat. and Sun. lunch.*

Steirer Eck. Some argue that this is Austria's top restaurant; others say it is overpriced. In any case, you can dine handsomely in classical elegance, among businesspeople at noon, amid politicians and personalities at night. Tables are set with flower arrangements and elegant crystal, with a flair that matches the food. Chef Helmut Österreicher is a genius at combining ideas and tastes; artichoke with lobster is a successful example, rack of wild boar with tiny sausages, another. The house wine list is overwhelming; you can ask for advice with the assurance that it will be good. *Rasumofskygasse 2, tel. 0222/713-3168. Reservations required. Jacket and tie required. AE. Closed weekends.*

Vier Jahreszeiten. The InterContinental's restaurant is an excellent if conservative choice for both the ample noontime buffet and evening dining. The atmosphere is elegant without being overdone. Service, too, is attentive but discreet, the wine list impressive but not overwhelming. The delicate roast lamb is consistently delicious; so is the fillet of beef with raw mushrooms. For dessert, ask for a *Mohr im Hemd*, literally, a moor in a shirt, a chocolate sponge-cake confection with chocolate sauce and whipped cream. *Johannesgasse 28, tel. 0222/71122-143. Reservations advised. Jacket and tie required. AE, DC, MC, V.*

Zu den Drei Husaren. The Three Hussars was for years Vienna's gourmet temple; like a culinary Dorian Gray, the house remains embalmed in its draped red velvet and gold. If you don't mind the heavy hand (which occasionally carries over to the

Vienna Dining

food and service), you may enjoy this touch of "old" Vienna, evening piano music included. Celebrities still celebrate evenings here, lunchtime is for business, and both are for tourists. Beware the enticing but unpriced hors d'oeuvre trolley; a single dip here can double your bill. The Husaren does best with standards: *Leberknödelsuppe* (liver-dumpling soup), Wiener schnitzel, roast beef, and the like. *Weihburggasse 4, tel. 0222/ 512–1092. Reservations advised at lunch, required in the evening. Jacket and tie required. AE, DC, MC, V. Closed mid-July–mid-Aug.*

Expensive

Hauswirth. Following a change in management and chefs, Hauswirth is struggling with some success to defend its former excellent reputation. The turn-of-the-century ambience remains friendly without being overbearing. Emphasis is now more toward basic Viennese cuisine, although some of the offerings—such as chicken liver parfait, bacon of wild boar, and guinea hen in morel sauce—are exotic and tasty. Ample open wines are available as accompaniment. *Otto-Bauer-Gasse 20, tel. 0222/587–1261. Reservations recommended. Closed weekends.*

★ **Imperial Café.** In the Imperial Hotel, the café is much more than just a (very good) meeting spot for coffee or *Torte;* both lunch and after-concert supper are popular and reasonably priced. The rooms are understated by local standards; crystal and velvet are evident but not overdone. The city's politicians, attorneys, and business types gather here for solid Viennese fare, selecting either from the choice daily specialties, which generally include a superb cream soup, or relying on such standards as *Leberknödelsuppe* and *Tafelspitz*, Viennese boiled beef. In summer, the terrace outside is pleasant but noisy. The wine list includes French and German selections, but many prefer an open wine by the glass. *Kärntner Ring 16, tel. 0222/ 501–10389. Reservations recommended. Jacket and tie advised. AE, DC, MC, V.*

König von Ungarn. In the hotel of the same name, the wood-paneled restaurant, with its comfortable atmosphere, is jammed at noon with businesspeople who come to deal and to sample the roast meats from the carvery trolley. When the relatively small space is packed, service can get lax. *Schulerstr. 10, tel. 0222/512–5319. Reservations required at lunch, advised in the evening. Jacket and tie advised. MC. Closed Sat.*

★ **Sirk.** This comfortable restaurant in traditional style is ideal for a light lunch or an evening snack. The sidewalk terrace is perfect for afternoon coffee and dessert, but for more privacy, take a table upstairs; those overlooking the Opera are best, but you'll have to fight Vienna's power brokers for one of them at noon. The daily menu is excellent value, or you might choose the rare roast beef with black-mushroom sauce. The post-opera menu is consistently good. *Kärntner Str. 53, tel. 0222/51516– 552. Reservations required at lunch, recommended at dinner. Jacket and tie advised. AE, DC, MC, V.*

★ **Steinerne Eule.** The Stone Owl, with its elegant but warm surroundings, is an outstanding choice for an evening out. Try the turbot in a saffron cream sauce or the breast of duck in honey-pepper sauce. Don't overlook the house-baked bread. *Halbgasse 30, tel. 0222/932250. Reservations required. Jacket and tie advised. MC. Closed Sun. and Mon.*

Zum Kuckuck. This intimate, wood-paneled restaurant, in a building many hundreds of years old, draws its clientele from the ministries in the neighborhood at noon. The kitchen does such variations on regional themes as fillet of pork Hungarian style (with a cabbage-tomato sauce) and fillet of venison in puff pastry. Try the outstanding whiskey-honey parfait for dessert. *Himmelpfortgasse 15, tel. 0222/512–8470. Reservations required. Jacket and tie advised. MC. Closed weekends.*

Moderate

Am Lugeck. At lunchtime you'll mingle with lawyers and businesspeople who appreciate the central location and the choice of Viennese food in an architecturally mixed but pleasant atmosphere. The modern grill-bar with a spiral stair is good for a quick snack; the great arched *Keller* rooms downstairs are more suited to a relaxed lunch or dinner. At the outdoor tables the generally good service tends to suffer. If you have the chance, choose any of the game dishes; the *Rehragout* (venison stew) is outstanding. The spareribs are more than ample. *Lugeck 7, tel. 0222/512–7979. Reservations advised. Jacket and tie advised; dress, outdoors: casual but neat. AE, DC, MC, V.*

Bastei Beisl. You'll find good basic Viennese cuisine in this unpretentious, friendly, pine-paneled restaurant. Try the *Zwiebelrostbraten*, a rump steak smothered in fried onions. The tables outside in summer add to the pleasure at noon or in the evening. *Stubenbastei 10, tel. 0222/512–4319. Reservations advised. Dress: casual but neat. AE, DC, MC. Closed Sun. and holidays; also Sat. during July and Aug.*

★ **Glacis-Beisl.** This restaurant, tucked beneath a section of the old city wall, is no longer the secret it once was, but the charm of the indoor rooms is still appealing, and its garden under grape arbors is unique. Alas, a proposed rebuilding of the Messepalast into a museum threatens the existence of this fascinating corner of Vienna. The menu is long; ask the waiter for help. You'll find most of the Viennese standards, but the place seems right for grilled chicken (*Brathendl*) and a mug of wine. *Messepalast (follow signs to the rear right corner), Messeplatz 1, tel. 0222/930–7374. Reservations required for the garden in summer. Dress: informal but neat. Closed Sat. lunch, Sun., and Jan.–Mar.*

Gösser Bierklinik. The rooms go on and on in this upstairs (more formal) and downstairs (preferred) complex that dates back four centuries. The fare is as solid as the house; you know the Wiener schnitzel here will be first class. The salad bar is new. And there's a menu in English. The beer, of course, is Austrian, from the Gösser brewery in Styria. You certainly may have wine if you prefer, although it is not in the same class with the beer. *Steindlgasse 4, tel. 0222/535–6897. Reservations advised, particularly at lunch. Jacket and tie advised upstairs; downstairs dress, casual but neat. AE, DC, MC, V. Closed Sun.*

★ **Gösser Brau.** This vast *Keller* with a (dummy) copper brewing vat is a noontime hangout of businesspeople from the city center who appreciate the good food and generally prompt service. Go for the game when it's available. *Rehrücken* (rack of venison) is a specialty. The appropriate accompaniment is Gösser beer, of course. *Elisabethstr. 3, tel. 0222/587–4750. Reserva-*

tions suggested at noon. Jacket and tie advised. AE, DC, MC, V.

★ **Martinkovits.** If you have time, head out to this typical "old Vienna" wine restaurant in the shadow of the Sievering vineyards, for grilled chicken of a quality and flavor you'll not soon forget. And the wines are excellent. The rooms inside are pleasant, but the garden is sheer delight. *Bellevuestr. 4, No. 39A bus from U2/U4 Heiligenstadt, Windhabergasse stop, tel. 0222/321546. Reservations advised on weekends. Dress: casual but neat. Closed Mon. and Tues. Closed Wed.–Fri. lunch. Check for winter closing months.*

★ **Ofenloch.** Unique for its turn-of-the-century ambience, this restaurant features waitresses in costume and the menu in miniature newspaper form. The fare is based on original recipes. A garlic fan will find the *Vanillerostbraten*, a rump steak prepared not with vanilla but with garlic, delicious. The misleading name came about because in early days, no one would admit to ordering anything with garlic. *Kurrentgasse 8, tel. 0222/533–8844. Reservations required. Jacket and tie advised. AE, MC, V.*

★ **Römischer Kaiser.** Spending a summer evening overlooking the Danube and part of the city in this idyllic garden setting under huge old trees is what Vienna is all about. Service is attentive, and you'll want to stay forever. The Beefsteak Tartare is excellent; if you don't like beef raw, choose one of the meats or fish from the outdoor charcoal grill. *Neustift am Walde 2, tel. 0222/441104. Reservations advised. Jacket suggested. MC, V. Closed Tues. and Wed.*

Stadtbeisl. The smallish dark-paneled rooms are packed at noon, as is the summer "garden" amid the ivy outside. Take the game in season, otherwise try one of the good Viennese standards. *Naglergasse 21, tel. 0222/533–3323. Reservations advised. Jacket advised inside, casual but neat outside. V.*

Zu den Drei Hacken. This is one of the last of the old *Gasthäuser* in the center of town; Schubert, among other luminaries of the past, is alleged to have dined here. You will find excellent Viennese fare, from schnitzel to Tafelspitz. The outdoor "garden" is attractive, but jammed in summer. *Singerstr. 28, tel. 0222/512–5895. Reservations advised. Dress: casual but neat. AE, DC, Closed Sat. evening, Sun.*

Zu ebener Erde und im ersten Stock. This gem of a historic house has an upstairs/downstairs combination: In the tiny room upstairs, done in old Vienna decor, the cuisine is adventurous, with such dishes as breast of duck with julienne zucchini and stuffed leg of hare, but you'll find old Viennese favorites as well. There's simpler (and cheaper) fare on the ground floor. *Burggasse 13, tel. 0222/936254. Reservations required. Jacket and tie required. AE, DC, V. Closed Sun. and Mon.*

Zum Laterndl. The atmosphere in the sidewalk "garden" is magical at night; the wood-paneled rooms inside comfortably carry the patina of the years. The food is good standard Viennese, with game in season. The venison is excellent; so, too, are the open wines. *Landesgerichstr. 12, tel. 0222/434358. Reservations advised. Dress: informal but neat. Closed weekends, holidays.*

Inexpensive

★ **Figlmüller.** If you'll accept the style of the house (you sit at a series of benches elbow-to-elbow with the other guests), this is *the* spot for Wiener schnitzel—one that overhangs the plate. (Waiters understand the doggie-bag principle.) Other choices are somewhat limited, and you'll have to take wine or mineral water with your meal because no beer or coffee is served. But Figlmüller is an experience you'll want to repeat. *Wollzeile 5, tel. 0222/512–6177. Reservations advised. Dress: casual but neat. No credit cards. Closed weekends.*

Gigerl. This charming and original wine restaurant offers a hot and cold buffet, specializing in vegetable and pasta dishes; try the macaroni salad or the *Schinkenfleckerl*, a baked noodle and ham dish. They go remarkably well with the light wines that the costumed waitresses keep pouring into your glass. In winter the rooms can get smoky and stuffy; in summer, the outside tables are delightful. *Rauhensteingasse 3/Blumenstockgasse 2, tel. 0222/513–4431. Reservations advised. Dress: casual but neat. AE, DC, MC, V. Evenings begin at 4 PM.*

★ **Göttweiger Stiftskeller.** In this traditional, basic restaurant, look for grilled and fried chicken, for schnitzel variants, tasty liver dishes such as Leberknödelsuppe, plus occasional surprises like oxtail soup. The food helps compensate for the rather unexciting rooms. The wines, on the other hand, are outstanding. *Spiegelgasse 9, tel. 0222/512–7817. Reservations not required. Dress: casual but neat. No credit cards. Closed weekends.*

★ **Gulaschmuseum.** The original idea behind this modern restaurant is literally dozens of tasty variants on the theme of goulash. They're just right for an in-between-meals snack, although most of the goulashes served are filling enough for a complete meal. *Schulerstr. 20, tel. 0222/512–1017. Reservations not required. Dress: casual but neat. AE.*

Naschmarkt. In this attractive cafeteria the food is good, of excellent value, and of far more variety than at the next-door McDonald's. Look for the daily specials on the blackboard. You'll also find good soups (chilled gazpacho on hot summer days), sandwiches, a salad bar, and a nonsmoking area. *Schwarzenbergplatz 16, tel. 0222/505–3115. Reservations not required. Dress: casual. No credit cards. Also at Schottengasse 1, tel. 0222/533–5186. Schottengasse is closed Sun. evening.*

Reinthaler. The atmosphere is thick enough to cut in this convenient "neighborhood" establishment, full of regulars. The fare is genuine Viennese: schnitzel, chicken, roast pork with *Knödel* (bread dumpling), and such. The ivy-fenced tables outside in summer are particularly popular. *Glückgasse 5, tel. 0222/512–3366. Reservations not required. Dress: casual. No credit cards. Closed Fri. evening and weekends.*

Stadtkeller. This self-service basement cafeteria offers good value in plain surroundings. The Wiener schnitzel is one of the cheapest in town, but you may fare better with the grilled chicken. *Singerstr. 6, tel. 0222/512–1269. Reservations not required. Dress: casual. No credit cards.*

★ **Trzesniewski.** "Unpronounceably good" is the (correct) motto of this tiny sandwich shop, a Viennese tradition for decades. If a quick snack will suffice, three or four of the open sandwiches and a *Pfiff* (⅛ liter) of beer, or a vodka, may be just the needed pickup. Share one of the few tables, or stand up at one of the counters. You'll be surprised at the elegance of many of the customers. *Dorotheergasse 1, tel. 0222/512–3291. Reservations not required. Dress: casual. No credit cards. Closed Sat. evening and Sun.*

Wine Taverns

In-town wine restaurants cannot properly be called *Heurige*, since they are not run by the vintner, so the term is "wine restaurant," or "cellar" (*Keller*). Many of them extend a number of levels underground, particularly in the older part of the city. Mainly open in the evening, they are intended primarily for drinking, though you can always get something to eat from a buffet, and increasingly, full dinners are available. Some of the better wine restaurants follow: no credit cards except where noted.

Antiquitäten-Keller. The fare is authentic Viennese cuisine, surrounded by authentic antiques and the strains of classical music. *Magdalenenstr. 32, tel. 0222/566–9533. Reservations advised. Jacket and tie required. AE, DC, MC, V. Moderate.*

★ **Esterhazykeller.** This maze of rooms offers some of the best Keller wines in town plus a hot-and-cold buffet. *Haarhof 1, tel. 0222/533–3482. Reservations advised on weekends. Jacket recommended. Stüberl closed Sat., Sun. lunch; Keller closed weekends. Moderate.*

★ **Melker Stiftskeller.** Down and down you go, into one of the friendliest Kellers in town, where *Stelze* (roast knuckle of pork) is a popular feature, along with outstanding wines by the glass. *Schottengasse 3, tel. 0222/533–5530. Reservations advised. Jacket recommended. Evenings only, closed Sun. Moderate.*

Piaristen Keller. The atmosphere, with live music, is sufficiently genuine that you can overlook the occasionally lax service. This is a dining Keller; the food is good and the house wines are excellent. *Piaristengasse 45, tel. 0222/429152. Reservations advised. Jacket and tie suggested. AE, DC, MC, V. Evenings only. Moderate.*

Augustinerkeller. This upstairs Keller is open at noontime as well. The grilled chicken is excellent. *Augustinerstr. 1/ Albertinerplatz, tel. 0222/533–1026. Reservations not required. Dress: casual but neat. Inexpensive.*

Zwölf Apostel-Keller. You pass a huge wood statue of St. Peter on the way down to the two underground floors in this cellar in the oldest part of Vienna. The young crowd comes for the good wines and the atmosphere, and there's buffet food as well. *Sonnenfelsgasse 3, tel. 512–6777. Reservations advised on weekends. Dress: casual but neat. Inexpensive.*

Heurige

These taverns in the wine-growing districts on the outskirts of the city vary from the simple front room of a vintner's house to ornate establishments. (The name means "new wine," and that's what is chiefly served.) The true Heuriger is open for only a few weeks a year to allow the vintner to sell a certain quantity of his production tax-free for consumption on his own premises. The commercial establishments keep to a somewhat more regular season, but still sell only wine from their own vines.

The choice is usually between a "new" and an "old" white wine and a red, but you can also ask for a milder or sharper wine according to your taste. Most Heurige are happy to let you sample the wines before ordering. You can also order a *Gespritzter*, half wine and half soda water. The waitress will bring you the wine, usually in quarter-liter mugs, but you collect your own food from the buffet. The wine tastes as mild as lemonade, but it packs a punch. If it isn't of good quality, you will know by a raging headache the next day.

Summer and fall are the seasons for visiting the *Heurige*, though often the more elegant and expensive establishments, called *Noble-Heuriger*, stay open year-round. No credit cards except where noted.

Heurige are concentrated in several outskirts of Vienna: Stammersdorf, Grinzing, Sievering, Nussdorf, Neustift, and a corner of Ottakring. Perchtoldsdorf, just outside Vienna, is also well known for its wine taverns.

Our favorite district is Stammersdorf, across the Danube. Try **Robert Helm.** *Stammersdorfer Str. 121, tel. 0222/391244. Reservations advised on weekends and in winter. Dress: casual but neat.*

The Grinzing district today is mainly for tourists, with a very few exceptions; one is **Zum Martin Sepp,** where the wine, food, service, and ambience are excellent. *Cobenzlgasse 32, tel. 0222/ 323233. Reservations suggested on weekends. Jacket advised. DC.*

In Sievering try **Haslinger.** *Agnesgasse 3, tel. 0222/441347. Reservations advised on weekends. Dress: casual but neat.*

In Neustift, **Wolff** has a gorgeous garden and outstanding food, as well as good wine. *Rathstr. 46, tel. 0222/442335. Reservations advised. Jacket suggested.*

In Nussdorf seek out **Schübl-Auer.** *Kahlenberger Str. 22, tel. 0222/372222. Reservations not required. Dress: casual but neat. Closed Jan., July.* In good weather, try **Stift Schotten,** with a superb garden under huge old trees. *Hackhofergasse 17, tel. 0222/371575. Reservations not required. Dress: casual but neat. Closed Jan., Feb.*

Cafés

The typical Viennese café, with polished brass or marble-topped tables, bentwood chairs, supplies of newspapers, and tables outside in good weather, is a fixed institution of which there are literally thousands. Many people take breakfast in the cafés, students do homework, businesspeople conclude deals, billiards is played, and bridge clubs meet. Everybody has his favorite; some people even have a regular table that is reserved for them every day. All cafés serve pastries and light snacks in addition to beverages. Many offer a menu or fixed lunch at noon, but be aware that some can get rather expensive. No credit cards except where noted.

When you want a quick (but excellent) coffee and dessert, look for an **Aida** café; they are scattered throughout the city. Here's a sampling of the best of the traditional cafés: **Alte Backstübe,** (Lange Gasse 34, tel. 0222/431101; MC, V; closed Mon.), in a gorgeous Baroque house, once a bakery, now a museum up front, and a café in back; **Bräunerhof** (Stallburggasse 2, tel. 0222/512–3893) has music on some afternoons; **Café Central** (Herrengasse 14, tel. 0222/535–4176; AE, DC, MC, V; closed Sun.) is where Stalin and Trotsky played chess; **Frauenhuber** (Himmelpfortgasse 6, tel. 0222/512–4323; closed Sat. evening and Sun.) has its original turn-of-the-century interior and a

good choice of desserts; **Haag** (Schottengasse 2, tel. 0222/533–
1810; closed Sun., June–Aug.), with crystal chandeliers and a
shaded courtyard garden in summer, serves snacks and desserts; **Landtmann** (Dr. Karl Lueger-Ring 4, tel. 0222/630621;
AE, DC, MC, V) is where government officials gather; **Museum**
(Friedrichstr. 6, tel. 0222/565202), original interior by the architect Adolf Loos, draws a mixed crowd and has lots of newspapers; **Schwarzenberg** (Kärntner Ring 17, tel. 0222/512–
7393), with piano music in late afternoons, is highly popular,
particularly its sidewalk tables in summer; **Tirolerhof**
(Tegetthofstr. 8/Albertinaplatz, tel. 0222/512–7833), with its
excellent desserts, is popular with students.

Café Hawelka (Dorotheergasse 12, tel. 0222/512–8230; closed
Mon., Sun. noon) deserves special mention; whole books have
been written here and about this gathering place. Its international clientele ranges from artists to politicians; Hawelka is
jammed any time of day, so you share a table (and the smoky
atmosphere).

Pastry Shops

Viennese pastries are said to be the best in the world. In all
shops you can buy them to eat on the premises as well as to take
out. **Kurkonditorei Oberlaa** (Neuer Markt 16, tel. 0222/513–
2936) has irresistible confections, cakes, and bonbons, as well
as light lunches and salad plates, served outdoors in summer.
Traditionalists and tourists with fat pocketbooks still go to
Demel (Kohlmarkt 14, tel. 0222/533–5516), where the value is
arguable but turn-of-the-century atmosphere prevails among
velvet and polished brass. **Gerstner** (Kärntner Str. 15, tel. 0222/
512–4963) is also recommended, and **Heiner** (Kärntner Str. 21–
23, tel. 0222/512–6863, and Wollzeile 9, tel. 0222/512–4838) is
dazzling for its crystal chandeliers as well as for its pastries.
Sluka (Rathausplatz 8, tel. 0222/427172) has special dietetic
desserts, snacks, and an appetizer buffet and serves outdoors
in summer.

Lodging

In Vienna's best hotels the staff seems to anticipate your
wishes almost before you have expressed them. Such service of
course has its price, and if you wish, you can stay in Vienna in
profound luxury. For those with more modest requirements,
ample rooms are available in less expensive but entirely adequate hotels. Pensions, mainly bed-and-breakfast establishments often managed by the owner, generally represent good
value. A number of student hostels are run as hotels in summer, offering about the most reasonable quarters of all. And
several apartment hotels accommodate those who want to stay
longer.

When you have only a short time to spend in Vienna, you will
probably want to stay in the inner city (the 1010 postal code) or
fairly close to it, within walking distance of the most important
sights, restaurants, and shops. Although most of the hotels
there are in the upper categories, excellent and reasonable accommodations can be found in the Eighth District, which bor-
ders the First and puts you close to the major museums. You'll
also find a group of moderate and inexpensive hotels in the

Mariahilfer Strasse–Westbahnhof area, within easy reach of the city center by streetcar.

For the high season, Easter through October, and around the Christmas–New Year holidays, make reservations a month or more in advance. Vienna is continually the site of some international convention or other, and in March and September, when the semiannual trade fair is on, the city fills up quickly.

Our hotel categories correspond more or less to the official Austrian rating system, with five stars the equivalent to our Very Expensive category. All rooms have bath or shower unless otherwise stated; color television is usual in the top two categories; breakfast is included with all *except* the highest category. Highly recommended lodgings are indicated by a star ★.

Category	Cost*
Very Expensive	over AS2,200
Expensive	AS1,200–AS2,200
Moderate	AS850–AS1,200
Inexpensive	under AS850

All prices are for a standard double room for two, including local taxes (usually 10%) and service (15%).

Very Expensive

Ambassador. This superbly located dowager (from 1866) wears well. An air of decadent elegance radiates from the red velvet and crystal chandeliers in the high-ceiling guest rooms. The trade-off is room air conditioners and rather stuffy period furniture. But what was once good enough for Mark Twain—yes, he stayed here, but long before the renovations of 1990–91—is still very good, and you will know instantly that you are in Vienna. Unless you want the excitement of a direct view into the lively pedestrian Kärntner Strasse, ask for one of the quieter rooms on the Neuer Markt side. *Neuer Markt 5/Kärntner Str. 22, A–1010, tel. 0222/514660. 107 rooms. Facilities: restaurant, bar, TV on request. AE, DC, MC, V.*

★ **Bristol.** This hotel has one of the finest locations in Europe, on the Ring next to the opera house. The accent here is on tradition, from the brocaded walls to the Biedermeier period furnishings in the public rooms and many of the bedrooms. The house dates to 1896; renovations have left no trace of the fact that the Bristol was the U.S. military headquarters during the 1945–55 occupation. Like an old shoe, the hotel is seductively comfortable from the moment you arrive. The rooms on the Mahlerstrasse (back) side of the house are quieter, but the view isn't as spectacular as from rooms in front. *Kärntner Ring 1, A–1010, tel. 0222/515160. 152 rooms. Facilities: Korso, one of the 2 restaurants, is rated Vienna's best; American bar, sauna, exercise room. AE, DC, MC, V.*

de France. From the glass-fanned canopy entrance, the decor speaks of friendly efficiency. After the chic 1988 renovations, you'd never guess from the inside that the de France building dates to 1873. Some of the older rooms, with their characteristic red velvet, crystal, and Oriental carpets, are in clever con-

Vienna Lodging

trast to the crisp blues and fresh white of the new design. And some of the traditional high ceilings have been retained. If you prefer modern, ask for a room in the new wing, added in 1988. The lofty maisonette (duplex) suites are sensational, with their living area and bathroom downstairs, sleeping area and toilet on a balcony. *Schottenring 3, A–1010, tel. 0222/345610. 183 rooms. Facilities: 2 restaurants (the Bistro is excellent for a light lunch), bar, sauna, theater-ticket office. AE, DC, MC, V.*

Hilton. The Art Deco public areas re-created for the opening in 1975 now look a bit dated, but the bedrooms are contemporary and a cut above the usual Hilton standard in size and individuality of decor. The suites are particularly spacious; who could resist breakfast on a suite balcony, with a 180-degree view of the city? The upper rooms are quietest; the no-smoking floor is so popular that you need to book at least a week in advance. The airport bus terminal is next door to the Hilton; the U3 and U4 subway lines, trains, and buses stop at the terminal across the street, yet you're within an easy walk of city center. *Am Stadtpark, A–1030, tel. 0222/717000. 620 rooms. Facilities: 2 restaurants (Rotisserie Prinz Eugen is outstanding), café, wine keller, Klimt lobby bar, sauna, fitness center. AE, DC, MC, V.*

Imperial. The hotel is as much a palace today as when it was completed in 1869. The emphasis is on "old Vienna" elegance and privacy; heads of state stay here when they're in town. Service is deferential; the rooms have high ceilings and are furnished in classic antiques and Oriental carpets. The bath areas, in contrast, are modern and inviting; many are as large as guest rooms in lesser hotels. The staff will adjust the hardness (or softness) of the beds to your specific wants. Don't overlook the ornate reception rooms to the rear or the formal marble staircase to the right of the lobby. *Kärntner Ring 16, A–1010, tel. 0222/501100. 158 rooms (nonsmoking rooms available). Facilities: 2 restaurants (the Café is excellent), piano bar. AE, DC, MC, V.*

InterContinental. This "first" among Vienna's modern hostelries (1964) has taken on the Viennese patina, and its public rooms, with glittering crystal and red carpets, suggest luxurious comfort. The guest rooms lean more toward the chain's norm, adequate though unexciting, but you will get either a view over the city park across the street (preferred) or over the city itself. The higher you go, the more dramatic the perspective. *Johannesgasse 28, A–1030, tel. 0222/711220. 498 rooms (nonsmoking rooms available). Facilities: 2 restaurants (Vier Jahreszeiten is recommended), 2 bars, sauna. AE, DC, MC, V.*

★ **Palais Schwarzenberg.** You will know from your first glimpse of the elegant facade that this is no ordinary hotel. Set in a vast formal park, the palace, built in the early 1700s, seems like a country estate, and you can even jog in the formal garden. Your room will be furnished in genuine (but surprisingly comfortable) antiques, with some of the Schwarzenberg family's art on the walls. The baths are modern, although you might miss a shower curtain. Each room is individual; duplex suites 24 and 25 have upstairs bedrooms and views over the park; Room 26 has exquisite furniture, gorgeous draperies, and a winding stair leading up to the bedroom. If you have any reason to celebrate, do it here; this is the genuine "old Vienna" at its most elegant. *Schwarzenbergplatz 9, A–1030, tel. 0222/784515. 38 rooms. Facilities: restaurant, bar, AE, DC, MC, V.*

Sacher. Few hotels in the world have featured so often in films or in history; you'll sense the musty atmosphere of tradition when you arrive. This is the house where the legendary cigar-smoking Frau Sacher reigned; Emperor Franz Josef was a regular patron. The Sacher dates to 1876; the patina remains (Room 329 exudes a sense of well-being) despite the elegant new baths installed in 1990. The corridors are a veritable art gallery, and the location directly behind the Opera House could hardly be more central. The staff is particularly accommodating; it has long been an open secret that the concierge at the Sacher could miraculously produce concert and opera tickets when all other possibilities were exhausted. The restaurant remains the great disappointment. *Philharmonikerstr. 4, A–1010, tel. 0222/514560. 125 rooms, 117 with bath (nonsmoking rooms available). Facilities: restaurant, café, 2 bars (the Blue is recommended). AE, MC, DC, V.*

Vienna Marriott. The metal-and-glass exterior gives the impression of a giant greenhouse, borne out by the inviting mini-jungle of green trees and plants in the vast atrium lobby. Some guests object to the perpetual waterfall in the bar/café area, but for Vienna the effect is certainly original. Despite the size, a friendly atmosphere pervades. For a hotel built in 1984, the rooms and suites are unusually spacious and furnished with extra attention to detail; the corner suites (number 24 on each floor) give a superb view out over the city park opposite. The upper rooms in back offer a panorama of the inner city; these and the rooms on the inner court are the quietest. You're an easy stroll from the city center. *Parkring 12a, A–1010, tel. 0222/51518. 304 rooms (nonsmoking rooms available). Facilities: 2 restaurants, café, 2 bars, sauna, pool, fitness room. AE, DC, MC, V.*

Expensive

Biedermeier im Sünnhof. This jewel of a hotel is tucked into a renovated 1820s house that even with all modern facilities still conveys a feeling of old Vienna. The rooms are compact but efficient, the public areas tastefully done in the Biedermeier style, and the service is friendly. The courtyard passageway around which the hotel is built has attracted a number of interesting boutiques and handicrafts shops, but at times there is an excess of coming and going as tour groups are accommodated. It's about a 20-minute walk or a six-minute subway ride to the center of the city. *Landstrasser Hauptstr. 28, A–1030, tel. 0222/755575. 204 rooms. Facilities: restaurant, bar. AE, DC, MC, V.*

Capricorno. In these intimate quarters on the four lowest floors of what is basically an office/apartment building, the mood is definitely Vienna, if not luxurious: The rooms have period furniture, and most overlook the Danube Canal. It's an ideal location, five minutes on foot from Stephansplatz, with subway and streetcar stops outside the door. The Danube city sightseeing boats dock across the street. Hotel services are limited (breakfast only), but the staff is unusually helpful, and good restaurants are nearby (even a McDonald's in the house). *Schwedenplatz 3–4, A–1010, tel. 0222/533–3104. 46 rooms. AE, DC, MC, V.*

Europa. The Europa had a face-lift in 1989, which almost worked, but the hotel cannot quite hide its 1957 birth year, and the garish blue-and-pink entry canopies don't help. But the rooms are comfortable without being luxurious and the baths are modern. You can't find a more central location. Rooms on the Neuer Markt side are quieter than those on Kärntner Strasse, and the best rooms are those on the corners. *Neuer Markt 3/Kärntner Str. 18, A–1010, tel. 0222/515940. 102 rooms. Facilities: restaurant, café, bar. AE, DC, MC, V.*

★ **König von Ungarn.** In a 16th-century house in the shadow of St. Stephen's cathedral, this hotel began catering to court nobility in 1815. (Mozart lived in the house next door when he wrote *The Marriage of Figaro*). A superb redesign has turned it into a modern hotel, and you could hardly hope for a happier result. The hotel radiates charm, from the greenery in the wood-paneled atrium lobby to the antiques of various periods and the pine country furnishings in the bedrooms. The rooms are not overly large, but each is individually and appealingly decorated. Those in back are somewhat quieter. *Schulerstr. 10, A–1010, tel. 0222/515840. 32 rooms. Facilities: restaurant, lobby bar. DC, MC, V.*

★ **Mailberger Hof.** This 14th-century house on a pedestrian street just off the Kärntner Strasse was once a Baroque town palace. In 1976 it was turned into an intimate family-run hotel with great success and is a favorite of stars at the nearby state opera. The rooms are so attractively decorated it's hard to imagine you're in a hotel; colors and furniture have been coordinated without fussiness to create a setting you won't want to leave. You'll have to book about a month ahead to get a room. *Annagasse 7, A–1010, tel. 0222/512–0641. 40 rooms. Apartments with kitchenettes are available by the month. Facilities: restaurant. AE, DC, V.*

★ **Opernringhof.** This establishment's spacious, comfortable rooms, furnished with real antiques of the mid-19th century, are only one reason why guests come back. The unusually friendly, personal attention of the owner, Susie Riedl, makes you feel as though you're the only guest. The hotel has Best Western affiliation. The rooms on the inner courtyard are quieter but have a dreary outlook; disregard the traffic noise (there's no air-conditioning, so you may want the windows open) and enjoy the extraordinary view of the Opera, diagonally across the Ring. *Opernring 11, A–1010, tel. 0222/587–5518. 35 rooms. AE, MC, DC, V.*

Moderate

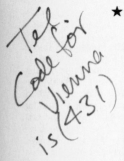
Tel. Code for Vienna is (431)

★ **Austria.** This older house, tucked away on a tiny cul-de-sac, offers the ultimate in quiet and is only five minutes' walk from the heart of the city. The high-ceiling rooms are pleasing in their combination of dark wood and lighter walls; the decor is mixed, with Oriental carpets on many floors. You'll feel at home here, and the staff will help you find your way around town or get opera or concert tickets. *Wolfengasse 3 (Fleischmarkt). A–1010, tel. 0222/515230. 51 rooms, 40 with bath or shower. AE, DC, MC, V.*

Fürstenhof. This turn-of-the-century block, directly across from the Westbahnhof, describes its large rooms as "old-fashioned comfortable," and you reach them via a marvelous hydraulic elevator. Furnishings are a mixed bag. The side rooms are quieter than those in front. *Neubaugürtel 4, A–1070, tel. 0222/933267. 60 rooms. AE, DC, MC, V.*

Ibis Wien. About an eight-minute walk from the Westbahnhof and easily identifiable by its bronze metal exterior, the Ibis offers its standard chain accommodations in contemporary rooms that are compact, complete, and very good value. The blue and blue-gray accents are refreshing against the white room walls. The rooms on the shady Wallgasse side are more comfortable; those on the upper floors have a superb panoramic view. You may have to contend with some tour groups. *Mariahilfer Gürtel 22–24/Wallgasse 33. A–1060, tel. 0222/565626. 341 rooms. Facilities: restaurant, Weinstube, garage. AE, DC, MC, V.*

★ **Kärntnerhof.** Behind the "Schönbrunn yellow" facade of this elegant 100-year-old house on a quiet cul-de-sac lies one of the friendliest small hotels in the center of the city. Don't let the dated and uninteresting lobby put you off; take the gorgeously restored Art Deco elevator to the rooms upstairs. They have just been done over in either brown or white reproduction furniture, and the baths are modern. Room 205, in its combination of blue and white, is stunning. The staff is adept at getting theater and concert tickets for "sold out" performances and happily puts together special outing programs for guests. For a small fee, parking can be arranged in the abbey courtyard next door. *Grashofgasse 4, A–1010, tel. 0222/512–1923. 43 rooms. AE, DC, MC, V.*

Pension Christine. This quiet pension, just steps from Schwedenplatz and the Danube Canal, offers mainly smallish modern rooms, warmly decorated with attractive dark-wood furniture set off against beige walls. Room 524 is particularly spacious and inviting. *Hafnersteig 7, A–1010, tel. 0222/533–2961. 33 rooms. MC.*

★ **Pension Pertschy.** Housed in a former town palace just off the Graben, this pension is as central as you can get. A massive arched portal leads to a yellow courtyard, around which the house is built. Anybody who has stayed in Room 220 with its stylish old blue ceramic stove (just for show) would be happy again with nothing less. Most rooms are spacious with antique furniture of mixed periods, but even the small single rooms are charming. Baths are good. Use the elevator, but don't overlook the palatial grand staircase. *Habsburgergasse 5, A–1010, tel. 0222/533–7094. 43 rooms. MC.*

★ **Pension Zipser.** This 1904 house, with an ornate facade and gilt-trimmed coat of arms, is one of the city's very best hotel values. It's in a fascinating district of small cafés, shops, jazz clubs, and excellent restaurants, yet within steps of the *J* streetcar line direct to the city center. The rooms are newly redone in browns and beige, with modern furniture to match; the baths are elegant and well lit. The balconies of some of the back rooms overlook tree-filled neighborhood courtyards. The friendly staff will help get theater and concert tickets. Book ahead a month or two to be sure of a room. *Lange Gasse 49, A–1080, tel. 0222/420828. 47 rooms. Facilities: coffee bar. AE, DC, MC, V.*

Schweizerhof. Occupying Floors 4, 5, and 6 of an Art Deco building in the heart of the city, this hotel will make you feel comfortably at home with its pleasantly mixed decor, parquet floors, and Oriental carpets. Ask for Room 527, with unusual and valuable handcarved pine country furniture. Corner Room 523 gives you a look at the Anker Clock; from corner Room 508, you can glimpse the spires of St. Stephen's Cathedral. *Bauernmarkt 22, A–1010, tel. 0222/533–1931. 55 rooms. AE, V.*

Wandl. The colorful facade (newly restored) identifies a 300-year-old house that has been in family hands as a hotel since 1854. You couldn't find a better location, tucked behind St. Peter's church, just off the Graben. The hallways are punctuated by cheerful, bright openings along the glassed-in inner court. The rooms are modern, but some are a bit plain and charmless, despite parquet flooring and red accents. Ask for one of the rooms done in period furniture, with decorated ceilings and gilt mirrors; they're palatial, if a bit overdone. *Petersplatz 9, A–1010, tel. 0222/534550. 138 rooms. Facilities: bar. No credit cards.*

Zur Wiener Staatsoper. The hotel's florid facade, with oversize torsos supporting its upper bays, is pure 19th-century Ringstrasse style. The rooms are less well defined in style, small yet comfortable. The baths are adequate. And you'll find yourself within steps of the Opera and the Kärntner Strasse. *Krugerstr. 11, A–1010, tel. 0222/513–1274. 22 rooms. AE, V.*

Inexpensive

★ **Hospiz.** This hotel, run by the Austrian YMCA, is two short blocks and four minutes from the Westbahnhof. Fully renovated in 1988, the house still shows some of its 1912 Art Deco origins. There's no elevator, baths and toilets are mainly "down the hall," but there is parking space. The rooms are compact and somewhat Spartan but utterly clean and a real bargain. *Kenyongasse 15, A–1070, tel. 0222/931304. 25 rooms. MC, V.*

Pension Aclon. On the third floor of a gray but gracious older building just off the Graben (with the famous Café Hawelka downstairs), this family-run hostelry (complete with sheepdog) is attractively done up in "old Vienna" style, with lots of plants, 19th-century furniture, dark woods, and elegant marble baths. Rooms on the inner court are quieter, though the street in front carries no through traffic. *Dorotheergasse 6–8, A–1010, tel. 0222/512–7949. 22 rooms. AE, DC, V.*

★ **Pension City.** You'll be on historic ground here: In 1791 the playwright Franz Grillparzer was born in the house that then stood here; a bust and plaques in the entryway commemorate him. On the second floor (the Viennese call it the mezzanine) of the present 100-year-old house about three minutes away from St. Stephen's Cathedral, the pension's rooms are newly outfitted in a successful mix of modern and 19th-century antique furniture against white walls. The baths are small but complete, and the amenities (minibars, TV, telephones) are remarkable at the price. *Bauernmarkt 10, A–1010, tel 0222/639521. 19 rooms. AE, DC, MC, V.*

Pension Edelweiss. One flight up, behind the drab facade of this turn-of-the-century apartment house, are comfortable rooms with contemporary furnishings, many quite spacious and many completely renovated in 1990. The front rooms are noisy, but the nearby streetcar is a convenience. It's under the same management as pensions Pertschy and Christine. *Lange Gasse 61, A–1080, tel. 0222/422306. 20 rooms. No credit cards.*

Pension Nossek. This family-run establishment on the upper floors of a 19th-century office and apartment building lies at the heart of the pedestrian and shopping area. The rooms have high ceilings and are eclectically but comfortably furnished; those on the front have a magnificent view of the Graben. *Graben 17, A–1010, tel. 0222/533–7041. 26 rooms, 16 with bath or shower. No credit cards.*

★ **Pension Suzanne.** This 1950s building on a side street is just steps away from the Opera. The rooms are smallish but comfortably furnished in 19th-century Viennese style; baths are modern, although short on shelf space. Suzanne has regular guests who book months in advance, so you'd be well advised to do the same. *Walfischgasse 4, A–1010, tel. 0222/513–2507. 24 rooms, 7 apartments with kitchenette. No credit cards.*

★ **Rathaus.** This friendly hotel, under the same management as the nearby Zipser, is in a 1908 building that has been attractively renovated: The spacious rooms have contemporary furnishings. You'll be within an easy walk of the main museums and close to public transportation. *Lange Gasse 13, A–1080, tel. 0222/434302. 40 rooms. No credit cards.*

Seasonal Hotels (Inexpensive–Moderate)

Student residences, which operate as hotels July–September, are an excellent bargain. They have single or double rooms, all, unless noted, with bath or shower. You can book any of the Rosenhotels by phoning 0222/597–0680. Credit cards in general are not accepted; exceptions are noted.

Academia (fairly luxurious). *Pfeilgasse 3A, A–1080, tel. 0222/431661–55. 368 rooms. Facilities: restaurant, bar. AE, MC, V.*
Alsergrund. *Alser Str. 33, A–1080, tel. 0222/4332–317 or 0222/512–7493. 58 rooms without bath.*
Auersperg (very inexpensive). *Auerspergstr. 9, A–1080, tel. 0222/4325490. 76 rooms. MC.*
Avis. *Pfeilgasse 4, A–1080, tel. 0222/426374. 72 rooms. Facilities: restaurant, bar. AE, MC, V.*
Haus Döbling (very inexpensive). *Gymnasiumstr. 85, A-1190, tel. 0222/347631 or 0222/344545. 308 rooms without bath.*
Josefstadt. *Buchfeldgasse 16, A–1080, tel. 0222/435211 or 0222/512–7493. 40 rooms without bath. MC, V.*
Panorama (slightly farther than most from the city center). *Brigittenauer Lände 224, A–1200, tel. 0222/351541. 270 rooms, 136 with shower. Facilities: restaurant, bar, sauna, parking.*
Rosenhotel Burgenland 1. *Wilhelm-Exner-Gasse 4, A–1090, tel. 0222/439122. 71 rooms. Facilities: restaurant, bar, garage. AE, MC, V.*
Rosenhotel Burgenland 2. *Mittelgasse 18, A–1060, tel. 0222/596–1247. 150 rooms. Facilities: restaurant, bar, garage. AE, MC, V.*
Rosenhotel Burgenland 3. *Bürgerspitalgasse 19, A–1060, tel. 0222/597–9475. 130 rooms. Facilities: restaurant, bar, garage. AE, MC, V.*
Rosenhotel Europahaus (well outside the center but clean, and with a lovely garden). *Linzer Str. 429, A–1140, tel. 0222/972536. 26 rooms. Facilities: parking.*
Rosenhotel Niederösterreich. *Untere Augartenstr. 31, A–1020, tel. 0222/353526. 100 rooms. Facilities: restaurant. AE, MC, V.*

The Arts and Nightlife

The Arts

Vienna is one of the main music centers of the world. Theater is good, although recent tendencies to experiment have taken even the traditional houses somewhat far afield: for example, a German version of Shakespeare barely identifiable with the original. Contemporary music gets its hearing, but it's the "hometown" standards—the works of Beethoven, Brahms, Haydn, Mozart, Schubert—that draw the Viennese public. A monthly program, put out by the city tourist board and available at any travel agency or hotel, gives a general overview of what's going on in opera, concerts, jazz, theater, and galleries, and similar information is posted on billboards and fat advertising columns around the city.

Most theaters now reserve tickets by telephone against a credit card; you pick up your ticket at the box office with no surcharge. The same applies to concert tickets. Ticket agencies charge a minimum 20% markup and generally deal in the more expensive seats. Expect to pay (or tip) a hotel porter or concierge at least as much as a ticket agency. You might try **Vienna Ticket Service** (Postfach 160, A-1060, tel. 0222/587–9843), **Kartenbüro Flamm** (Kärntner Ring 3, A-1010, tel. 0222/512–4225), or **Cosmos** (Kärntner Ring 15, A-1010, tel. 0222/515330).

Tickets to the state theaters (Opera, Volksoper, Burgtheater, or Akademietheater) can be charged against your credit card (AE, DC, MC, V). You can order them by phone up to six days before the performance (tel. 0222/513–1513) or buy them in person up to seven days in advance at the central box office. *Theaterkassen, back of the Opera, Hanuschgasse 3, in the courtyard, tel. 0222/514440. AE, DC, MC, V. Open weekdays 8–6, Sat. 9–2, Sun. 9–noon.*

You can also write ahead for tickets. The nearest Austrian National Tourist Office can provide you with a schedule of performances and a special ticket order form. Send the form (no payment is required) to the ticket office (Kartenvorverkauf Bundestheaterverband, Goethegasse 1, A–1010 Vienna), which will mail you a reservation card; when you get to Vienna, take the card to the main box office to pick up and pay for your tickets.

Opera   The **Staatsoper,** one of the world's great houses, has been the scene of countless musical triumphs and a center of unending controversies over how it should be run and by whom. (When Lorin Maazel was unceremoniously dumped as head of the opera not many years ago, he pointed out that the same house had done the same thing to Gustav Mahler a few decades earlier.) A performance takes place virtually every night from September through June, drawing on the vast repertoire of the house, with emphasis on Mozart and Verdi. (Opera here is nearly always performed in the original language, even Russian.) Check for possible out-of-(opera)-season performances by the Volksoper company in "the big house on the Ring" in July and August. And guided tours of the opera house are held year-round. The opera in Vienna is a dressy event. Evening dress and black tie, though not compulsory, are recommended for first-night performances and in the better seats. Jeans, even designer jeans, are frowned upon, even in standing room.

Light opera and operetta are performed at the **Volksoper,** outside the city center at Währingerstrasse and Währinger Gürtel (third streetcar stop on No. 41, 42, or 43 from "downstairs" at Schottentor on the Ring). Prices here are significantly lower than in the main opera, and performances can be every bit as rewarding. Mozart is sung here, too, but in German, the language of the house. If *Kiss Me, Kate* is on, it too is sung in German, and it's a good romp at that.

You'll find musicals and operetta also at the **Theater an der Wien** (Linke Wienzeile 6, tel. 0222/588300), the recently renovated **Raimundtheater** (Wallgasse 18, tel. 0222/599770), and **Ronacher** (Seilerstätte/Himmelpfortgasse, tel. 0222/513–8565). Opera and operetta are performed on an irregular schedule at the **Kammeroper** (Fleischmarkt 24, tel. 0222/512–0100–31).

In summer, chamber opera performances by the Kammeroper ensemble are given in the exquisite **Schlosstheater** at Schönbrunn Castle. Ticket agencies will have details.

Music   Vienna is the home of four full symphony orchestras: the great Vienna Philharmonic and the Vienna Symphony, the broadcasting service's ORF Symphony Orchestra, and the Niederösterreichische Tonkünstler. There are also hundreds of smaller groups, from world-famous trios to chamber orchestras.

The most important concert halls are in the buildings of the Gesellschaft der Musikfreunde, called the **Musikverein** (*Dumbastr. 3; ticket office at Karlsplatz 6, tel. 0222/505–8190. AE, DC, MC, V. Open weekdays 9–6, Sat. 9–noon*) and the **Konzerthaus** (*Lothringerstr. 20, tel. 0222/712–1211. AE, DC, MC, V. Open weekdays 9–6, Sat. 9–1*). Both houses contain several halls; tickets bear their names: **Grosser Musikvereinssaal, Brahmssaal,** or **Kammersaal** in the Musikverein; **Grosser Konzerthaussaal, Mozartsaal,** or **Schubertsaal** in the Konzerthaus.

Concerts are also given in the small **Figarosaal** of Palais Palffy (Josefsplatz 6, tel. 0222/512–5681), the concert studio of the broadcasting station (Argentinierstr. 30a, tel. 0222/50101–881), and the **Bösendorfersaal** (Graf Starhemberg-Gasse 14, tel. 0222/656651).

Although the **Vienna Festival** (late May to mid-June) wraps up the primary season, the summer musical scene is bright, with something going on every day. Outdoor symphony concerts are given twice weekly in the vast arcaded courtyard of the Rathaus (entrance on Friedrich Schmidt-Platz). You can catch musical events in the Volksgarten and in the Schwarzenberg, Rasumofsky, and Trautson palaces; at Schönbrunn they're part of an evening guided tour.

Mozart concerts are performed in 18th-century costumes and powdered wigs in the Mozartsaal of the Konzerthaus; operetta concerts are held in the Musikverein and the Hofburg; tickets are available through hotels and travel and ticket agencies.

Church music, the Mass sung in Latin, can be heard on Sunday morning during the main season at **St. Stephen's;** in the **Franciscan church, St. Michael's;** and, above all, in the **Augustinerkirche.** At the latter, the schedule is posted on the door. The Friday and Saturday newspapers carry details. St. Stephen's also has organ concerts most Wednesday evenings from early May to late November.

The **Vienna Choirboys** sing at 9:15 AM Mass in the **Hofburgkapelle** from mid-September to late June. Written requests for seats (standing room is free but limited) should be made at least eight weeks in advance to Hofmusikkapelle Hofburg, A–1010 Vienna. You will be sent a reservation card, which you exchange at the box office (in the Hofburg courtyard) for your tickets. Tickets are also sold at ticket agencies and at the box office every Friday at 5 PM, but you should be in line by 4:30. Each person is allowed a maximum of two tickets.

Theater   Vienna's **Burgtheater** (Dr. Karl Lueger-Ring 2, A–1010 Vienna; *see* above for ticket details) is the leading German-language theater of the world; for an actor to play the Burg means supreme achievement. It specializes in classical works: Goethe, Schiller, Grillparzer, Nestroy, plus translations of Shakespeare, Congreve, Wilde, Molière, and others. The Burg's smaller house, the **Akademietheater** (Lisztstr. 1) draws on much the same group of actors, for classical and modern plays. Both houses are closed during July and August.

The **Theater in der Josefstadt** (Josefstädterstr. 26, tel. 0222/402–5127) stages classical and modern works year-round in the house once run by the great producer and teacher Max Reinhardt. **Volkstheater** (Neustiftgasse 1, tel. 0222/932776) gives dramas, comedies, and folk plays; **Kammerspiele** (Rotenturmstr. 20, tel. 0222/533–2833) does modern plays.

For theater in English (mainly standard plays), head for **Vienna's English Theater** (Josefsgasse 12, tel. 0222/402–1260) or the equally good **International Theater** (Porzellangasse 8, tel. 0222/316272).

Dance   Other than the ballet companies in the opera and Volksoper, Vienna offers nothing in the way of regular dance. The ballet evenings that are on the opera-house schedules are more of a fill-in than a serious attempt to offer good dance. Efforts to get an annual dance festival under way are making progress, so check schedules; the situation can only get better.

Film   Film has enjoyed a recent renaissance, with viewers seeking original rather than German-dubbed versions. Look for films in English at **Burgkino** (Opernring 19, tel. 0222/587–8406)—in summer, Carol Reed's classic *The Third Man* with Orson Welles is a regular feature; **de France** (Hessgasse 7, tel. 0222/345236); and **Top-Kino** (Rahlgasse 1, tel. 0222/587–5557). In the film listings, *OmU* means original language with German subtitles.

The **Filmmuseum** in the Albertina (Augustinerstr. 1, tel. 0222/533–7054; screenings Mon.–Sat. 6 and 8 PM; AS 45) shows original-version classics like *Birth of a Nation, A Night at the Opera*, and *Harvey* and organizes retrospectives of the works of artists, directors, and producers. The monthly program is posted outside, and guest memberships for a week are available. It is closed July, August, and September.

Nightlife

Bars and Lounges   Vienna has blossomed in recent years with delightful and sophisticated bars. Head for the Bermuda Triangle, an area in the First District roughly defined by Judengasse, Seitenstättengasse, Rabensteig, and Franz-Josefs-Kai. Here you will find dozens of bars, both intimate and large, like **Salzamt, Krah-Krah,** and **Ma Pitom**. Around Concordiaplatz and in the Heinrichsgasse, **Puerto** and **Domicil** are highly popular. Back toward Stephansplatz, on the Bäckerstrasse, check out **Weinorgel, Oswald & Kalb;** on Blutgasse, **Chamäleon;** on Singerstrasse, the **Galerie Bar. The American Bar** on Kärntner Durchgang has an original Adolf Loos turn-of-the-century interior.

Cabaret Cabaret has a long tradition in Vienna. **Simpl** (Wollzeile 36, tel. 0222/512–4742) continues earning its reputation for barbed political wit but has had to give way to some newcomers at **K&K** (Linke Wienzeile 4, tel. 0222/587–2275) and **Kabarett Niedermair** (Lenaugasse 1A, tel. 0222/408–4492). To get much from any of these, you'll need good German plus knowledge of local affairs and dialects.

Casinos Try your luck at the casino **Cercle Wien** (Kärntner Str. 41, tel. 0222/512–4836) in a former town palace. The Austrian casinos are state operated, so you'll get as fair a chance as anywhere.

Discos The disco scene is big in Vienna, and the crowd seems to follow the leader from one "in" spot to the next. A few continually draw full houses. Try **Atrium** (Schwarzenbergplatz 10, tel. 0222/505–3594); **Queen Anne**, still very much "in" (Johannesgasse 12, tel. 0222/512–0203); and **U–4**, popular with a mixed group, early thirties and under (Schönbrunner Str. 222, tel. 0222/858307).

Jazz Clubs Vienna is increasingly good for jazz, and though places where it can be heard tend to come and go, each seems to be known to the other. Nothing gets going before 9 PM. Try **Duke's** (Gumpendorferstr. 9, tel. 0222/568710); **Jazzland** (Franz-Josefs-Kai 29, tel. 0222/533–2575); **Miles Smiles** (Lange Gasse 51, tel. 0222/428–4814); **Opus One** (Mahlerstr. 11, tel. 0222/513–2075); **Papa's Tapas** Schwarzenbergplatz 10, tel. 0222/505–0311); and **Roter Engel** (Rabensteig 5, tel. 0222/535–4105).

Nightclubs Vienna has no real nightclub tradition, although there are a number of clubs in town. Most of the ones with floor shows are horribly expensive and not very good. The two where you run the least risk are **Casanova,** where singles can sit reasonably peacefully at the upstairs bar (Dorotheergasse 6, tel. 0222/512–9845; open daily till 4 AM), and **Moulin Rouge** (Walfischgasse 11, tel. 0222/512–2130; open Mon.–Sat. 10 PM–6AM).

The leading night spots for dancing are the **Eden Bar,** which always has a live band and is for the well-heeled mature crowd (Liliengasse 2, tel. 0222/512–7450; open 10 PM–4 AM); the **Splendid Bar,** which draws a mixed crowd (Jasomirgottstr. 3, tel. 0222/533–3430, open to 4 AM); **Chattanooga,** which often has a live band and has a younger crowd (Graben 29, tel. 0222/533–5000); and **Volksgarten** (in the Volksgarten, Burgring 1, tel. 0222/630518), where a mixed younger set comes, particularly in summer, for outdoor dancing.

Excursions from Vienna

Baden

This short tour takes you to Baden through the band of rolling wooded hills called the Vienna Woods (Wienerwald) that border Vienna on the west. The hills are skirted by vineyards forming a "wine belt," which also follows the valleys south of Vienna. You can visit this area easily in a day's outing, either by car or by public transportation, or you can spend the night in Baden, Mödling, or Alland for a more leisurely tour, visiting Mayerling, Heiligenkreuz, and a few other sights in the area.

Tourist Information Get information in Vienna before you start out, at the tourist office of Lower Austria (Heidenschuss 2, tel. 0222/533–4773).

Other tourist offices are for Perchtoldsdorf (tel. 0222/8676–3434); Mödling (tel. 02236/26727); Gumpoldskirchen (tel. 02252/62421); Baden (tel. 02252/8680–0310).

Escorted Tours   This is one of the standard routes offered by the sightseeing-bus tour operators in Vienna, and it usually includes a boat ride through the "underground sea" grotto near Mödling. For details, check with your hotel or **Cityrama** (tel. 0222/534130) or **Vienna Sightseeing Tours** (tel. 0222/712–4683).

Getting Around   You can get to Baden directly from Vienna by bus or, far more
By Bus or Train   fun, interurban streetcar in about 40 minutes; the bus departs from the Ring directly opposite the Opera; the streetcar, from the Ring across from the Bristol Hotel. It is possible, with advance planning, to go on to Mayerling and Heiligenstadt on post office buses (tel. 0222/71101), but schedules are infrequent, and driving is preferable.

By Car   Head for Liesing (23rd District), then take the Wiener Strasse to Perchtoldsdorf; from there, follow the signs south to Mödling and Baden. From Baden, take Route 210 (marked "Helenental") to Mayerling and on to Alland; return to Vienna via route 11, stopping in Heiligenkreuz en route.

Exploring   *Numbers in the margin correspond with points of interest on the Vienna Excursions map.*

❶ Just over the Vienna city line is **Perchtoldsdorf,** a picturesque market town with many wine taverns; a 13th-century Gothic parish church; and the symbol of the town, an imposing stone defense tower completed in 1511. Locally known as Pedersdorf, this is a favorite excursion spot for the Viennese, who come mainly for the good local wines. Continue south 8 km (5 mi) to
❷ **Mödling,** founded in the 10th century, where you'll find another Gothic parish church; a Romanesque 12th-century charnel house (where the bones of the dead were kept); and the town hall, which has a Renaissance loggia.

A few km east of Mödling—about 16 km (10 mi) south of Vien-
❸ na—is **Schloss Laxenburg,** a complex consisting of a large Baroque Neues Schloss (New Castle), a small 14th-century Altes Schloss (Old Castle), and an early 19th-century neo-Gothic castle set into the sizable lake. The large park is full of birds and small game, such as roe deer and hare, and is decorated with statues, cascades, imitation temples, and other follies. The Altes Schloss was built in 1381 by Duke Albrecht III as his summer residence, and several Habsburg emperors spent summers in the Neues Schloss, which now houses the International Institute of Applied Systems Analysis. Opposite is the large Baroque Convent of the Charitable Sisters.

❹ West of Mödling on Route 11 is the **Seegrotte Hinterbrühl,** a fascinating but now somewhat commercialized underground sea, created years ago when a mine filled up with water (Grutschg. 2, tel. 02236/26364). You can take a motorboat trip on the lake and look at the reflections through the arched caverns of the mine. Not far is the "Höldrichsmühle," a mill that's now a restaurant, made famous by Franz Schubert's song about the linden tree.

Back in Mödling, we follow the "wine road" through the lush vineyard country to the famous wine-producing village of
❺ **Gumpoldskirchen,** the home of one of Europe's pleasantest white wines. Vintners' houses line the main street, many of

them with the typical large wooden gates that lead to the vine-covered courtyards where the Heuriger (wine of the latest vintage) is served by the owner and his family at simple wooden tables with benches. Gumpoldskirchen also has an arcaded Renaissance town hall, a market fountain made from a Roman sarcophagus, and the castle of the Teutonic knights, whose descendants still own some of the best vineyard sites in the area.

Continuing on the wine road brings you to the famous spa of **Baden.** Since antiquity, Baden's sulphuric thermal baths have attracted the ailing and the fashionable from all over the world. When the Romans came across the springs, they dubbed the town *Aquae;* the Babenbergs revived it in the 10th century, and when the Russian Czar Peter the Great visited in 1698, Baden's golden age began. Austrian Emperor Franz II spent the summers here; every year for 12 years before his death in 1835, the royal entourage moved from Vienna for the season. In Baden, Mozart composed his "Ave Verum"; Beethoven spent 15 summers here and wrote large sections of his Ninth Symphony and *Missa Solemnis;* here Franz Grillparzer wrote his historical dramas; and Josef Lanner, both Johann Strausses (father and son), Carl Michael Ziehrer, and Karl Millöcker composed and directed many of their waltzes, marches, and operettas in Baden.

The loveliest spot in Baden, and the main reason for a visit, is the huge and beautiful **Kurpark,** where many outdoor public concerts still take place. Operetta is given under the skies in the Summer Arena (the roof closes if it rains); in winter, it is performed in the Stadttheater. People sit quietly under the old trees or walk through the upper sections of the Kurpark for a view of the town from above. The old Kurhaus, now enlarged and renovated, incorporates a convention hall. The ornate casino, with its 19th-century decor, is a marvelous sight.

The six spa buildings are built directly over the 15 springs, which pour forth 8 million liters (1.76 million gallons) of the water every day. The water is about body temperature and is considered a particularly good cure for rheumatic diseases. Outdoors there are two thermal-water swimming complexes, the larger with five pools and a water temperature of 32° C (just under 90° F).

Route 210 takes you through the quiet Helenental Valley west of Baden to **Mayerling,** scene of a suicide pact in 1889 between the 30-year-old Habsburg heir, Crown Prince Rudolf, Emperor Franz Josef's only son, and his 17-year-old mistress, Baroness Marie Vetsera. The mystery surrounding the tragedy is still a juicy subject for speculation. In an attempt to suppress the scandal—the full details are not known to this day—the baroness's body was smuggled back into the city by carriage, propped up between two uncles. The Mayerling story surfaces regularly in books, films, and tabloid-newspaper gossip. The hunting lodge is no longer there; it was replaced by a Carmelite convent, built by the bereaved emperor.

About 4 km (2.5 mi) northeast of Mayerling, in the heart of the southern section of the Vienna Woods is **Heiligenkreuz,** a magnificent Cistercian abbey with a famous Romanesque and Gothic church, founded in 1135 by Leopold III. The church itself is lofty and serene, with beautifully carved choir stalls (the Cistercians are a singing order) surmounted by busts of Cistercian saints. The cloisters are interesting for the Chapel of the Dead, where the brothers lie in state guarded by four gesticulating skeletons holding candelabra. The chapterhouse contains the tombs of Babenberg rulers.

Dining and Lodging
Alland

Marienhof. Close to both Mayerling and Heiligenkreuz, this stylish building set in a beautiful park has simple but immaculate rooms. The **Kronprinz** restaurant serves outstanding, adventuresome fare, and there's a simpler and cheaper restaurant as well. *A–2534, tel. 02258/2378. 25 rooms. Facilities: restaurant (reservations not required, jacket and tie advised). No credit cards. Closed Sun. evening and Mon. Expensive.*

Baden

Sauerhof. "Schönbrunn yellow" marks this appealing country house that's been elegantly renovated, with rooms in "old Vienna" style. The hotel caters to seminars and group activities. Nevertheless, the restaurant is excellent (try the veal steak with mushrooms, or for dessert, the famous house crêpes). *Weilburgstr. 11–13, A–2500, tel. 02252/41251. 83 rooms. Facilities: restaurant (reservations not required, jacket and tie advised, open for lunch Sun. only), bar, indoor pool, tennis. AE, DC, MC, V. Very Expensive.*

Krainerhütte. This friendly house, in typical alpine style, with balconies and lots of natural wood, is family run. The rooms are attractively furnished in country style. *Helenental, A–2500, tel. 02252/4451. 60 rooms. Facilities: restaurant, indoor pool, sauna, solarium, tennis, DC, MC, V. Expensive.*

Mödling

Rosenhotel. The inside of this modern block, with its rustic decor, is far pleasanter than you'd expect from the plain outside. The rooms are simple but comfortable. *Guntramsdorferstr. 10a, A–2340, tel. 02236/85123. 50 rooms. Facilities: restaurant, bar. Moderate.*

Perchtoldsdorf

Jahreszeiten. This elegant, formal restaurant is now in the capable hands of Günter Winter, who achieved an excellent reputation with Hauswirth in Vienna. The menu offers international cuisine with an Austrian flair. Beyond the kitchen, the atmosphere, like the tables, is set to perfection, and the menu is supplemented by wines from an outstanding cellar, international as well as local. *Hochstr. 17, tel. 0222/864763. Reservations required. Jacket and tie advised. AE, DC, MC, V. Closed Mon. and early Aug. Very Expensive.*

Carnuntum and Rohrau

As the Romans moved up the Danube, they set up installations and fortresses along the way, mainly on the south side of the river. The Roman ruins in Vienna have long since been covered by later generations of buildings and can now be seen only in the handful of underground museums in the First District. But about 20 km (12 mi) east of the airport, one of the more impressive Roman camps, Carnuntum, has been extensively excavated, and in an easy day trip by car or public transportation, you can see this ancient community and the nearby towns of Rohrau and Bruck an der Leitha.

Escorted Tours

With the opening of Czechoslovakia, more tours may be offered to the eastern part of Lower Austria, but for the moment this is one area you'll probably have to explore on your own.

Getting Around
By Train or Bus

The suburban rail line from Wien-Mitte (Landstrasser Hauptstr.) stops at Petronell, with service about once an hour.

Carnuntum is about a 10-minute walk from the Petronell station. You can also take a post office bus, from the Wien-Mitte bus station, which drops you right at the ruins. From Petronell, a bus runs to Rohrau (check schedules), and from Rohrau, you can either return to Petronell or take a bus on to Bruck an der Leitha and from there a bus or train back to Vienna.

By Car In leaving the city, follow signs to "Airport/Bratislava" (A–4). Leave the divided highway at the airport for the more scenic Route 9, which will be marked to Hainburg. At Petronell, you will have to take a sharp right off the new road, but signs are clear for the Roman ruins (Carnuntum). From Petronell, take Route 211 to Rohrau and on to Bruck an der Leitha; from there, Route 10 takes you back to Vienna.

Exploring The Roman town and military camp of **Carnuntum** was the larg-
9 est garrison on the Roman "Amber Road" leading south from the Baltic Sea. At its peak it had a civilian population of 30,000 and boasted two amphitheaters. The settlement collapsed following a defeat by the Germans in the third century. You can take a guided tour (tel. 02165/2480; admission: AS25 adults, AS15 children; open Apr.–Oct., daily 9–5) or you can wander through the excavations, arranged as an open-air museum, with the remains of Roman houses, the amphitheater that once held 25,000 people, and the Heidentor (Heathen Gate), in a nearby field. New buildings are being completed to house the artifacts found in the course of the diggings, many of which are now on display in the Museum Carnuntinium in Bad Deutsch-Altenburg, 4½ km (2.8 mi) east. The Danube Museum in the great castle at Petronell contains some relics from the excavations (it is the only part of the castle open to visitors).

10 About 8 km (5 mi) south of Petronell is **Rohrau,** the birthplace of the composers Franz Josef (1732–1809) and Michael (1737–1806) Haydn. The compact straw-roofed house in which the family with 12 children lived is now a museum that gives a good idea of country life of the time (tel. 02164/2268; admission: AS20 adults, AS10 children; open Tues.–Sun. 10–5). Down the road is the 16th-century **Harrach Castle,** with an entry bridge (over the former moat) and a lake at the back. The art gallery contains the largest private collection in Austria (dating to 1668) with works by Rubens, Van Dyck, Breughel, and many Spanish and Italian artists. Haydn's mother was a cook at the castle, and Count Harrach became one of Haydn's first patrons. *Tel. 02164/22530. Admission: AS40 adults, AS20 children. Open Apr.–Oct., Tues–Sun. 10–5.*

Time Out **Schlosstaverne.** The restaurant tucked into the front corner of the castle serves substantial portions of good country food and wines from the region. Service slows somewhat when tour groups appear. The terrace is particularly inviting on a warm, sunny day. *Tel. 02164/2487. Reservations advised on weekends. Dress: casual but neat. No credit cards. Closed Mon., in winter. Inexpensive.*

11 If you return to Vienna via **Bruck an der Leitha,** take time to look around this walled community, which until 1921 marked the border with Hungary. Note the town square, with the 15th-century Holy Trinity church and the town hall with its arcaded court and Rococo balcony.

The Waldviertel

The "Forest District" north of the Danube and to the northwest of Vienna was long dormant, out of the mainstream and cut off from neighboring Czechoslovakia by a sealed border. Today, with the collapse of communism in Czechoslovakia and the re-opening of many crossing points, the Waldviertel has reawakened. Here gentle hills bearing stands of tall pine and oak are interspersed with small farms and friendly country villages. The region can be seen in a couple of days, longer when you pause to explore the museums, castles, and other attractions. Zwettl and Raabs an der Thaya make good bases for discovering this area away from the major tourism routes, where facilities are more modest and much less expensive.

Tourist Information The tourist office for Lower Austria in Vienna (Heidenschuss 2, tel. 0222/533–4773) has ample material on the Waldviertel. Other tourist offices within the region are those at Gars am Kamp (tel. 02985/2680), Horn (tel. 02982/265614), Zwettl (tel. 02822/2233), Gmünd (tel. 02852/53212), Waidhofen an der Thaya (tel. 02842/233117), and Raabs an der Thaya (tel. 02846/365).

Escorted Tours The Waldviertel remains undiscovered for organized tourism; for the time being, visitors are on their own.

Getting Around
By Bus or Train The main rail line from Vienna to Prague passes through the Waldviertel, making the region accessible by train. In addition, post office buses cover the area fairly well and with reasonable frequency. Bus hubs are Horn, Waidhofen, and Zwettl. An express bus service runs between Vienna and Heidenreichstein via Waidhofen an der Thaya.

By Car Signs for Prague will head you in the right direction out of Vienna. At Stockerau take Route 4 to Horn, Route 38 west to Zwettl, an unnumbered road to Weitra, Route 41 to Gmünd and Schrems, Route 30 north to Heidenreichstein, Route 5 to Waidhofen an der Thaya, an unnumbered road via Gross Siegharts to Raabs an der Thaya, Route 30 to Riegersburg, an unnumbered road to Hardegg. Return on Route 30 to Geras, Route 4 to Horn, Route 34 down the Kamp valley past Langenlois, and Route 3 back to Vienna.

Exploring The successful Austrian field marshall Radetzky (1766–1858) is buried at Heldenberg in the tiny village of **Kleinwetzdorf,** in elegant but lugubrious surroundings. His tomb, arranged for by a wealthy uniform supplier, is set in a park studded with dozens of larger-than-life busts of Austrian royalty and nobility. The small castle has a Radetzky museum. *Tel. 02956/2619. Admission: AS30 adults, AS60 family. Open May–Oct., weekends 10–5.*

Time Out **Restaurant Naderer** at the top of the hill above Maissau is an ideal stop for coffee: The house cakes are particularly good. A full meal can be enjoyed in summer on the terrace overlooking the valley.

At **Horn** are remnants of the impressive fortification walls built in 1532 as a defense against the invading Turks. Note the painted Renaissance facade on the house (1583) at Kirchenplatz 3.

About 5 km (3 mi) outside Horn, at **Altenburg** on Route 38, **Altenburg abbey** was built in 1144 and rebuilt in 1645–1740 after its destruction by the Swedes. The library and the frescoed ceilings are glorious. *Tel. 02982/3451. Admission: AS35 adults, AS15 children. Open (with guided tours) Easter–Oct., daily 9–noon and 1–5.*

Almost 25 km (15 m) west of Altenburg, the castle at **Ottenstein,** now a hotel-restaurant, has a number of impressive reception rooms and parts dating to 1178. Ottenstein defied the Swedes only to be devastated by the Russians in 1945. Sports enthusiasts will find boating and swimming in the reservoir-lake and golf at Niedergrünbach. The ruined **Lichtenfels castle** nearby can be explored.

Zwettl is known for the vast **Cistercian abbey** dating to 1138 about 2¼ km (1½ mi) west of the town. Later renovations added the glorious Baroque touches. *Tel. 02822/531–8117. Admission: AS35 adults, AS20 children. Open (with guided tours) May–Oct., Mon.–Sat. 10–noon and 2–4, Sun. 11–noon and 2–4.*

About 2 km (1 mi) north of Zwettl on Route 36, a fascinating **museum of medicine and meteorology** is housed in a cloister chapel built in 1294. Exhibits follow the development of medicine from earliest times to the present, and the courtyard garden of medicinal herbs adds another dimension to the history. *Tel. 02822/53180. Admission: AS40 adults, AS15 children. Open May–early Nov., Tues.–Sun. 10–6.*

Time Out | In the Zwettl abbey the **Stiftsrestaurant,** a spacious tavern complex, serves good Austrian country fare such as grilled chicken and roast pork with bread dumpling. The beer is fresh from the nearby brewery.

About 7½ km (almost 5 mi) west of Zwettl (follow signs to Rosenau), **Rosenau castle** is an impressive renaissance structure built in 1590 with later Baroque additions. The castle was ravaged by the Soviets in 1945, then rebuilt as a hotel and museum complex housing the unique **Freemasonry museum,** with a secret room once used for lodge ceremonies that was discovered during the renovations. Displays show the ties of Haydn and Mozart to freemasonry, and many exhibit labels are in English, reflecting the origins of the brotherhood. *Tel. 02822/8221. Admission: AS40 adults, AS30 senior citizens, AS20 children. Open mid-Apr.–mid-Nov., daily 9–5.*

On the main road, turn west 20 km (12½ mi) to **Weitra,** a small town stunning for its ornate painted houses (Sgraffiti) dating from the 17th and 18th centuries. A charming small brewery here has been in business since 1321! And the tradition is well founded: in 1645, 33 citizens held the right to operate a brewery.

Gmünd lies 16 km (10 mi) north of Weitra on Route 41, a town that was divided when the border with Czechoslovakia was established. The actual line passes through a few houses and backyards, but with the barbed-wire defenses removed, the border is now a harmless affair. Railroad fans have a field day here; the Czechs still use some steam locomotives for switching, and on the Austrian side Gmünd is one of the main points on the narrow-gauge Waldviertler Bahn, which runs occasional steam excursions (tel. 02852/4120 or 02852/4386). The nature park to the northeast of the center, open to the public all year, includes a geological open-air museum and a stone marking the 15th meridian east of Greenwich.

North of Schrems a detour west from Route 30, on Route 303, leads to Neunagelberg, a center of glassmaking since 1740. Among the glassworks you can visit is *Glasstudio Zalto* (tel. 02859/237). Another, *Stölzle Kristall* (tel. 02859/531), has a showroom and factory outlet.

At **Heidenreichstein** on Route 30, the massive moated **castle** with its corner towers has never been captured since it was built in the 15th century; some of the walls, 3 meters (10 ft) thick, went up in the 13th century. *Tel. 02862/2336. Admission (with guided tour): AS30 adults, AS15 children. Open mid-Apr.–mid-Oct., Tues.–Sun. 9–noon and 2–5.*

Route 5 leads east to **Waidhofen an der Thaya,** a three-sided walled defense city typical of the 13th century. Fires destroyed much of the early character of the town, but the town square, rebuilt at the end of the 19th century, has a pleasing unity of character. The town is dominated by its Baroque parish church; the Rococo chapel to Mary includes a madonna of 1440 and distinguished portraits marking the stations of the cross. Outside the city walls, the **Bürgerspitalkapelle** has a side altar with a Gothic carved-wood relief of Mary and child and 13 assistants, from about 1500.

An unnumbered road continues east 21 km (13 mi) via Gross-Siegharts to **Raabs an der Thaya,** an attractive village watched over by an 11th-century castle perched dramatically on a rock outcropping and reflected in the river below. *Tel. 02846/659. Admission AS20. Open May–Oct., daily 9–noon and 1–4.*

The intriguing ruins of the Kollmitz castle to the southeast of Raabs can be explored, and a bit farther along are the ruins of Eibenstein castle, another link in the defense chain along the border with Bohemia.

Route 30 leads to Drosendorf, with a castle built in 1100 and a town center typical of a small walled community. Farther along—27 km (17 mi) from Raabs—**Riegersburg castle** was originally moated, then the substantial edifice was given a Baroque rebuilding in 1731 and restored again after heavy damage inflicted by the Russians in 1945. Note the window variations and the figures that ornament the roofline. *Tel. 02916/332. Admission (on guided tour only): AS58 adults, AS27 children. Combination ticket with Hardegg: AS95. Open Apr.–June, Sept.–Oct., daily 9–5; July–Aug., daily 9–7.*

About 6 km (4 mi) east of Riegersburg on an unnumbered road, **Hardegg castle** stands mightily on a rock promontory high above the Thaya river, challenging Czechoslovakia. (The river midstream marks the boundary; as recently as 1990, the pedestrian bridge was unpassable, the border sealed, and Czech border defenses concealed in the woods opposite.) The earliest parts of the castle date to 1140. The armory and armament collection, chapel, and the museum's exhibits on the emperor Maximilian in Mexico are alone worth the visit. In addition, the kitchen and other working rooms of the castle give a real feeling of the daily life of an earlier era. *Tel. 02949/8225. Admission: AS50 adults, AS45 senior citizens, AS27 children. Open Apr.– June, Sept.–Nov., daily 9–5; July–Aug., daily 9–6.*

From Hardegg, retrace your steps on Route 30 to Geras, where the impressive abbey has a marvelous Baroque interior. Continue south on Route 4 to Horn and take Route 34 south to Rosenburg and on through the Kamp river valley.

The castle at **Rosenburg** dates to 1200 and dominates the north entrance to the valley. Its interesting features include the jousting field, the reception rooms, and the Renaissance balconies and small courtyards incorporated into the design. *Tel. 02982/2911. Admission (with guided tour): AS50 adults, AS35 children. Falconry demonstration daily at 11 and 3; combination ticket AS80 adults, AS60 children. Open Apr.–mid-Nov., daily 9–5.*

The scenic Kamp valley technically belongs to the Waldviertel, though for the amount of wine produced here, it might as well be a part of the Weinviertel, the wine district to the east. The villages along the route—Gars am Kamp, Schönberg am Kamp, Zöbing, and Langenlois—are all known for excellent wines, mainly varietal whites. Castle ruins dot the hilltops above the vineyards; the area has been populated since well before 900 BC.

Route 34 takes you through more vineyards to Kollersdorf, where Route 3 east will return you to Vienna.

Dining and Lodging
Grafenegg
★

Schlosstaverne Grafenegg. Behind the golden facade of the elegant tavern waits a friendly and welcoming atmosphere. Rooms are comfortably furnished in beiges and reds. The restaurant offers game in season and local cuisine with international touches. The strawberries in early summer taste even better outdoors on the sunny dining terrace. *A–3485 Haitzendorf, tel. 02735/2616. 6 rooms. Facilities: restaurant (reservations advised on weekends). No credit cards. Closed Jan.–Feb. Moderate.*

Kirchberg am Wagram
★

Gut Oberstockstall. A former cloister houses this country inn where the rustic setting indoors is charming and the courtyard garden idyllic in summer. The menu promises lamb, duck, game in season, and tempting desserts such as grilled apricots—all to the accompaniment of the house's own wines. *Tel. 02279/2335. Reservations advised. Dress: casual chic. No credit cards. Closed Sun.–Tues.; mid-Dec.–Feb., last 2 weeks in Aug. Expensive.*

Langenlois

Brundlmayer. This country Heuriger offers outstanding wines from one of Austria's top vintners as well as a tasty hot and cold buffet, all in a rustic setting or in the Renaissance courtyard. The simple but delicious fare includes *Schinkenfleckerl*, a baked dish of noodles and ham. *Walterst. 14, tel. 02734/2883. Reservations advised in winter. Dress: casual chic. No credit cards. Closed Mon.–Wed.; Jan.–Feb. Moderate.*

Raabs an der Thaya
★

Hotel Thaya. A family-run hotel directly on the river, the Thaya offers modern rooms in beiges and dark wood in the new annex. Rooms overlooking the river are the favorites. The restaurant prepares such solid local specialties as roast pork and veal. *Hauptstr. 14, A–3820 Raabs an der Thaya, tel. 02846/ 2020. 25 rooms. Facilities: restaurant, bar, beer garden, disco,* *sauna, solarium, fitness room, parking. No credit cards. Moderate.*

★ **Pension Schlossblick.** This small modern pension has a homey atmosphere in its spacious lounge and cheery breakfast room. The beige-and-red rooms on the town side looking through the trees to the castle are the nicest. *Eduard Breit-Str. 7, A–3820 Raabs an der Thaya, tel. 02846/437. 13 rooms. Facilities: restaurant for hotel guests, parking. No credit cards. Inexpensive.*

Rosenau **Schloss Rosenau.** Set in an elegant palace, this small hotel offers country quiet and modern rooms furnished in period style. The wood-paneled restaurant is one of the best in the area, featuring garlic soup, bread soup, and lamb or game in season. In summer food seems to taste even better on the sunny outdoor terrace. *A–3924 Rosenau, tel. 02822/8221. 18 rooms. Facilities: restaurant (reservations advised on weekends), indoor pool, sauna, solarium, fishing. AE, DC, MC, V. Closed mid-Jan.–Feb. Moderate.*

The Weinviertel

The "Wine District," the rolling countryside north of Vienna, earns its name from the ideal terrain and climate here for wine. Both reds and whites come from the region, bounded by the Danube on the south, the Thaya river and the reopened Czech border on the north, the March river and Czechoslovakia to the east. No well-defined line separates the Weinviertel from the Waldviertel to the west; the Kamp river valley, officially part of the Waldviertel, is an important wine region. Whether wine, crops, or dairying, this is farming country, its broad expanses of vineyards and farm crops broken by patches of forest and neat villages. A tour by car, just for the scenery, can be made in a day; you may want two or three days to savor the region and its wines—generally on the medium-dry side. Don't expect to find here the elegant facilities you found elsewhere in Austria; prices are low by any standard, and village restaurants and accomodations are mainly *Gasthäuser* that meet local needs. This means that you'll rub shoulders over a glass of wine or a beer with country folk, a rugged specie different from that you find in most parts of the nation.

Tourist Information The tourist office for Lower Austria in Vienna (Heidenschuss 2, tel. 0222/533–4773) has basic information on the Weinviertel. Other tourist offices within the region are those at Poysdorf (Liechtensteinstr. 1, tel. 02552/3515), Retz (Herrenplatz 30, tel. 02942/2700), Laa an der Thaya (Rathaus, tel. 02522/5010), Mistelbach (Hauptplatz 6, tel. 02572/2787), Poysdorf (Singerstr. 2, tel. 02552/220017), and Gänserndorf (Rathausplatz 1, tel. 02282/26501).

Escorted Tours The Weinviertel has yet to be exploited by tour operators, and visitors are on their own.

Getting Around
By Bus or Train Bus service to and through the area is good, with direct services available between Vienna and Retz, Laa an der Thaya, and Poysdorf as well as buses between the region's larger towns. Trains run from Vienna to Mistelbach, and to Gänserndorf and beyond to Bernhardsthal on the Czech border.

By Car Roads are good and well marked. Head out of Vienna to Stockerau on Route 3 or the autobahn A22/E49/E59, following the signs to Prague. After Stockerau, turn north on Route 303 to beyond Hollabrun, then Routes 2 and 30 to Retz. From Retz, backtrack on Route 30 to Route 45 and head east to Laa an der Thaya. Then follow Route 46 to Staatz, Route 219 to Poysdorf, Route 7/E461 south beyond Gaweinstal, Route 220 to Gänserndorf, and Route 8 back to Vienna.

Exploring   Like Linz, **Korneuburg** is a center of Austrian shipbuilding; many Danube passenger ships, including those under USSR and other flags, were built here. The massive Gothic-style town hall dominates the main square, though other buildings are far older. The Augustine church has a *Last Supper* (1770) by the Austrian painter Maulpertsch as part of the altar.

Schloss Schönborn at **Göllersdorf** was laid out in 1712 by that master of baroque architecture, Lukas von Hildebrandt. Today the castle is in private hands, but the harmony of design can be appreciated from the outside.

Retz, at the northwest corner of the Weinviertel, is known for its red wines. Here you can tour Austria's largest wine cellar, tunneled 20 m (65 ft) under the town, and at the same time taste wines of the area. Some of the tunnels go back to the 13th century, and at the end of the 15th century each citizen was permitted to deal in wines and was entitled to storage space in the town cellars. Efforts to use the cellars for armaments production during World War II failed because of the 88% humidity. The temperature remains constant at 8–10°C (47–50°F). Entrance to the cellars is at the Rathauskeller. *Tel. 02942/2700 or 02942/2379. Guided tour (includes a commemorative glass and a wine sample): AS40 adults, AS15 children. Tours Mon.–Sat. 2 PM, Sun. 10, 11, 2, 3.*

The Retz town square is an attractive mixture of Sgraffito (painted) facades, Biedermeier, and other styles. Most buildings date to 1660 or later; during the Thirty Years' War the Swedes occupied Retz and left only 28 buildings standing. The Dominican church (1295) at the southwest corner of the square survived, and it is interesting for its long, narrow design.

To the northwest of the center, outside the walls on a hillcrest at Kalvarienberg 1, the windmill—the town's emblem—dates to 1830 and was in commercial use to 1927 as a gristmill and is still operational.

Retrace your way south on Route 30 to Route 45 and turn east to **Laa an der Thaya,** once an isolated town but increasingly a commercial center for Czechoslovakian shoppers now that the border is open. (As long as you have your passport with you, you should be able to cross the border and return without complication.) Laa boasts a **Beer Museum,** located in the town fortress, that traces the history of beer (the nearby Hubertus brewery has been in business since 1454) and maintains an imposing collection of beer bottles. *Tel. 02522/5010. Admission: AS15 adults, AS10 children. Open May–Sept., weekends 2–4.*

Time Out   If a coffee break seems in order, **Café Weiler,** upstairs on the main square at Stadtplatz 2, has outstanding cakes and pastries.

Driving Route 46 from Laa, you'll find that the impressive hilltop castle ruin at **Staatz** loses significance the closer you get. It's possible to wander through the ruin, but little is left of the onetime fortress other than a pile of stone and a strategic view of the countryside.

Route 219 leads to **Poysdorf** and the heart of the Weinviertel. Poysdorf vintages, mainly whites, rank with the best Austria has to offer. The town museum includes a section on viticulture and wine making. *Brunner Str. 9, tel. 02552/220025. Admission: AS20 adults. Open Easter–Nov., Sun. 10–noon and 2–4.*

South of **Gänserndorf,** the **auto safari park** allows visitors to drive through recreated natural habitats of live wild animals, many of which (lions and tigers) are hardly indigenous to Austria. The adventure takes five to six hours. *Siebenbrunner Str., tel. 02282/7261. Admission: AS135 adults, AS80 children. Open Palm Sunday–Nov., weekdays 9:30–4:30, weekends 9–5.*

Nearby at **Strasshof** the **Heizhaus** is a fascinating private collection of dozens of steam locomotives and railroad cars stored in a vast engine house. Enthusiasts have painstakingly rebuilt and restored many of the engines, which are operated on weekends. The complex includes transfer table, water towers, and coaling station, and visitors can climb around among many of the locomotives awaiting restoration. *Sillerstr. 123, tel. 02287/3027. Admission (with parking and guided tour): AS50 adults, AS25 children. Open Apr.–Sept., Sun. 10–4.*

Route 8 returns you to Vienna, passing through one of Austria's few oil fields, where operating pumps patiently pull up crude to be piped to the refinery about 20 km (12½ mi) south.

Dining and Lodging
Deutsch Wagram
Marchfelderhof. This sprawling complex with its eclectic series of rooms decorated with everything from antiques to hunting trophies has been undergoing renovation, but its character is unlikely to change. Nor is the menu, which pretends to grander things. The standards—Wiener Schnitzel, roast pork, lamb—are more successful than the more expensive efforts at innovation. *Tel. 02247/2243. Reservations advised. Jacket and tie advised. AE, DC, MC, V. Closed late Dec.–early Feb. Expensive.*

Laa an der Thaya
★
Restaurant Weiler. Light woods and country accessories set the tone in this family-run restaurant, and in summer dinner is served in the outdoor garden. The delicate cream of garlic soup is worth a visit, and a house specialty is game in season. For dessert, the cakes of the house are displayed in a showcase. *Staatsbahnstr. 60, tel. 02522/379. Reservations advised on weekends. Dress: casual neat. No credit cards. Closed Mon. and late June–mid-July. Moderate.*

Mistelbach
Zur Linde. This friendly restaurant with the rustic decor is setting higher standards for such traditional fare as roast pork, flank steak, and fresh game in season. But the major attraction here is the remarkable range of wines from the neighborhood at altogether reasonable prices. *Bahnhofstr. 49, tel. 02572/2409. Dress: casual but neat. AE, MC, V. Closed Mon. dinner; mid-Jan.–mid-Feb. Moderate.*
Gasthof Goldene Krone. This friendly, traditional house offers simple but adequate accommodation. Rooms are quaintly old-fashioned yet comfortable, and guests are in the heart of the Weinviertel for excursions. *Oberhofer Str. 15, A–2130, tel. 02572/27295. 22 rooms. Facilities: restaurant, bar, garage. No credit cards. Inexpensive.*

Poysdorf
Schreiber. Choose the shaded garden under huge trees or the country rustic decor indoors. The typical Austrian fare—roast

pork, stuffed breast of veal, boiled beef, filet steak with garlic—is commendable, as is the house-made ice cream. The wine card lists more than 60 area labels. *Bahnst. 2, tel. 02552/2348. Dress: casual but neat. No credit cards. Closed Wed. lunch, Thurs.; mid-Jan.–mid-Feb. Moderate.*

Winzerstadl. Local wines and such specialties as roast pork with caraway, and smoked ham, are the fixtures at wine restaurants. This is a typical Weinviertel house, where in summer diners relax in the garden under huge chestnut trees. *Brunner Str. 7, tel. 02552/2772. Dress: casual but neat. No credit cards. Closed Mon., Tues.; Nov.–Apr. Moderate.*

4 The Danube Valley

Vienna to Linz

Introduction

*by George W.
Hamilton*

In this chapter we follow the course of the Danube upstream
from Vienna as it winds through Lower Austria (Niederösterreich) and a bit of Upper Austria (Oberösterreich) to Linz, past
castles and industrial towns, the vineyards of the Weinviertel,
and apricot and apple orchards. This is a wonderful trip in early
spring, when the fruit trees are in bloom, or in fall after the
grape harvest, when the hillside vineyards turn reddish blue
and a crisp autumn chill settles over the Danube at dusk. This is
where Lorelei lured sailors to the shoals, where Richard the
Lionheart was locked in a dungeon for years, where marvelous
castles suddenly appear at a turn in the road.

Linz, Austria's third-largest city (and perhaps its most under-
rated) is a key industrial center. It's a fine town for shopping;
the stores are good, prices more reasonable than in Vienna or
the big resorts, and it's fun just to wander the narrow streets of
the old city. Concerts and opera at Linz's modern *Brucknerhaus* can be every bit as good as those in Vienna or Salzburg. From Linz, we explore several nearby towns and return
along the Danube's south bank, visiting the great abbey at
Melk (setting for the historical novel and film *The Name of the
Rose)*, the Göttweig abbey above the river opposite Krems, and
the abbey at Klosterneuburg.

The Danube, rising in Germany's Black Forest and emptying
into the Black Sea, is our focal point: The route that brought
the Romans to the area and contributed to its development remains one of Europe's important waterways, with three national capitals on its banks—Vienna, Budapest, and Belgrade.
Many of the hilltop castles along the route were built to give an
overview of this vital channel; the cities developed as ports for
the salt, wood, ores, and other cargo it carried; and the railroads and highways of today largely parallel its course. (The
Danube, not the latitudes, determines the names: Upper Austria is upstream, Lower Austria is downstream.)

Essential Information

Important Addresses and Numbers

**Tourist
Information**

For general information on the area, check with the district
tourist offices for **Lower Austria** (Heidenschuss 2, A–1010 Vienna, tel. 0222/533–4773), **Upper Austria** (Schillerstr. 50, A–
4010 Linz, tel. 0732/663021), and **Styria** (Herrengasse 16, A–
8010 Graz, tel. 0316/835–2410). Tourist offices for the towns
are:

Bad Hall (Kurhaus, A–4540, tel. 07258/20310)
Dürnstein (Parkplatz Ost, A–3601, tel. 02711/360, 02711/200)
Eferding (A–4070 Eferding, tel. 07272/555520)
Freistadt (Hauptplatz 12, A–4240, tel. 07942/2974)
Grein (Hauptstr. 3, A–4360, tel. 07268/680)
Klosterneuburg (Niedermarkt, A–3400, tel. 02243/2038)
Krems/Stein (Undstr. 6, A–3500, tel. 02732/82676)
Melk (Linzer Str. 3–5, A–3390, tel. 02752/2307)
Pöchlarn (Regensburger Str. 11, A–3380, tel. 02757/231040)
St. Polten (Rathausplatz 1, A–3100, tel. 02742/53354)
Steyr (Stadtplatz 27, A–4400, tel. 07252/23229)

Tulln (Stadtgemeinde, Nussallee 4, A–3430, tel. 02272/42850)
Wachau (Undstr. 6, A–3500 Krems, tel. 02732/85620)
Waidhofen an der Ybbs (Obere Stadtplatz 28, A–3340, tel. 07442/251–1165)
Weissenkirchen (Gemeinde Weissenkirchen, A–3610, tel. 02715/2232.

Arriving and Departing

You can travel to and from Vienna from most parts of the world (*see* Chapter 3, Vienna, Arriving and Departing by Plane). Linz is served mainly by Austrian Airlines, plus Lufthansa, KLM, Swissair, and Air France. Regular flights connect it with Vienna, Amsterdam, Düsseldorf, Frankfurt, London, Milan, Paris, and Zurich. The Linz airport (tel. 07221/72700–0) is in Hörsching, about 12 km (7.5 mi) southwest of the city. *See also* Chapter 3, Vienna: Arriving and Departing by Car, Train, Boat and Bus.

Getting Around

By Car A car is certainly the pleasantest way to make this trip. Roads are good and well marked, and if at any point you should be in a hurry, you can switch over to the A-1 autobahn, which parallels the general east–west course of the route. (*See* Chapter 1, Renting and Leasing Cars.)

By Train Every larger town and city on this tour can be reached by train—assuming you have the time—but the train misses the Wachau valley along the Danube's south bank. The rail line on the north side of the river literally clings to the bank in places, but service on that line is infrequent. You can combine rail and boat transportation along this route and have the best of both, taking the train upstream and crisscrossing your way back on the river. From Linz, the delightful LILO interurban line (tel. 0732/54376) makes the run up to Eferding, and you can also get to Bad Hall by train.

By Bus If you link them together, bus routes will get you to the main points of this trip and even to the hilltop castles and monasteries, assuming you have the time. If you coordinate your schedule to arrive at a point by train or boat, you can usually make reasonable bus connections to outlying destinations. In Vienna you can book bus tours (*see* Guided Tours, below); in Linz, ask at the municipal bus station (Bahnhofplatz 12, tel. 0732/1671.)

By Boat Taking the heart of this tour by boat is one of the highlights of an Austrian trip. Large river boats with sleeping accommodations ply the route between Vienna and Linz and on to Passau on the German border. Smaller day boats go between Vienna and the Wachau valley, and there you can change to local boats that crisscross the river between the colorful towns. Bridges across the river are few along this stretch, so boats are essential transportation; service is frequent enough that you can cross the river, visit a town, catch a bus or the next boat to the next town, and cross the river farther up- or downstream. You can take a day trip from Vienna and explore one of the stops, such as Krems, Dürnstein, or Melk. Boats run from May to late September. For information on boat schedules, contact DDSG/ Danube Steamship Company (Handelskai 265, A–1020 Vienna,

tel. 0222/217100 or Regensburger Str. 9, A–4010 Linz, tel.
0732/770–01115).

By Bicycle A bicycle trail parallels the Danube from considerably southeast of Vienna to Passau. The tourist offices of the towns along
the way (*see* Tourist Information, above) have information,
maps, and recommendations for sightseeing and overnight and
mealtime stops.

Guided Tours

Tours out of Vienna take you to Melk and back by bus and boat
in eight hours, with a stop at Dürnstein. Bus tours operate
year-round, but the boat runs only April–October. **Cityrama/
Gray Line,** *Börsegasse 1, tel. 0222/534130; adults AS690, children AS300, lunch not included;* **Vienna Sightseeing Tours,**
*Stelzhammergasse 4/11, tel. 0222/712–4683); adults AS870,
children AS480, lunch and hotel transfer included.*

Day boat trips with loudspeaker announcements in English
run daily from mid-April to late October. Contact the DDSG/
Danube Steamship Co. (Handelskai 265, tel. 0222/217100).

In Linz two-hour guided city sightseeing tours leave the
DDSG/Danube Steamship Co. landing quay (Niebelungen-
brücke) daily, May–October, at 2:15. For information and tickets, check with Tourist Information (Hauptplatz 34, Linz, tel.
0732/2393–1777).

Exploring the Danube Valley and Linz

This trip can be done in as little as three days, allowing one day
along the north Danube side (Tour 1), a day in Linz and surroundings (Tours 2 and 3), and a day to return along the south
shore (Tour 4). You could also happily spend six or more days:
adding time in Eferding and Freistadt, a day in Kremsmünster
and Steyr, a day for Waidhofen an der Ybbs, and perhaps returning by ship.

Highlights for First-time Visitors

Burg Kreuzenstein (*see* Tour 1)
Dürnstein castle ruins (*see* Tour 1)
Freistadt (*see* Tour 3)
Carved wood altar at Kefermarkt (*see* Tour 3)
The library at the great abbey at Melk (*see* Tour 4)
100-year-old open streetcars in Linz (*see* Tour 2)
Stift Göttweig (*see* Tour 4)
Town square in Steyr (*see* Tour 3)
Weinkolleg Kloster Und (*see* Tour 1)

Tour 1: The North Bank of the Danube, the Wachau

*Numbers in the margin correspond with points of interest on
the Danube Valley maps.*

If you're taking the tour by train, take streetcar D to the Franz
Jozefs Bahnhof. If you're driving, the trickiest part may be
getting out of Vienna. Follow signs to Prague to get across the

Danube. Avoid the right-hand exit marked Prague, which leads to the autobahn, and continue ahead, following signs for Prager Strasse and turning left at the traffic light. Prager Strasse (Route 3) heads you toward Langenzersdorf and Korneuburg.

Korneuburg is a center of Austrian shipbuilding, where river passenger ships and barges and transfer cranes are built for the Soviet Union. Stop for a look at the imposing neo-Gothic city hall (1864), which dominates the central square and towers over the town.

1 Continue on Route 3 about 3 km (2 mi) beyond Korneuburg, and atop a hillside to your right you'll spot **Burg Kreuzenstein,** a fairyland castle with turrets and towers. Using old elements and Gothic and Romanesque bits and pieces brought here for the purpose, Count Wilczek built Kreuzenstein, from 1879 to 1908, on the site of a destroyed castle, to house his Late Gothic collection. You wouldn't suspect the building wasn't absolutely authentic if the tour guides weren't so honest. You'll see rooms full of armaments, the festival and banquet halls, library, chapel, even the kitchens. You can also reach Kreuzenstein via the suburban train *(S-Bahn)* to Leobendorf and a ¾ hour hike up to the castle. *Leobendorf bei Korneuburg, tel. 02262/66102. Admission: AS50 adults, AS30 children. Open for guided tours Mar.–Nov., Tues.–Sun. 9–5 (last tour at 4).*

2 Route 3 continues past Stockerau, through a lush meadow and woodland area, and after about 33 km (21 mi), at Grafenwörth, you'll see signs pointing to your right to **Schloss Grafenegg.** The moated Renaissance castle dating to 1533 was stormed by the Swedes in 1645 and rebuilt from 1840 to 1873 in the English Gothic Revival style. Greatly damaged during the 1945–55 occupation, it was extensively restored in the 1980s. Look for such fascinating detail as the gargoyle waterspouts, and don't miss the chapel. *Haitzendorf, tel. 02735/220527. Admission: AS50 adults, AS15 children. Open May–Oct., Tues., Thurs. 1–5, weekends and holidays 10–5, depending on scheduled exhibitions.*

Time Out The **Schlosstaverne** in Haitzendorf (tel. 02735/2616) offers excellent food in a delightful setting, either in the Biedermeier dining room or under an umbrella in the garden. In season, you'll find game; otherwise, turn to the excellent Austrian standards such as *Tafelspitz.*

3 Return to Route 3 or follow signs over the back roads to **Krems.** This Renaissance town is closely tied to Austrian history; here the ruling Babenbergs set up a dukedom in 1120, and the earliest Austrian coin was struck in 1130. In the Middle Ages, Krems looked after the iron trade, while neighboring Stein traded in salt and wine. Today the area is the center of a thriving wine production. Krems over the years became a center of culture and art, and today it is an attractive city to wander through, with narrow streets and irregular squares in a pedestrian zone.

Among the sights of Krems–Stein is the **Steiner Tor,** the massive square gate protected by two stubby round towers, once set into the wall of the moated city. The oldest part of town is to the east. Follow along the Obere and Untere Landstrasse, and you'll spot dozens of eye-catching buildings in styles ranging

Lower Danube Valley

Upper Danube Valley

MÜHLVIERTEL

INNVIERTEL

NIBELUNGAU

Danube (Donau)

Danube (Donau)

SOUTH BANK
TOUR CONTINUES
ON MAP ABOVE

Melk **43**
Pöchlarn
Maria Taferl
Wördorf
Ottenschlag
Arbesbach
St. Georgen a. Walde
Mönchdorf
Hochrachsthal
Kefermarkt **33**
Freistadt **32** **33**
Pregarten
Gallneukirchen
Ottensheim
Pöstlingberg **31**
Feldkirchen
Pupping
Asbach **36**
Hartkirchen **35** **34** Eferding
Pöting
Altenfelden
Schlögen
Grieskirchen
Wallern
Hörsching
Wels
Meggenhofen
Tambach

Persenbeug **9**
Ybbs an der Donau **42**
Wieselburg
Purgstall
Randegg
Scheibbs
Grein **10**
Dornach
Amstetten
Waidhofen an der Ybbs **41**
Baumgartenberg **11**
Strengberg
Perg
Haag
Seitenstetten Markt
Steyr **39**
Mauthausen
Enns **40**
Linz **12 — 30**
Ebelsberg
Traun
Kronstorf
Sterning
Bad Hall
St. Florian **37**
Neuhofen a.d.K.
Kremsmünster **38**

Enns

Ybbs

Traun

119
124
123
124
125
127
129
131
129
137
137
135
138
122
122
122
121
337
115
139
3
3
3
1
1
1
36
25
22
A1
A1
A1
A2

6 miles
9 km
0

N

from Gothic to Renaissance to Baroque. It's easy to pick out the heavy Gothic **Piaristenkirche,** begun in 1470, with its distinctive square tower and central peak and minitowers at each corner. The main altar and most of the side altars incorporate paintings by the local artist Martin Johann Schmidt (1718–1801), popularly known as Kremser Schmidt, whose translucent works you will repeatedly come across in the course of this trip. Close by is the parish church of **St. Veit,** completed in 1630. The interior is surprisingly spacious; Kremser Schmidt did the ceiling frescoes.

The 14th-century former Dominican cloister, farther along the street, now serves as the **city museum,** with a wine museum that holds tastings; notice the arcade with its variety of pillars. *Tel. 02732/801338. Admission: AS20 adults, AS10 children. Open Easter–late Oct., Tues.–Sat. 9–noon and 2–5; Sun., holidays 9–noon.*

On the entry portal of the **Bürgerspitalkirche** at Obere Landstrasse 15, you'll see Friedrich III's legend *AEIOU,* standing for *Austria Erit In Orbe Ultima,* literally, "Austria extends to the ends of the earth."

④ Between Krems and Stein, in a beautifully restored Capucin cloister in the tiny town of **Und,** is the **Weinkolleg Kloster Und.** The building also houses the tourist office and a small wine museum, where you can taste (and buy) more than 100 Austrian wines. *Undstr. 6, Krems–Stein, tel. 02732/73073. Admission (with tasting): AS120. Open daily 11–7.*

⑤ In **Stein,** the former 14th-century **Minoritenkirche,** just off the main street in the pedestrian zone, now serves as a museum with changing displays. A few steps farther on, an imposing square Gothic tower identifies the 15th-century St. Nicholas parish church, whose altar painting and ceiling frescoes were done by Kremser Schmidt. The upper part of the Gothic charnel house (1462), squeezed between the church and the hillside, has been converted to housing. Notice, too, the many architecturally interesting houses in Stein, among them the former tollhouse, with rich Renaissance frescoes. Stein was the birthplace of Ludwig Köchel, the cataloguer of Mozart's works, which are referred to by their "Köchel number" from the index.

⑥ Moving along Route 3, you'll see **Dürnstein** ahead, distinguished by its prominent Baroque church and castle ruin on the hill overlooking the town. In the tower of this castle Richard I of England, was imprisoned (1192–93), until he was rescued by Blondel, the faithful minnesinger. It's said that Blondel, while wandering the area trying to find where his king was imprisoned, heard the sound of his master's voice completing the verse of a song he was singing. The town is small; leave the car at one end and walk the narrow streets. A 30-minute rather steep climb to the ruins will earn you a breathtaking view up and down the Danube valley and over the hills to the south. The gloriously Baroque former **Stiftskirche,** from the early 1700s, sits on a cliff overlooking the river. More than 100 tiny angels decorate the heavens of its ceiling, and couples come from near and far to be married in the romantic setting.

⑦ Tucked among vineyards, just around the bend in the Danube, is **Weissenkirchen,** a picturesque town that was fortified against the Turks in 1531. A fire in 1793 laid waste to much of the town, but the 15th-century parish church of **Maria**

Himmelfahrt, built on earlier foundations, largely survived the conflagration. You can compare styles and eras here: The south nave dates to 1300, the middle nave to 1439, the chapel to 1460. The madonna on the triumphal arch goes back to the Danube school of about 1520; the Baroque touches date to 1736; and to complete the picture, the Rococo organ was installed in 1777. On the Marktplatz, check out the 15th-century *Teisenhoferhof*, which has a charming Renaissance arcaded courtyard. The building now houses the Wachau museum and contains many paintings by Kremser Schmidt. *Tel. 02715/2268. Admission: AS20 adults, AS10 children. Open Apr.–Oct., Tues.–Sun. 10–5.*

About 4 km (2½ mi) farther along Route 3 is **St. Michael** at Wösendorf, noted for the Late Gothic parish church dating to 1500, with its choir roof ridge ornamented by curious ceramic deer, horses, and hares. They are copies; the originals are in the museum in Krems. The church's Baroque interior has traces of late 16th-century frescoes. The charnel house contains mummified remains from 1150 to 1300 and a rather grotesque altar made of skulls.

❽ Less than 1 km (½ mi) farther, a road swings off to the right into **Spitz,** set like a jewel in the surrounding vineyards and hills. One vineyard, the "thousand bucket" hill, is said to produce a thousand buckets of wine in a good year. A number of interesting houses in Spitz go back to the 16th and 17th centuries. The Late Gothic 15th-century parish church contains Kremser Schmidt's altar painting of the martyrdom of St. Mauritius. Note the carved wood statues of Christ and the 12 apostles dating to 1380, on the organ loft.

Just beyond Spitz and above the road is the ruin of the castle Hinterhaus, to which you can climb. A side road here marked to Ottenschlag (Route 217) leads up the hill, and about 4 km (2½ mi) farther on, to **Burg Ranna,** a well-preserved castle surrounded by a double wall and dry moat. The original structure dates to 1114–25, the St. George chapel possibly even earlier. *Ober-Ranna 1, Mühldorf, tel. 02713/8221. Admission: AS19. Open May–Nov., Sat. 3–5, Sun. and holidays 2–6.*

You can return on a back road to Route 3 at Aggsbach. The views are now mainly of the other side of the Danube, as you look across at Schönbühel and Melk. Shortly after Weitenegg the Wachau ends, and you come into that part of the Danube valley known as the Niebelungenau, where the mystical race of dwarfs, the Niebelungen of legend, are supposed to have settled for a while.

Crowning a hill on the north bank is the two-towered **Maria Taferl,** a pilgrimage church with a spectacular outlook. It's a bit touristy, but the church and the view are worth the side trip. About 4 km (2½ mi) up a back road is **Schloss Artstetten,** a massive square castle with four round defense towers at the corners. This is the burial place of Archduke Franz Ferdinand and his wife Sophie, whose double assassination in 1914 in Sarajevo was one of the triggers that set off World War I. *Tel. 07413/8302. Admission: AS50 adults, AS 26 children. Open Apr.–Nov., daily 9–5:30.*

❾ The Niebelungenau ends at **Persenbeug,** a small town with an important castle (viewable only from the outside) and a number of attractive Biedermeier houses. The castle, which sits directly over the Danube, was the birthplace in 1887 of Austria's last emperor and still belongs to the Habsburg family.

 About 19 km (12 mi) upstream you'll come to **Grein,** a picturesque town with a castle set above the Danube. The river bend below, known for years as "the place where death resides," was one of the most dangerous stretches of the river until the reefs were blasted away in the late 1700s. In Grein, take time to see the intimate Rococo **Stadttheater** in the town hall, built in 1790 by the populace and still occasionally used for concerts or plays. *Rathaus. Admission: AS10 adults, AS5 children. Tours Apr.–late Oct., daily 9, 10:30, 2:30.*

Time Out **Café Blumensträussl** (Stadtplatz 6) is a lovely spot for coffee and cake, amid the Viennese Biedermeier decor in winter or outdoors in the garden in summer. The *Mozarttorte* is renowned, as are the delicious goodies served during strawberry season. You can also get soup and snacks.

At Dornach the road leaves the Danube, and about 6 km (just under 4 mi) farther you'll find **Baumgartenberg,** which is worth a visit for its ornate Baroque parish church and the unusual chancel supported by a tree trunk.

Just before **Mauthausen** the road and the river again come together, and from the south the Enns river, one of six main tributaries, joins the Danube. Mauthausen, which has some interesting 16th-century houses, is better known today as the location of the Nazi concentration camp *KZ Lager*, northwest of the town. It has been preserved as a memorial to those who died here and in other such camps. Seventeen countries, including the United Kingdom, the Soviet Union, and France, have given monuments. There's a map and booklet in English. *Marbach 38, tel. 07238/2269. Admission: AS15 adults, AS5 children. Open Feb.–Mar., daily 8–3; Apr.–Sept., daily 8–5; Oct.–mid-Dec., daily 8–3; closed mid-Dec.–Jan.*

From Mauthausen it's 27 km (17 mi) to **Linz.** Route 3 takes you across the Danube south of the city and then into the center.

Tour 2: Linz

Numbers in the margin correspond with points of interest on the Linz map.

The capital of Upper Austria, set where the Traun river flows into the Danube, has a fascinating old city core and an active cultural life. In 1832 it had a horse-drawn train to Czechoslovakia that was the first rail line on the Continent. It is also the center of Austrian steel and chemical production, both started by the Germans in 1938. In the past, these industries made Linz a dirty city; with pollution controls now in place, Linz has been proclaimed cleaner than Vienna or Graz.

The heart of the city has been turned into a pedestrian zone; either leave the car at your hotel or use the huge new parking garage under the main square in the center of town. Streets in the center are narrow and mostly one-way, but distances are not great, and you can take in the highlights in the course of a two-hour walking tour.

Start at the Tourist Information Office (Hauptplatz 34, tel. 0732/2393–1777) and pick up the "Linz from A–Z" booklet in

⑬ English. Here you're on the main square at the **Altes Rathaus,** the Old City Hall. Although the original 1513 building was mainly destroyed by fire and replaced in 1658–59, its octagonal corner turret and lunar clock, as well as some vaulted rooms, remain, and you can detect traces of the original Renaissance structure on the Rathausgasse facade. The present exterior dates from 1824. The approach from Rathausgasse 5, opposite the Keplerhaus, leads through a fine arcaded courtyard. On the facade here you'll spot portraits of Emperor Friedrich III, the mayors Hoffmandl and Prunner, the astronomer Johannes Kepler, and the composer Anton Bruckner.

⑭ One of the symbols of Linz is the 20-meter (65-ft) Baroque **Pillar to the Holy Trinity** in the center of the square. Completed in 1723 of white Salzburg marble, the column offers thanks by an earthly trinity, the provincial estates, city council, and citizens, for deliverance from the threat of war (1704), fire (1712), and plague (1713).

⑮ Turn right on the west side of the square into the Klosterstrasse. On your left at the end of the block is the **Minorite Church,** once part of a monastery. The present building dates to 1752–58 and has a delightful Rococo interior with side altar paintings by Kremser Schmidt and the main altar by Bartolomeo Altomonte. (Open Oct.–June, Mon.–Sat. 7:30–11, Sun. 7:30–noon; July–Sept., daily 7:30–4.) The adjoining early Renaissance monastery buildings with the distinctive tower are ⑯ now the **Landhaus,** seat of the provincial government. Look inside to see the inner arcaded courtyard with the 1852 Planet Fountain and the Hall of Stone on the first floor, above the barrel-vaulted hall on the ground floor. The beautiful Renaissance doorway (1570) is made of red marble. Around the corner at ⑰ Altstadt 17 is the three-story Renaissance **Mozart Haus,** with a later Baroque facade and portal, where Mozart wrote his *Linz* symphony in 1783. Inside is a fine 17th-century three-story arcaded courtyard.

⑱ Headed down Altstadt toward the river, you'll pass the **Waaghaus,** bought by the city in 1524, at one time the public weighing office and now an indoor market. Emperor Friedrich ⑲ III is said to have died in the **Kremsmünstererhaus** (Altstadt 10) in 1493. The building was done over in Renaissance style in 1578–80, and a story was added in 1616, with two turrets and onion domes. There's a memorial room to the emperor here; his heart is entombed in the Linz parish church, but the rest of him is in St. Stephen's cathedral in Vienna. *Tel. 0732/2393–1912. Open by appointment.*

⑳ Just around the corner to your left, in Tummelplatz, you come to a massive four-story building with two inner courtyards, the **Linz Castle,** rebuilt by Friedrich III about 1477 (and much restored since), literally on top of a castle that dates to 799. Note the **Friedrichstor,** the Friedrich gate, with the same AEIOU monogram we saw earlier in Krems. The castle houses the Upper Austrian provincial museum, with weapons, musical instruments, nativity scenes, Upper Austrian art, and prehistoric and Roman relics. *Tummelplatz 10, tel. 0732/774419. Admission: AS25. Open Tues.–Fri. 9–5, weekends and holidays 10–4.*

㉑ Up the Herrenstrasse, at the corner of Bischofstrasse, you'll find the **Bischofshof** (1721), with its fine wrought-iron gate-

Alter Dom, **28**
Altes Rathaus (Old
City Hall), **13**
Bischofshof, **21**
Carmelite Church, **23**
Deutschordens-
kirche, **25**
Elisabethinen-
kirche, **27**

Johannes Kepler
House, **30**
Kremsmünsterer-
haus, **19**
Landhaus, **16**
Linz Castle, **20**
Minorite Church, **15**
Mozart Haus, **17**

Neuer Dom, **22**
Nordico (City
Museum), **26**
Pillar to the Holy
Trinity, **14**
Pöstlingbergbahn, **31**
Stadtpfarrkirche, **29**
Ursuline Church, **24**
Waaghaus, **18**

㉒ way. The massive **Neuer Dom** (New Cathedral) in Baumbach-strasse is to your right diagonally across Herrenstrasse. The bishop of Linz in 1862 engaged one of the architects of the Cologne cathedral to develop a design in neo-Gothic French-cathedral style and ordered that its tower not be higher than that of St. Stephen's in Vienna. At 134 meters (440 ft), it is shorter by a scant 2 meters. The 1633 statues of Saint Peter and Saint Paul on the high altar came from the parish church in nearby Eferding. The crypt contains a large nativity scene. *Open daily 7:30–7.*

From Herrenstrasse, cross left through Rudigierstrasse and walk north one block in the pedestrian Landstrasse to the Harrachstrasse, where magnificent Baroque churches sit on ㉓ either side: the **Carmelite Church,** modeled on St. Joseph's in ㉔ Prague (open daily 7–noon, 3–6:30), and the **Ursuline Church,** with double-figured towers, one of the identifying symbols of Linz (open daily 8–6). Go down the Harrachstrasse to see the ㉕ former **Deutschordenskirche** (Seminary Church, 1723), a beautiful yellow and white Baroque treasure with an elliptical dome, designed by Johann Lukas von Hildebrandt, who also designed its high altar. *Open May–Sept., daily 7–6; Oct.–Apr., daily 7–5.*

Down the Dametzstrasse, at the corner of Bethlehemstrasse, ㉖ you'll find the **Nordico,** the city museum (1610), whose collection follows local history from pre-Roman times to the mid-1880s. *Bethlehemstr. 7, tel. 0732/2393–1912. Admission free. Open weekdays 9–6, weekends 1–5.*

㉗ Farther up the Bethlehemstrasse is the **Elisabethinenkirche,** built in the mid-18th century. Note the unusually dynamic colors in the dome fresco by Altomonte. Turn down the Elisabethstrasse and head west along the Museumstrasse into Graben (straight ahead, don't turn right, although that's also ㉘ called Graben) to reach the Baroque **Alter Dom,** the old cathedral (1669–78), whose striking feature is the single nave, together with the side altars. Anton Bruckner was organist here from 1856 to 1868. *Open daily 7–noon and 3–7.*

Continue around the corner in the Domgasse to come to the ㉙ **Stadtpfarrkirche** (city parish church), which dates to 1286 and was rebuilt in Baroque style in 1648. The tomb in the right wall of the chancel contains Friedrich III's heart. The ceiling frescoes are by Altomonte, the figure of Johann Nepomuk (a local saint) in the chancel is by Georg Raphael Donner, in a setting by Hildebrandt. *Open Mon.–Sat. 8–7, Sun. 9–7.*

Head back toward the main square via the Rathausgasse. At ㉚ **No. 5,** the astronomer **Johannes Kepler** lived from 1622 to 1626; Linz's first printing shop was established in this house in 1745.

For a splendid view over Linz and the Danube, take the run up ㉛ the **Pöstlingberg** on the electric **Pöstlingbergbahn.** To reach the base station for the railway, take streetcar line 3 across the river to Urfahr, Linz's left bank. The cars take 16 minutes for the 2.9-km (nearly 2-mi) trip, making a 255-meter (840-ft) climb in the process. When it was built in 1898, it boasted the steepest incline of any noncog railway in Europe. In summer, the old open-bench cars are used. *Tel. 0732/28010. Round-trip fare: AS28 adults, AS14 children 6–15, two children under 6 free. Service daily all year, every 20 min, 5:30 AM–8:20 PM.*

A treat at the top for children is the fairy-tale-grotto railroad, which runs through a colorfully illuminated imaginary world. *Admission: AS25 adults, AS12 children under 15. Open Sat. before Easter–Nov., daily 9–5:45.*

The twin-towered Baroque pilgrimage church (1748) at the summit is another Linz landmark. The zoo on Pöstlingberg is still in the development stage, but it has some 600 animals. *Windflachweg 19, tel. 0732/237180. Admission: AS15 adults, AS5 children. Open Oct.–Mar., daily 10–4; Apr.–Sept., daily 10–6; closed Dec. 24–26, 31, and Jan. 1.*

Also in Urfahr is the exceptional **Neue Galerie,** one of Austria's best modern-art museums, which has a fine, well-balanced collection, mainly by contemporary artists. *Blütenstr. 15, Urfahr, tel. 0732/2393–3600. Admission: AS30 adults, AS10 children. Open Mon.–Wed., Fri., Sat. 10–6, Thurs. 10–10, Sun. 10–1.*

Tour 3: Short Excursions from Linz

Numbers in the margin correspond with points of interest on the Danube Valley maps.

The **Mühlviertel** (mill district in the agricultural, not industrial, sense) north of Linz to the Czechoslovak border is made up of meadows and gentle wooded hills interspersed with towns whose appearance has changed little since the Middle Ages. To the west of Linz, south of the Danube, lies the **Innviertel,** named for the Inn river (which forms the border with Germany before it joins the Danube), a region of broad fields and meadows, of enormous woodland tracts, ideal for cycling, hiking, and riding. To the south, the hilly landscape with its many streams and forested areas begins the foothills of the Austrian Alps, also a countryside for fishing, hiking, and riding.

32 To get to **Freistadt,** a beautifully preserved walled city in the eastern part of the Mühlviertel, cross the Danube to Linz–Urfahr and turn right onto Freistädter Strasse (Route 125/E55).

Freistadt developed as a border defense city on the salt route into Bohemia (now Czechoslovakia), which accounts for the wall, towers, and gates. Look at the Late Gothic **Linzertor,** the Linz gate, with its steep wedge-shaped roof, and the **Böhmertor,** on the opposite side, leading to Bohemia. If you have the time, walk around the wall to get an impression of how a city in the Middle Ages was conceived and defended; it will take you about a half hour. The city's central square, aglow with pastel facades, is virtually the same as that of 400 years ago, with no jarring modern buildings; only the parked cars intrude into the picture.

Wander through the side streets and alleys back of the central square and note the architectural details; many of the arcades contain interesting small shops. The 15th-century parish church of St. Catherine's was redone in Baroque style in the 17th century but retains its slender tower with the unusual balconies with railings on all four sides. The Late Gothic castle to the northeast of the square now houses the Mühlviertel district museum (Heimathaus); the display of painted glass (for which the nearby town of Sandl is famous) in the chapel and the hand tools in the tower are especially interesting. *Tel. 07942/2274.*

Admission: AS10 adults, children free. Guided tours only.
May–Oct., Tues.–Sat. 10 and 2; Sun., holidays, 10; Nov.–
Apr., Tues.–Fri. 10; Tues. and Thurs. also at 2.

33 On the way back from Freistadt, detour slightly east to **Kefermarkt,** about 10½ km (6½ mi) south. Here in the Late Gothic St. Wolfgang's church is one of Europe's great anonymous art treasures, a 13-meter- (42-ft-) high winged altar intricately carved from linden wood.

34 About 26 km (16¼ mi) west of Linz on Route 129 lies **Eferding,** a centuries-old community with an attractive town square. The double door in the south wall of the 15th-century church of St. Hippolyte is a gem of Late Gothic stonecutting, with the madonna and child above flanked by Saints Hippolyte and Agyd. Inside, note the Gothic altar with its five reliefs and the statues of Saints Wolfgang and Martin. Several of the gravestones in the church have unusual motifs from the Bible. Also visit the *Spitalskirche* (originally built in 1325) and note the Gothic frescoes in the Magdalen chapel, which date to about 1430.

Take Route 130 north from Eferding to Pupping, and if you like to explore ruins, follow signs for the turnoff on the left to **Schaunberg's** castle ruin. Otherwise, continue 3 km (2 mi) up
35 the road from Pupping to the parish church at **Hartkirchen,** to see fine Baroque wall and ceiling frescoes that create the illusion of space and depth. And 2 km (1 mi) farther (Route 131), on
36 the Danube, is **Aschach,** a small village that was once a river toll station, with gabled-roof burgher houses, a castle, and a Late Gothic church.

37 Southeast of Linz lies **St. Florian,** best known for the great abbey where Anton Bruckner (1824–96) was organist for 10 years and where he is buried. Take the road south to Kleinmünchen and Ebelsberg, or for a most romantic approach, try the **Florianer Bahn,** a resurrected electric interurban tram line, which runs museum streetcars on Sunday and holidays 6 km (nearly 4 mi) from Pichling to St. Florian (tel. 0732/485323, 821722, or 07435/4075). You enter the abbey complex via a magnificent figured gate that encompasses all three stories. A large and elegant staircase leads to the upper floors, and the major rooms are grouped around the inner courtyard. Guided tours include these and the imperial suite. In the splendid abbey church, where the ornate decor is somewhat in contrast to much of Bruckner's music, the Krismann organ (1770–74) is one of the largest and best of its period. *Tel. 07224/89030. Admission: AS40 adults, AS15 children. Guided tours only, 1½ hrs. Apr.–Oct., daily at 10, 11, 2, 3, 4.*

38 Take Route 139 southwest (or the train) from Linz to the vast Benedictine abbey at **Kremsmünster,** established in 777, one of the most important cloisters in Austria. Inside the church is the Gothic memorial tomb of Gunther, killed by a wild boar, whose father, Tassilo, duke of Bavaria, vowed to build the abbey on the site. Note the Baroque decor added in the 18th century and the frescoes and paintings. There are magnificent rooms: the **Kaisersaal** and the frescoed library with more than 100,000 volumes, many of them manuscripts. On one side of the **Prälatenhof** courtyard are four elegant fish basins amid splendid Baroque statuary, and opposite is the **Abteitrakt,** whose art collection includes the Tassilo chalice, from about 765. The eight-story observatory houses an early museum of science.

The "mosque" garden house from 1640 has Oriental decoration. *Tel. 07583/275216. Admission: AS35 adults, AS15 children. Guided tours only when 5 or more are interested; tours are run Easter–Nov., daily at 9, 10, 11, 1, 2, 3, and 4, including observatory May–Nov.; tours Nov.–Easter by prior arrangement.*

Where Route 139 joins Route 122, cut south to **Bad Hall,** known for its saline-iodine curative springs. Tassilo, who founded Kremsmünster, gave the springs to the abbey in 777, but the town is now an independent spa.

About 17 km (10½ mi) farther along Route 122, at the confluence of the Steyr and Enns rivers, you'll come to **Steyr,** a stunning Gothic market town. Today the main square is lined with pastel facades, many with Baroque and Rococo trim, all complemented by the castle that sits above. On the Enns side, steps and narrow passageways lead down to the river. So many of the houses are worthy of attention that you have to take your time and explore. The **Bummerlhaus** at No. 32, in its present form dating to 1497, has a Late Gothic three-story effect. The Steyrertalbahn, a narrow-gauge museum railroad, wanders 17 km (10½ mi) from Steyr through the countryside. (For information, tel. 07252/26569).

Tour 4: The South Bank of the Danube, the Wachau

South of the Danube is a district of gentle countryside crossed by the valleys of rivers that rise in the Alps and eventually feed the Danube. Little evidence remains today, in this prosperous country of small-industry and agriculture, that the area was heavily fought over in the final days of World War II. Neither mass tourism nor commerce has spoiled its tranquil life.

The return trip east starts at **Enns.** A settlement has existed continuously here at least since AD 50; the Romans set up a major encampment shortly after that date. From 1945 to 1955, the Enns river east of the city marked the border between the Soviet occupation zone and the U.S. zone.

Enns is dominated by the 56-meter (184-ft) square city tower (1565–68) that stands in the town square. A number of Gothic buildings in the center have Renaissance or Baroque facades. Visit the **St. Laurence basilica,** built on the foundations of a far earlier church, west of the town center, to see the glass-enclosed layers of earlier civilizations that the archaeologists discovered as they uncovered a part of the floor. And outside, look for the Baroque carved-wood Pontius Pilate disguised as a Turk, alongside a hand-bound Christ, on the balcony of the old reliquary.

Take the A1 autobahn or Route 1 east from Enns to just before Amstetten, where Route 121 cuts south paralleling the Ybbs river and the branch rail line for about 25 km (16 mi) to **Waidhofen an der Ybbs.** This appealing river town developed early as an industrial center, turning Styrian iron ore into swords, knives, sickles, and scythes. These weapons proved successful in the defense against the Turks in 1532; in remembrance, the hands on the north side of the town tower clock remain at 12:45 (your watch is right and the clock isn't). In 1871, Baron Rothschild bought the collapsing castle and assigned Friedrich Schmidt, architect of the Vienna city hall, to rebuild it in neo-Gothic style. Stroll around the two squares in the

Altstadt to see the Gothic and Baroque houses, and to the Graben on the edge of the old city, for the delightful Biedermeier houses and the churches and chapels.

Make your way back to the Danube via Routes 31 and 22 east, then Route 25 north through the beer-brewing town of Wieselburg to **Ybbs an der Donau.** Or retrace your steps up Route 121 and take the autobahn. Floods and fires have left their mark here, but many 16th-century and Renaissance houses remain, their courtyards vine covered and shaded. Look particularly at the houses around the main square. The parish church of St. Laurence has interesting old tombstones, a gorgeous gilded organ, and a Mount of Olives scene with clay figures dating to 1450. Note, too, that Ybbs boasts one of Austria's finer restaurants, Villa Nowotni (*see* Dining and Lodging, below).

From Ybbs, backtrack about 2 km (1 mi) on Route 25 to Route 1, then head northeast for about 1½ km (1 mi) until you come to a road on the left marked to Sarling and Sausenstein. Follow that road to **Pöchlarn,** the birthplace of the artist Oskar Kokoschka, whose dramatic and colorful oils are in museums around the world. His birthplace is now a museum that has special exhibits every year. *Regensburger Str. 39, tel. 02757/7656. Admission: AS30. Open mid-June–mid-Sept., Wed.–Sun. 10–noon and 2–5.*

Continuing eastward through Pöchlarn brings you back to Route 1. About 4 km (2½ mi) on, you'll glimpse the magnificent **Melk** abbey ahead, on its promontory above the river, one of the great views in all Austria. The ideal time for this approach is mid- to late afternoon, when the sun sets the abbey's ornate yellow facade aglow.

Melk by any standard is a Baroque masterpiece. Here the story of *The Name of the Rose* took place, and in fact as in fiction, the monastery did burn in 1297, in 1683, and again in 1735. The Benedictine abbey was established in 1089; the building you see today dates to 1736, although earlier elements are incorporated. A tour of the building will include the main public rooms: the magnificent library, with more than 70,000 books and 2,000 manuscripts and a superb ceiling fresco by the master Paul Troger; the marble hall, whose windows on three sides enhance the ceiling frescoes; the glorious spiral staircase; and the church of Saints Peter and Paul, an exquisite example of Baroque. Note the side altars and the portraits of the saints; the artist Paul Troger was active here, too. The pulpit and even the confessionals are glorious; the organ loft is breathtaking. *Abt. Berthold Dietmayr-Str. 1, tel. 02752/23120. Admission: AS50 adults, AS30 children. Open Mar.–Oct., daily 9–noon, 1–4; June–Sept., daily 9–5; guided tours hourly last about 50 min.*

Time Out   The **Stiftsrestaurant** here offers standard fare, but the abbey's excellent wines elevate a simple meal to an experience—particularly on a sunny day on the terrace. The roast chicken is good and combines superbly with the dry white wines. *Closed Nov.–May.*

From Melk, take Route 33 along the south bank, and you're back in the Wachau again. About 4 km (2½ mi) along, you'll come to **Schönbühel an der Donau,** whose unbelievably picturesque castle, perched on a cliff overlooking the Danube, is unfortunately not open to visitors.

Past **Aggsbach Dorf** you'll spot, on a hill to your right, the romantic ruin of 13th-century Aggstein castle, reportedly the lair of pirates who preyed on river traffic. As you continue northeast, you'll have lovely views of the towns across the river.

Mautern, opposite Krems, was a Roman encampment mentioned in the tales of the Niebelungen. The old houses and the castle are attractive, but contemporary Mautern is known for one of Austria's top restaurants, in an inn run by Lisl Bacher; in nearby Klein-Wien there's another—also superb—run by her sister (*see* Dining and Lodging, below).

㊹ You're bound to have seen **Stift Göttweig** as you came along the riverside road: The vast Benedictine abbey high above the Danube valley watches over the gateway to the Wachau. To reach it, go along Route 33, turn right into the highway south (marked to Stift Göttweig and St. Pölten), and turn right again (marked to Stift Göttweig) at the crest of the hill. Göttweig was redone outside in the mid-1700s in classic style, which you'll note from the columns and balcony and relatively plain side towers. Inside, it is a monument to Baroque art, with marvelous ornate decoration against the gold, brown, and blue. The stained-glass windows behind the high altar date to the mid-1400s. The public rooms of the abbey are splendid, particularly the Kaiserzimmer (Emperor's rooms), in which Napoleon stayed in 1809, reached via the elegant Emperor's staircase. Depending on the schedule of exhibitions, rooms may or may not be open to view. In postwar years, surprising treasures turned up in the Göttweig library, including original musical scores by Haydn and Mozart. *Furth bei Göttweig, tel. 02732/855810. Admission:AS30 adults, AS15 children. Guided tours only, Easter–Oct., daily at 10, 11AM and 2, 3, 4PM.*

Time Out   The terrace of the **Stiftsrestaurant** on the abbey grounds offers not only good local cuisine but, on a good day, a spectacular view. It's a great spot for lunch, coffee, or a drink. You might try—and buy by the bottle—the excellent wines produced by the abbey.

㊺ You may want to make a detour 20 km (12½ mi) south to **St. Pölten,** Lower Austria's capital. The old center of the city, now mainly a pedestrian zone, shows a distinctly Baroque face: The originally Romanesque cathedral on Domplatz has a rich Baroque interior; the Rococo Franciscan church at the north end of the Rathausplatz has four altar paintings by Kremser Schmidt. The Institute of English Maidens (a former convent) in nearby Linzer Strasse is one of the finest Baroque buildings in the city. The church contains frescoes by master Paul Troger.

Take the Wiener Strasse (Route 1) out of St. Pölten headed east for 12 km (8 mi) to Kapelln, then turn left to **Herzogenburg.** In the great Augustine cloister here, the buildings date mainly to the mid-1700s. Fischer von Erlach was among the architects who designed the abbey. The church, dedicated to Saints George and Stephen, is ornate Baroque; the organ loft is a beauty. *Tel. 02782/3112. Admission: AS30 adults, AS10 chil-*

dren. Open Apr.–Oct. Guided tours only (about 1 hr) 9–noon
and 1–5.

Head north on Route S33 or the parallel road, marked to
Traismauer, and pick up Route 43 east. If you're ready for back
roads (too well marked for you to get lost), cut off to the left to
Oberbierbaum (Upper Beer Tree) and then on to Zwentendorf
(there's a fascinating black madonna in the side chapel of the
parish church here). If you follow Route 43, it will land you on
Route 1 at Mitterndorf; drive east and after 4 km (2½ mi), turn
left off Route 1 onto Route 19, marked for Tulln.

 At **Tulln,** you'll spot a number of charming Baroque touches in
the attractive main square. There's a new museum to honor the
artist Egon Schiele (1890–1918) who was born here, although
you'll find his best works in Vienna. *Donaulände 26, tel. 02272/
4570. Admission: AS30 adults, AS15 children. Open Tues.–
Sun. 9–noon and 2–6.*

The Romanesque parish church of St. Stephen on the Wiener
Strasse is noteworthy for its west door and the six figures
carved in relief circles on each side (presumably the 12 apostles). Beside the church, the unusual combined chapel (upstairs) and charnel house (below) is in a structure that
successfully combines late Romanesque and early Gothic.

Drive east on Route 14 and turn left at St. Andrä-Wördern to
hug the Danube shoreline en route to **Greifenstein.** Atop the hill
there, another castle with a spectacular view looks up the Danube and across to Stockerau. Its earliest parts date to 1135, but
most of what you see stems from a thorough but romantic renovation in 1818. The view is worth the climb, even when the castle is closed. *Kostersitzgasse 5, tel. 02242/2353. Currently
closed.*

As you come down into **Klosterneuburg,** the great Augustine
abbey dominates the scene. It has changed many times since it
was established in 1114, most recently in 1892, when Friedrich
Schmidt, architect of Vienna's city hall, added neo-Gothic features to its two identifying towers. Klosterneuburg was unusual in that until 1568 it had both men's and women's orders in the
same abbey.

In the abbey church, look for the carved wood choir and oratory
and the large 17th-century organ. Among Klosterneuburg's
treasures are the beautifully enameled 1181 Verdun Altar in
the Leopold chapel, stained-glass windows from the 14th and
15th centuries, Romanesque candelabra from the 12th century,
and gorgeous ceiling frescoes, in the great marble hall. In the
wine cellar there's a huge cask over which people slide. The exercise, called *Fasslrutsch'n,* is indulged in during the *Leo-
poldiweinkost,* the wine tasting around Saint Leopold's day,
November 15. The abbey foundation owns vast properties in
Austria, including many vineyards whose wines are excellent.
*Stiftsplatz 1, tel. 02243/621–0212. Admission: AS30 adults,
AS10 children; guided tours only (about 1 hour) every half-
hour, Mon.–Sat. 9–11 and 1:30–5; Sun. and holidays 11,
1:30–5.*

Time Out Stop at **Café Veit** (Niedermarkt 13) for a light snack, coffee
(house roasted), or tea (25 varieties). Try the potato soup or the

semolina dumpling soup and finish off with an excellent apple strudel.

About 3 km (2 mi) down the road, off to the right tucked under Leopoldsberg, is the charming small vintner's village of **Kahlenberg**, an excellent spot to stop and sample the local wines. And you're now on the outskirts of Vienna, where our trip began.

What to See and Do with Children

Burg Kreuzenstein (*see* Tour 1, above).

The trip up the **Pöstlingberg** (*see* Tour 2, above) the fairytale grotto and the zoo.

The museum at **Schloss Ebelsberg** in Linz (take the Wiener Strasse from Blumauerplatz near the main rail station, or Streetcar 1 to Simonystrasse and change to Bus 11 to Ebelsberg) shows weapons, from the breech loader to the automatic rifle, and has a collection of old-time cars and motorcycles. *Schlossweg 7, Ebelsberg, tel. 0732/307632. Admission: AS38 adults, AS20 children. Open June–Sept., weekends and holidays 10–noon, 1–5.*

The **Florianer Bahn** from Pichling to St. Florian (*see* Tour 3, above).

The **Steyrertalbahn** (*see* Tour 3, above).

The castle at **Kremsegg**, on Route 139 near Kremsmunster, has a collection of old-fashioned cars and motorcycles. *Tel. 07583/247. Admission: AS50 adults, AS20 children. Open Sat. 1–5, Sun., holidays 10–noon, 1–5; July–Aug., daily 10–noon, 1–5.*

In a moated castle north of **Pottenbrunn**, 6½ km (4 mi) east of St. Pölten, there's a museum (*Zinnfigurenmuseum*) of tin soldiers. Imagine a bird's-eye view of entire armies in battle; you'll see thousands of soldiers, at their places in the battles of Leipzig (1813), Berg Isel (Innsbruck, 1809), Vienna (1683), and World War I. *Pottenbrunner Hauptstr. 77, tel. 02785/2337. Admission: AS35 adults, AS10 children. Open Apr.–Oct., Tues.–Sun. 9–5.*

The **Feuerwehrmuseum** (Firefighters' Museum) in St. Florian displays equipment from the Baroque era to the present day. Saint Florian, the patron saint of firefighters and the guardian against fire, is easily recognized in Austrian churches as a figure pouring water from a bucket over a blazing house. *Stiftstr. 3, tel. 07224/219. Admission: AS20 adults, AS10 children. Open May–Oct., Tues.–Sun. 9–noon, 2–4.*

Off the Beaten Track

There's a marvelous *Heuriger* (wine garden) at Hollenburg, 1 km (½ mi) up the hill after the Routes 33 and S33 intersection, southeast of Krems, then about 5½ km (3½ mi) east—the turnoff is marked to Thallern. The setting is on a hill above the Danube, and there's even a castle ruin. The **Ruinenheuriger** is one of those seasonal places that's open when it's open, so call ahead. The wines come from the Geymüller vineyards; nearly everybody in the town appears to be a vintner. *Tel. 02732/2229.*

Steyr has an intriguing section of abandoned industrial buildings along the Steyr river (take Gaswerkgasse and turn down to the river). In the same area, you'll see workers' housing of 100 years ago; it was provided by the employer and was probably better than that which the workers would otherwise have had.

Shopping

If you want to shop for wine, you're in the ideal area. St. Pölten has a large selection of more standard items, and you will find good local souvenirs in Krems and Enns. Linz is a good place to shop; prices are generally lower than those in resorts and other large cities, and selections are good. The major shops are found in the main square and the adjoining side streets, in the Old Quarter to the west of the main square, in the pedestrian zone of the Landstrasse and its side streets, and in the Haupstrasse of Urfahr, over the Niebelungen bridge across the Danube. For local handmade items and good-quality souvenirs, try **Ö.Ö. Heimatwerk** (Landstr. 31, Linz, tel. 0732/773–3760), where you'll find silver, pewter, ceramics, fabrics, and some clothing. All kinds of stuff, from clothing to china, is sold (March–mid-November, Saturday 7–2) on the Hauptplatz (main square). In winter the **Flea Market** moves across the river next to the new city hall, left just over the bridge. The state-run "Dorotheum" auction house is at Fabrikstrasse 26 (tel. 0732/773132).

For antiques go to the old city, on the side streets around the main square. Try **Otto Buchinger** (Bethlehemstr. 5, tel. 0732/770117), **Richard Kirchmayr** (Bischofstr. 3a, tel. 0732/276–9843), **Kunsthandlung Kirchmayr** (Herrenstr. 23, tel. 0732/774667), **Ute Pastl** (Wischerstr. 26, Urfahr, tel. 0732/237306), and **Heinz Roland** (Khevenhüllerstr. 25, tel. 0732/663003). For jewelry, try **Pfaffenberger** (Landstr. 42, tel. 0732/772495) or **Wild** (Landstr. 49, tel. 0732/774105).

Sports and Fitness

Participant Sports

Bicycling
The trail along the Danube must be one of the great bicycle routes of the world. For much of the way (the exception being the Korneuburg–Krems stretch) you can take this trip by bike on both sides of the river. For details and information, *see* Getting Around, By Bicycle, above. Get the folder "Danube Cycle Track" (in English, from Niederösterreich-Information, Heidenschuss 2, A–1010 Vienna, tel. 0222/533–4773) for hints on what to see and where you'll find "cyclist friendly" accommodations, repairs, and other services. Some small hotels will even pick up you and your bike from the cycle path. You'll find bicycle rentals at Aggsbach–Markt, Dürnstein, Grein, Krems, Mautern, Melk, Persenbeug–Gottsdorf, Pöchlarn, Schönbühel/Aggsbach Dorf, Spitz, Weissenkirchen, and Ybbs.

The landscape around Linz is relatively level, and within the city there are 89 km (55 mi) of marked cycle routes. Get the brochure "Cycling in Linz" from the tourist office. You can rent a bike through the city (tel. 0732/239–31777; AS20 per day) and at Verein Arbeitsloseninitiative (Bischofstr. 7, tel. 0732/771986). In the areas of Eferding, St. Florian, through the

Enns river valley, and around Steyr, the territory is generally good for cycling, with gentle hills and special routes. Bicycles can be rented at the railroad stations in Freistadt (tel. 07942/2319), Kremsmünster (tel. 07583/218), and Steyr (tel. 07252/1700 or 07252/233210).

Canoeing The Danube in general is fast and tricky, so you're best off to stick to the calmer waters back of the power dams (at Pöchlarn, above Melk, and near Grein). You can rent a canoe at Pöchlarn. You can also canoe on an arm of the Danube near Ottensheim, about 8 km (5 mi) west of Linz. For information call Ruderverein Donau (tel. 0732/236250) or Ruderverein Ister-Sparkasse (tel. 0732/774888).

Fishing This is splendid fishing country. Check with the town tourist offices about licenses and fishing rights for river trolling and fly-casting in Aggsbach–Markt, Dürnstein, Emmersdorf, Grein, Kleinpöchlarn, Krems, Mautern, Mauthausen, Persenbeug–Gottsdorf, Pöchlarn, Schönbühel/Aggsbach Dorf, Spitz, Waidhofen/Ybbs, and Ybbs. In Linz, check **Fischereiverband** (Kärntnerstr. 12, tel. 0732/50507) or **Weitgasser** (Figulystr. 5, tel. 0732/56566).

In the streams and lakes of the area around Linz, you can fly-cast for rainbow and brook trout and troll for pike and carp. For details, contact the tourist offices or the numbers listed below: Aschach (Dreihann-Harrach'sche Gutsverwaltung, tel. 07273/6312), Bad Hall (Pfarrkirchen, Schloss Feyregg, tel. 07258/2591; Gasthof Schröck "Hofwirt," hotel guests only, tel. 07258/2274), Freistadt (Sportgeschäft Gutenbrunner, tel. 07942/2720; Sportgeschäft Juch, tel. 07942/2532), Kremsmünster (Gerhard Fleck, tel. 07583/6103), Steyr (Angelsportverein Steyr, tel. 07252/615443).

Golf An 18-hole, par-72 course at **Tillysburg,** near St. Florian, is open April to November, but you'll have to caddy for yourself. *Tillysburg, St. Florian bei Linz, tel. 07223/2873. Greens fee: AS300 weekdays, AS400 weekends.*

Health and To keep fit in Linz, try **Olympic** (Mozartkreuzung, tel. 0732/
Fitness Clubs 776156; open weekdays 10–9, Sat. 2–6, Sun. 10–2) or **Sportstudio California** (Landwiedstr. 119, tel. 0732/41157; open weekdays 10–9, weekends 10–2).

Hiking You could hardly ask for better hiking country: From the level ground of the Danube valley, hills rise on both sides, giving great views when you reach the upper levels. There are *Wanderwege* (marked hiking paths) virtually everywhere; local tourist offices have maps and route details, and in Linz you can get the booklet "Urban Hiking Paths in Linz." Around the city you might retrace the route of the Linz–Budweis horse-drawn tramway, continental Europe's first railway, or wander from one castle to another. You can arrange to hike in the Mühlviertel from Freistadt to Grein (information: tel. 0732/235020) and even get your pack transferred from hotel to hotel.

Jogging Runners also use the bicycle trail along the Danube. The place to jog in Linz is along the river bank on the far side of the Danube (Urfahr).

Skating Linz is an ice-skating city; from late October to late February, there's outdoor skating daily 2–5 and 6–9 (no evening skating on Thurs.), weekends and holidays also 9–noon, and indoors from late September to late April, Wednesday 9–noon, Saturday 2–5, Sunday 10–noon, 2–5, 6–9. Untere Donaulände 11, tel. 0732/778513.

Tennis You'll find tennis courts—indoors and out—throughout this area in nearly every town. Ask at the tourist offices in Aggsbach–Markt, Dürnstein, Grein, Krems, Maria Taferl, Mautern, Persenbeug–Gottsdorf, Pöchlarn, Spitz, Waidhofen/Ybbs, and Weissenkirchen. In Linz, contact the Upper Austrian Tennis Association (Waldeggstr. 16, tel. 0732/51250). The Novotel also has two clay courts (Wankmüllerhofstr. 37, tel. 0732/47281).

In the country around Linz, there are courts in Bad Hall (Kurverwaltung, tel. 07258/20310), Freistadt (Turn- und Sport-Union, tel. 07942/2570), Kremsmünster (Tennishallenbetrib, tel. 07583/395 and Tennis-Center Stadlhuber, tel. 07583/7498), and Steyr (Tennishof Rottenbrunner, tel. 07252/61219).

Water Sports and Swimming All along the Danube there are many water sports available (check with the tourist offices in Krems, Mautern, and Pöchlarn), but the Danube is not for swimming. Virtually every town has an outdoor pool, and some have them indoors as well. You'll find large pools at Artstetten, Dürnstein, Grein, Krems, Maria Taferl, Mauthausen, Melk, Pöchlarn, Schönbühel/Aggsbach–Dorf, Spitz, and Waidhofen/Ybbs. All are family facilities, with changing rooms and lockers; most have snack bars or restaurants, too. In Linz, the Kral Waterskiing School offers waterskiing and other water sports (Talgasse 14, 0732/231494). The closest swimming is at the Pleschinger lake; to get there, take the No. 1 tram to Urfahr/Reindlstrasse and the No. 32 bus to the lake. This is a pleasant spot for family swimming, although it tends to be crowded on sunny, warm weekends.

Spectator Sports

Soccer matches are played in Linz in the **Stadion** (Roseggerstr. 41, tel. 0732/56055 or 0732/660670). Tennis matches and other sports events are held at the adjacent **Stadthalle** (tel. 0732/57311). Hockey and skating competitions are held in the **Eishalle.** Buy tickets for sports events at Kartenbüro Ruefa (Landstr. 67, tel. 0732/662–6810. Open weekdays 8:30–noon, 2–6; Sat. 8:30–noon).

Dining and Lodging

Dining

The restaurants in this chapter are varied; there are sophisticated and stylish ones, as well as the plain and peasant type. Everywhere they capitalize on the river view, and outdoor dining is common. Many of the towns along both sides of the Danube will have country inns with dining rooms rather than separate restaurants. Prices include tax and a service charge, but you may want to leave a small additional tip.

Highly recommended restaurants are indicated by a star ★.

Category	Cost*
Very Expensive	over AS500
Expensive	AS300–AS500
Moderate	AS200–AS300
Inexpensive	under AS200

*per person for a typical three-course meal with a glass of house wine

Lodging

On this trip you might stay in a castle hotel, a standard city hotel, or a country inn. Distances are short between tours, so you can easily stay in one place and drive to another to try a different restaurant. Room rates include taxes and service and almost always breakfast (except in the most expensive hotels), but it is wise to ask. It is customary to leave a small (AS20) additional tip for the chambermaid.

Highly recommended lodgings are indicated by a star ★ .

Category	Cost*
Very Expensive	over AS1,500
Expensive	AS1,000–AS1,500
Moderate	AS700–AS1,000
Inexpensive	under AS700

*All prices are for a standard double room, including tax and service.

Aschach/Feldkirchen

Dining and Lodging ★
Faust Schlössl. Once a toll-collection station belonging to the Schaunberg family (ruins of the family castle are nearby), this castle, on the river directly across from Aschach, is said to be haunted and to have been built by the Devil in a single night for Dr. Faustus. Ignore the tale and enjoy simple but modern comfort in the converted castle among the towers and turrets. *Oberlandshaag 2, A–4082 Feldkirchen, tel. 07233/7402. 25 rooms. Facilities: restaurant (closed Tues.), outdoor pool, bicycle rental, fishing. No credit cards. Moderate.*

Zur Sonne. The welcome of the bright yellow facade carries over to the comfortable traditional decor inside. You're right on the Danube here, and the best rooms have a river view. The popular restaurant offers regional and traditional specialties and, of course, fish, including fresh trout. *Kurzwernhartplatz 5, A–4082 Aschach/Donau, tel. 07273/6308. 12 rooms, 6 with bath. Facilities: restaurant (closed Fri., Oct.–Easter), sauna. No credit cards. Moderate.*

Bad Hall

Dining and Lodging ★
Schlosshotel Feyregg. You'll be in an exclusive setting in this Baroque castle just outside town, the elegant summer residence of an abbot. The comfortable, spacious guest rooms on the ground floor are furnished in period style. *A–4540 Bad Hall/*

Feyregg-Pfarrkirchen, tel. 07258/2591. 14 rooms. Facilities: restaurant, bar, garage. No credit cards. Very Expensive.

Gasthof Mitter. In this traditional family-run *Gasthof*, you're in the heart of town, convenient to the train station and the spa facilities. The rooms are in a pleasant country style in light colors. The hotel restaurant offers local dishes, including lamb, and game in season. *Hauptplatz 1, A–4540, tel. 07258/23630. 20 rooms, 16 with bath. Facilities: restaurant (closed Mon.), bar, garage. No credit cards. Closed Jan. Moderate.*

Dürnstein

Dining **Loibnerhof.** Here, in an idyllic setting on the banks of the Danube, you'll dine on interesting variations on Austrian themes: ravioli with blood-sausage filling and various grilled fish or lamb specialties. The wines come from the restaurant's own vineyards. *Unterloiben 7, tel. 02732/82890. Reservations advised on weekends. Dress: casual. No credit cards. Closed mid-Jan.–mid-Feb. and Mon.–Tues. Expensive.*

Zum Goldenen Strauss. A onetime post station, long a simple *Gasthaus*, now has ambitions to be something more. You'll be offered enormous portions of very good Austrian fare, with a flair that helps compensate for the occasionally slow service. Try the garlic soup followed by *Tafelspitz*. The rooms inside are cozy, the terrace a delight. *Tel. 02711/267. No reservations. Dress: casual but neat. No credit cards. Closed Tues. and mid-Jan.–mid-Mar. Moderate.*

Lodging **Richard Löwenherz.** The superb vaulted reception and dining rooms of this former convent are beautifully furnished with antiques. Though spacious and comfortable, the balconied guest rooms in the newer part of the house are more modern in decor and furnishings. The restaurant is known for its regional specialties and local wines. *A-3601, tel. 02711/222. 40 rooms. Facilities: restaurant, bar, outdoor pool. AE, DC, MC, V. Closed Nov.–Feb. Very Expensive.*

★ **Schlosshotel Dürnstein.** If there's to be one big fling on your trip, it might well be here. This 17th-century early Baroque castle, on a rocky terrace with exquisite views over the Danube, offers dream accommodations, surrounds you with genuine elegance and comfort, and has a particularly friendly and helpful staff. The best rooms look onto the river, but all are unusually bright and attractive; of moderate size, they have pillows, comfortable chairs, and country antiques throughout. The kitchen has a good reputation and wines are from the area. Dining on the terrace is a memorable experience. *A-3601, tel. 02711/212. 37 rooms. Facilities: restaurant (reservations advised, jacket and tie advised), bar, outdoor pool, sauna, solarium, garage. AE, MC. Closed Nov.–Mar. Very Expensive.*

Sänger Blondel. Behind the yellow facade is a very friendly, typical, traditional family hotel, with elegant country rooms of medium size that have attractive paneling and antique decorations. The staff is particularly helpful and can suggest several excursions in the area. The hotel is known for its restaurant, which features local specialties and a wide range of salads and lighter dishes. You can even buy a loaf of the house bread or a jar of the apricot marmalade. *A-3601, tel. 02711/253. 16 rooms. Facilities: restaurant (reservations advised on weekends, jacket advised, closed Sun.) bicycle rental, garage. No credit cards. Restaurant and hotel closed mid-Dec.–Feb. Moderate.*

Eferding

Dining   **Dannerbauer.** Two km (1¼ mi) north of Eferding on the road to Aschach, right on the Danube, is one of the area's best restaurants. It serves species of fish you probably never heard of, poached, grilled, broiled, or fried. Many of the fish come from the river; some are kept in the house tanks, to ensure freshness. There are meat dishes, too, and game (delicious wild hare) in season, and the soups (try the nettle soup) are excellent. The place has a pleasant outlook with lots of windows. *Brandstatt bei Eferding, tel. 07272/2471. Reservations advised. Jacket suggested. DC. Closed Mon., Tues., and Feb. Expensive.*

Dining and Lodging   **Zum Goldenen Kreuz.** The golden facade indicates a typical country-style hotel, simple but with the charm of a family-run establishment. You'll sleep on fluffy feather beds. The restaurant is known for its good regional cuisine, and there are occasional specialty weeks. *Schmiedstr. 29, A–4070, tel. 07272/ 42470. 21 rooms. Facilities: restaurant (closed Sun. night). AE, DC, MC. Closed a few days at Christmas. Moderate.*

Enns

Dining and Lodging   **Lauriacum.** You might overlook this plain contemporary building, set as it is among Baroque gems in the center of town, but it's the best place to stay. The bright rooms offer modern comfort, and the quiet garden is a welcoming spot. *Wiener Str. 5–7, A–4470, tel. 07223/2315. 30 rooms. Facilities: restaurant, bar, sauna, tennis, garage. MC, V. Very Expensive.*

Freistadt

Dining and Lodging ★   **Deim/Zum Goldenen Hirschen.** This romantic 600-year-old house full of atmosphere fits perfectly into the old city and is a wonderful place to stay. The rooms are up to date and attractive. The stone-arched ceiling adds to the elegance of the dining room, where you'll find international and local specialties and game in season (closed Fri. in winter). *Böhmergasse 8, A–4240, tel. 07942/2258, 07942/2111. 23 rooms, 19 with bath. Facilities: restaurant. DC. Expensive.*

★   **Zum Goldenen Adler.** Here you'll be in another 600-year-old house; it has been run by the same family since 1807, so tradition runs strong. The medium-size rooms are modern and full of country charm; the service is exceptionally accommodating. The newly renovated garden, with a piece of the old city wall as background, is a delightful oasis. The restaurant is known for such excellent regional specialties as *Böhmisches Bierfleisch*, a cut of beef cooked in beer. The desserts are outstanding. *Salzgasse 1, A–4240, tel. 07942/2112, 07942/2556. 30 rooms. Facilities: restaurant (closed Tues. Apr.–Oct.), pub, outdoor pool, solarium, sauna, fitness room. MC. Moderate.*

Göttweig/Klein Wien

Dining ★   **Schickh.** This restaurant, tucked away among lovely old trees below the north side of the Göttweig abbey, is worth looking for. The variety of dishes, from lamb to lobster, is astonishing for a small place, and the creative ideas that come out of the kitchen have made it a draw for knowledgeable diners. (It's in friendly competition with Bacher in nearby Mautern; the two are run by a pair of sisters.) In summer you'll dine in the garden, probably rubbing elbows with the prominent of Vienna. There's a handful of guest rooms available for overnights. *Avastr. 2, A–3511 Klein-Wien/Furth bei Göttweig, tel. 02736/ 218. Reservations required. Jacket and tie advised. No credit cards. Closed Wed., Thurs. Very Expensive.*

Klosterneuburg

Dining **Stiftskeller.** These atmospheric underground rooms in a historic part of the abbey are an authentic cellar in every sense of the word: Some of the fine wines carry the Klosterneuburg label. You can sample them along with standard Austrian fare, from Wiener schnitzel to rumpsteak with onions. *Albrechtsberggasse 1, tel. 02243/2070. Dress: casual but neat. Reservations advised on weekends. No credit cards. Moderate.*

Korneuburg

Dining **Tuttendörfl.** This rustic-modern restaurant is attractive, if just for the terrace right on the Danube. The kitchen turns out standard Viennese fare, good but unexciting, and there's game in season. To get here, look sharp for the turnoff left from Route 3 (*not* the A–22 autobahn) marked "Tuttendörfl," about 1½ km (1 mi) west of the Bisamberg intersection and traffic light. *Tuttendörfl 6, tel. 02262/2485. Reservations suggested on weekends. Jacket advised. No credit cards. Closed Sun., Mon., and Jan. Expensive.*

Krems/Stein

Dining and Lodging ★ **Alte Post.** You're allowed to drive into the pedestrian zone to this romantic old house in the heart of the old town, next to the Steinener Tor (west gate). The rooms are in comfortable country style, but the real feature here is dining on regional specialties or having a glass of local wine in the arcaded Renaissance courtyard. The staff is particularly friendly, and cyclists are welcome. *Obere Landstr. 32, A–3500 Krems, tel. 02732/82276. 25 rooms, 5 with bath. Facilities: restaurant, bicycle rental, garage. No credit cards. Moderate.*

Am Förthof. An inn has existed on the riverside site of this modern hotel for hundreds of years. The rooms are comfortable and balconied; those on the front have a view of the Danube and Göttweig abbey across the river—and the sounds of the traffic. The dining room offers good regional cuisine, and breakfasts are particularly recommended. *Förthofer Donaulände 8, A–3500, tel. 02732/83345, 02732/81348. 22 rooms. Facilities: restaurant, outdoor pool, sauna, solarium, bicycle rental. DC, MC. Moderate.*

Langenlebarn

Dining ★ **Zum Roten Wolf.** In an unpretentious but attractive rustic restaurant (one of Austria's top three dozen), the stylishly elegant table settings complement the outstanding food. Try any of the lamb variations or the breast of duck. The service is especially friendly; ask for advice on the wines. You can get here by local train from Vienna; the station is virtually at the door. *Bahnstr.*

58, tel. 02272/2567. Reservations required. Jacket and tie recommended. AE, DC, MC, V. Closed Mon., Tues. Expensive.

Linz

Dining **Allegro.** Upstairs here in Linz's top restaurant, you'll find distinctive table settings and outstanding cuisine and service in a
★ modern-elegant wood and rose-colored setting. Many of the dishes emphasize the careful treatment of local and regional fare; the lentil soup with sour cream garnished with grilled frankfurter bits is an example. The fish dishes and lamb are particularly praiseworthy—but you can hardly go wrong. Ask for advice on the food as well as the wines. The abundant cheese tray is excellent. *Schillerstr. 68, tel. 0732/669800. Reservations required. Jacket and tie required. AE. Closed Sat., Sun., except Sat. evening in Oct.–Apr.; closed early Aug. Very Expensive.*

★ **Kremsmünsterer Stuben.** In a beautifully restored house in the heart of the old city you'll find an attractive wood-paneled restaurant offering everything from regional specialties to a seven-course dinner. You might choose from saddle of hare or fillet of venison as a main course as you relax in the comfortable, traditional ambience. *Altstadt 10, tel. 0732/782111. Reservations advised. Jacket and tie required. AE, DC. Closed Mon., two weeks in Jan., two weeks in Aug. Very Expensive.*

Vogelkäfig. This excellent restaurant across the river, on the edge of the city, gives the impression of a country estate; with its many bird cages, the atmosphere is a bit exotic. The intriguing variations on local specialties are surprising, but they do work; how about onion soup garnished with an apple dumpling? *Neulichtenberg 13, tel. 0732/234037. Reservations recommended. Jacket and tie advised. AE, DC, MC, V. Closed Sun. eve., Mon. Expensive.*

Wolfinger. Upstairs in this house that's been beautifully restored to expose the old timbers is a restaurant that features both local dishes (excellent soups and a renowned Tafelspitz) and Italian fare. This is a favorite gathering place for Linz businesspeople. *Hauptplatz 19, tel. 0732/773–2910. Reservations advised. Jacket and tie recommended. AE, DC, MC, V. Closed Sun. Expensive.*

Tautermann. Downstairs you can choose from the café's prizewinning cakes and pastries and enjoy them with coffee at the wrought-iron tables upstairs. *Klammstr. 14, tel. 0732/779686. No reservations. Dress: casual but neat. No credit cards. Closed Tues. Moderate.*

★ **Traxlmayr.** This is one of Austria's great coffeehouses in the old tradition, with the patina of age, where you can linger all day over one cup of coffee, reading the papers in their bentwood holders, and then have a light meal. All Linz gathers on the terrace in summer. Ask for the specialty, *Linzer Torte*, with your coffee. *Promenade 16, tel. 0732/773353. Reservations unnecessary. Dress: casual but neat. No credit cards. Closed Sun. Moderate.*

Zum Klosterhof. This complex in the former Kremsmünster abbey gives you a choice of upstairs and downstairs rooms that range from fairly formal to rustic-country to completely informal. The fare is traditional Austrian, and the beverage of choice is Salzburger Stiegl beer. *Landstr. 30, tel. 0732/773–3730. Reservations usually not necessary. Dress: jackets or casual, depending on the room. AE, DC, MC, V. Moderate.*

Dining and Lodging

Schillerpark. This very modern complex (glass outside, marble inside) puts you close to the south end of the pedestrian zone but still reasonably near the center and the sights. The casino is in the same building. The rooms have clean lines, with contemporary furnishings. *Rainerstr. 2–4, tel. 0732/554050. 111 rooms. Nonsmoking floor. Facilities: 2 restaurants (1 in the casino), 2 bars (1 in the casino), café, sauna, solarium, garage. AE, DC, MC, V. Very Expensive.*

Dom-Hotel. Behind the plain facade on a quiet side street near the new cathedral and the city center is a modern hotel with its own garden. The rooms are compact but attractive, in natural woods and shades of blue. *Baumbachstr. 17, tel. 0732/778441. 44 rooms. Facilities: restaurant, bar, sauna, solarium, parking. AE, DC, MC, V. Expensive.*

Spitz. This ultramodern neo–Art Deco hotel in Urfahr is an easy walk across the bridge from the city center. The rooms are smallish but comfortable, and some have a view over the new city hall to the main city. *Paladino*, its restaurant, is earning a good reputation. *Karl-Fiedler-Str. 6, tel. 0732/236–4410. 56 rooms. Facilities: restaurant (closed Sun.), bar, sauna, solarium, garage. AE, DC, MC, V. Expensive.*

Trend. You'll be directly on the Danube in this multistory modern hotel, next to the Brucknerhaus concert hall and within reasonable walking distance of the center. The rooms are compact-modern and attractively decorated; ask for an upper room on the river side for the superb views. The excellent restaurant is packed with businesspeople at lunchtime. *Untere Donaulände 9, tel. 0732/76260. 176 rooms. Facilities: restaurant, bar, nightclub, café, indoor pool, sauna, solarium, fitness room, garage. AE, DC, MC, V. Expensive.*

Drei Mohren. This has been an inn since 1595, and the rooms are well worn, but they have up-to-date baths. It's all in the heart of the old city within a block of the pedestrian zone. *Promenade 17, tel. 0732/772626. 27 rooms, 24 with bath. Facilities: restaurant, bar. AE, DC, V. Moderate.*

Prielmayerhof. This attractive, traditional house is not central, but bus No. 21 will take you the eight blocks to the pedestrian zone or the main rail station. The Oriental-carpeted rooms are larger than those in the newer hotels, and the baths are fully up to standard. *Weissenwolfstr. 33, tel. 0732/774131. 32 rooms, 30 with bath. Facilities: restaurant, bar. AE, DC, MC, V. Moderate.*

★ **Wolfinger.** This charming, traditional hotel in an old building in the heart of the city is a favorite of regular guests, certainly, in part, because of the friendly staff. You couldn't be more central. The medium-size rooms have been recently modernized, with comfortable new furniture and bright fabrics. Those on the front are less quiet but give you a first-hand view of city activities. The restaurant is excellent (*see* Dining, above). *Hauptplatz 19, tel. 0732/773–2910. 27 rooms, 23 with bath. Facilities: restaurant, wine stube. AE, DC, MC, V. Moderate.*

Zum Schwarzen Bären. This fine, traditional house near the center of the old city, a block from the pedestrian zone, was the birthplace of the tenor Richard Tauber (1891–1948). The rooms are smallish and well worn, but the baths (mostly with shower) are modern, if compact. *Herrenstr. 9–11, tel. 0732/772–4770. 36 rooms, 29 with bath. Facilities: restaurant, bar, wine stube. AE, DC, MC, V. Moderate.*

Maria Taferl

Dining and Lodging **Krone–Kaiserhof.** Two hotels under the same family management share each other's luxurious facilities. The Krone looks out over the Danube valley, the Kaiserhof has views of the nearby Baroque pilgrimage church. The rooms are done a bit slickly in a country style in both houses. Every Sunday in July and August there's a buffet with live dance music, on Wednesdays a *Heuriger* buffet (new wine and cold dishes) with zither music. *A–3672 Maria Taferl, tel. 07413/63550, 07413/3250. 65 rooms. Facilities: 2 restaurants, bar, indoor and outdoor pools, sauna, solarium, fitness room, minigolf, garage. No credit cards. Expensive.*

Mautern

Dining **Landhaus Bacher.** Lisl Bacher's creative, light cuisine here has
★ elevated this attractive country restaurant to one of the top dozen in the country. The light-flooded rooms are elegant but not stiff, and there's an attractive garden. A recent menu offered crabmeat salad, breast of pigeon, and spring lamb. Ask for advice on wines; the choice is wide. You can buy a copy of Mrs. Bacher's cookbook, although it costs about as much as a meal. Note that there are a few small and cozy rooms for overnight guests in an adjoining guest house. *Südtirolerplatz 208, tel. 02732/829370 or 02732/85429. Reservations required. Jacket and tie advised. DC, V. Closed Mon., Tues. and mid-Jan.–mid-Feb. Very Expensive.*

Melk

Dining and Lodging **Stadt Melk.** This traditional hotel in the heart of town offers plain but adequate accommodations in smallish rooms, but the main feature here is the excellent and attractive restaurant. The cuisine ranges from regional traditional to creative light; try one of the cream soups and stuffed chicken breast to enjoy the contrasts; dishes here are individually prepared. *Hauptplatz 1, A–3390, tel. 02752/2475. 16 rooms. Facilities: restaurant (reservations advised, jacket advised) garage. AE, V. Expensive.*

Goldener Ochs. Here in the center of town you're in a typical village *Gasthof* with the traditional friendliness of a family management. The rather small rooms were renovated in 1990, and the restaurant offers solid standard fare. *Linzer Str. 18, A–3390, tel. 02752/2367. 35 rooms, 25 with bath. Facilities: restaurant (closed Sat., Sun. Nov.–Apr.) wine cellar, sauna. AE, DC, MC, V. Moderate.*

Persenbeug

Dining **Donaurast.** You look through lots of glass over the Danube, about 2 km (1 mi) below Persenbeug, as you dine. Various river fish are specialties here, and interesting meat dishes such as wild boar, roast chicken, or Tafelspitz. Finish up with any of the excellent desserts or the selection of Austrian cheese. There are rooms as well, should you decide to stay overnight. *Wachaustr. 28, Persenbeug/Metzling, tel. 07412/2438. Dress: informal. Reservations not required. No credit cards. Closed Tues. in Nov., Dec., also Wed. in Mar.–May, Oct.; closed mid-Jan.–end Feb. Moderate.*

St. Pölten

Dining **Galerie.** Stock from the antique shop next door flows over to lend atmosphere to this stylish small restaurant. In contrast to the antiques, the kitchen strives to do new things—generally successfully—with Austrian standards like pork fillet. *Fuhrmanngasse 1, tel. 02742/51305. Reservations advised. Jacket and tie advised. AE, DC, MC. Closed Sun., Mon. Expensive.*

Spitz

Dining **Mühlenkeller.** You're really in an old mill here, and the cellar rooms go back to the 11th century. This is as much a *Heuriger* as it is a restaurant, open mainly in late afternoon and evening; wines come from neighboring vineyards. In summer you've the choice of the inside courtyard or the garden. Huge portions are served of local specialties like roast pork and Tafelspitz. *Auf der Wehr 1, tel. 02713/2352. No reservations. Dress: informal. No credit cards. Closed Wed., mid-Dec.–mid-Jan. Moderate.*

Dining and Lodging **Wachauer Hof.** This appealing traditional house, set near the vineyards, has been under family management for generations. You can enjoy the wines in the *Gaststube*, the shaded garden, or the restaurant, which offers basic Austrian fare. The medium-size rooms have comfortable chairs, ample pillows, and rustic decor in reds and browns. *Hauptstr. 15, A–3620, tel. 02713/ 2303. 32 rooms, 15 with bath. Facilities: restaurant. AE, MC. Closed mid-Nov.–Palm Sunday. Moderate.*

Steyr

Dining **Rahofer.** You'll have to search out this attractive intimate Italian restaurant in one of the passageways off the main square down toward the river. The choice is limited but of excellent quality; try the Saltimbocca. Soups and desserts are praiseworthy. *Stadtplatz 9, tel. 07252/24606. Reservations advised. Dress: casual but neat. AE, DC, MC, V. Closed Sun., Mon. Moderate.*

Dining and Lodging
★ **Minichmayr.** From this traditional hotel the view alone—out over the confluence of the Enns and Steyr rivers, up and across to Schloss Lamberg—will make your stay memorable. Add to that the especially homey rooms, a friendly staff, and an excellent restaurant offering creative, light cuisine and regional specialties, and there's little more to want, except easier parking. Ask for rooms on the river side. *Haratzmüllerstr. 1–3, A– 4400, tel. 07252/23410. 51 rooms. Facilities: restaurant, sauna, solarium. AE, DC, MC, V. Expensive.*

★ **Mader/Zu den Drei Rosen.** In this very old family-run hotel with small but pleasant modern rooms, you're right on the picturesque town square. The restaurant offers solid local and traditional fare, with outdoor dining in a delightful garden in the ancient courtyard. *Stadtplatz 36, A–4400, tel. 07252/23358. 53 rooms. Facilities: restaurant (closed Sun.), garage. MC, V. Moderate.*

Tulln

Dining and Lodging
★ **Zur Rossmühle.** Starting with the cheerful yellow facade, elegance is the byword in this attractively renovated hotel on the town square. From the abundant greenery of the reception

area to the table settings in the dining room, you'll find pleasing little touches. The rooms are in modern Baroque decor. For sheer pleasure, take lunch in the courtyard garden; here, as in the more formal dining room, you'll find Austrian standards and ambitious creations by the aspiring young chef. You'd do well with any of the excellent open wines on the list. *Hauptplatz 12–13, A–3430, tel. 02272/2411. 55 rooms. Facilities: restaurant (reservations advised, jacket and tie advised), bar, sauna, riding. AE, DC, MC, V. Closed Mon. and Jan. Expensive.*

Waidhofen an der Ybbs

Dining **Türkenpfeiferl.** "Family atmosphere" is served at this attractive, family-run restaurant, along with excellent creative, light cuisine and regional standards. Try the breast of chicken or lamb in a spiced crust. Note the attention to details: The bread is house baked. The garden is particularly pleasant for summer dining, and children are welcome. *Hoher Markt 23, tel. 07442/3507. Reservations recommended. Jacket advised. DC, MC. Closed Mon. and first week in July. Moderate.*

Weissenkirchen

Dining **Jamek.** Josef Jamek is known for his outstanding wines, his
★ wife Edeltraud for what she and her chefs turn out in the kitchen of this excellent restaurant, which is, in fact, their home. The combination makes for memorable dining in a rustic-elegant atmosphere. You dine in a succession of tastefully decorated rooms with 18th-century touches. Creative variations on typical Austrian specialties are emphasized; lamb and game in season are highlights. *Joching 45, tel. 02715/2235, 02715/2414. Reservations required. Jacket and tie advised. No credit cards. Closed Sun., Mon.; mid-Dec.–mid-Feb.; first week in July. Very Expensive.*

Florianihof. This is one of those restaurants that's packed on pleasant weekends; come during the week if possible. The dark-wood paneling in the succession of rooms is imposing and lends an illusion of elegance to this simple place. Check the *Rostbraten* (rumpsteak), roast pork, or grilled chicken. *Wösendorf 74, tel. 02715/2212. Reservations advised. Dress: casual but neat. No credit cards. Closed Thurs. and Jan.–Feb. Expensive.*

Kirchenwirt. The fare here is dependably Austrian: You'll find Tafelspitz, roast pork, *Kaiserfleisch* (corned pork), and other standards, all well prepared and served in the cozy rooms done in dark wood. *Weissenkirchen 17, tel. 02715/2332. Reservations advised on weekends. Dress: casual but neat. No credit cards. Closed Mon., Tues. in winter; closed mid-Dec.–mid-Jan. Expensive.*

Prandtauerhof. The Baroque facade is the work of Jakob Prandtauer, the architect responsible for many buildings in the area. Ornate details are carried over into the cozy guest rooms and the inner court; a sense of history pervades the house. The kitchen delivers excellent traditional cuisine with such creative touches as pork medallions in a light Gorgonzola sauce. You'll find fish and game in season, and the wines come from the house vineyards. *Joching 36, tel. 02715/2310. Reservations recommended. Jacket and tie advised. MC. Closed Tues., Wed. and mid-Feb.–mid-Mar. Expensive.*

Lodging **Raffelsbergerhof.** This stunning Renaissance building (1574),
★ once a shipmaster's house, has been tastefully converted into a
hotel with every comfort. The rooms are attractively decorated
without being overdone. The family management is particularly friendly, and there's a quiet garden to complement the *ge-
mütlich* public lounge. *A-3610 Weissenkirchen, tel. 02715/2201.
12 rooms. MC. Closed Nov.–Apr. Expensive.*

Ybbs an der Donau

Dining **Villa Nowotni.** Dining in this gorgeous Art Deco house makes
★ you feel almost as though you'd been personally invited.
Evelyn Nowotni looks after the attractive rooms while her husband, Franz, handles the kitchen. The cuisine is basically Austrian with imaginative touches, such as the steamed corned leg
of venison or breast of duck stuffed with fillet of beef. Six open
wines are offered in addition to a wide range of bottled wines.
And children are welcome in this gourmet temple; there's a
great meadow playground behind the villa. *Trewaldstr. 3, tel.
07412/2620. Reservations required. Jacket and tie advised.
AE, DC, MC, V. Closed Sun. eve. Oct.–May and Mon. year-
round. Expensive.*

The Arts and Nightlife

In the smaller towns and cities covered in this chapter, the arts
tend to come to life in summer. Nightlife is not bad in Linz and
St. Pölten, and each town or group of towns has a hangout
where the crowd gathers, but this is family country for vaca-
tioners, and nightlife will usually consist of sitting around a table with a glass of wine.

The Arts

In Linz, the tourist office's monthly booklet "Was ist los in Linz
und Oberösterreich" (What's On in Linz and Upper Austria)
will give you details of theater and concerts. Two ticket agencies are **Linzer Kartenbüro** (Herrenstr. 4, tel. 0732/776127) and
Ruefa (Landstr. 67, tel. 0732/662–6810).

Music Summer concerts are held in June and July at the abbeys at
Kremsmünster and St. Florian (tel. 0732/775230). A chamber-
music festival takes place at Schloss Tillysburg in July (tel.
0732/778800). From June to September, a series of concerts on
the Bruckner organ is given on six Sunday afternoons at 4 in
the church at St. Florian (tel. 07224/8903). Melk also offers a
series of concerts around Pentecost, and concerts are held at
Grafenegg during the summer. Get details and dates from the
town or regional tourist offices.

In Linz, concerts and recitals are held in the **Brucknerhaus,** the
modern hall on the banks of the Danube. From mid-September
to early October, it's the center of the International Bruckner
Festival. *Untere Donaulände 7, tel. 0732/775230. Box office
open weekdays 10–6.*

Opera During July, the operetta festival in **Bad Hall** presents a different work each week (tel. 07258/2255–35).

The **Linz** opera company is excellent and often more willing to
mount venturesome works and productions than those in Vien-

na or even Graz. Most performances are in the **Landestheater** (tel. 0732/777655), some in the Brucknerhaus.

The **Stadttheater** (tel. 02742/520260 or 02742/541830) in **St. Pölten** includes operetta and occasionally opera in its repertoire. Check with the tourist office for schedules and times.

Theater   In **Linz,** plays (in German) in the classical tradition and some operas are performed at the **Landestheater;** in the **Kammerspiele** you'll find more contemporary plays. Several smaller "cellar" theaters also offer drama; the tourist office will have information. *Landestheater: Promenade 39, tel. 0732/777655. Box office open Tues.–Fri. 10–12:30 and 4½ hrs before performances; Sat. 10:30–12:30; Mon., weekends, and holidays, 6 PM to performance; Kammerspiele: Promenade 39, tel. 0732/777855. Box office open same hours as Landestheater.*

The theater in **St. Pölten** is quite good for a provincial house; classical and contemporary plays in German are presented. *Stadttheater, Rathausplatz 11, tel. 02742/520260 or 02742/541830. Box office open Tues.–Sun. 11–1, 5–6:30.*

Summer theater is held on the grounds next to the abbey in **Melk** during July and August, and **Grein** puts on a summer festival; call the tourist office for details.

Nightlife

Linz is a far livelier town than most Austrians realize, and the local population is friendlier than in Vienna or Salzburg and much less cliquish than in the top resort towns.

Cabaret   Linz has no cabaret in the Viennese tradition, but there's striptease at **Bambi-Diele** (Landwiedstr. 140, tel. 0732/84516) from 9 PM on.

Casinos   The Linz casino, with roulette, blackjack, poker, and slot machines, is in the **Hotel Schillerpark,** and the casino complex includes a bar and the **Rouge et Noir** restaurant. *Rainerstr. 2–4, tel. 0732/54487. Open daily except Good Friday, Nov. 1, and Dec. 24, 3 PM–3 AM. Admission: AS170, includes four AS50 tokens. Passport required. Jacket and tie advised.*

Bars and Lounges   Linz has not lagged behind other Austrian cities in developing its own "Bermuda triangle." Around the narrow streets of the old city (Klosterstrasse, Altstadt, Hofgasse) are dozens of fascinating small bars and lounges, and as you explore, you'll probably meet some Linzers who can direct you to the current "in" location. In St. Pölten, try the **New York Pub & Steakhouse** (Kugelgasse 6, tel. 02742/52829) for a start.

Discos   St. Pölten is the place for disco activity, and the **Fabrik,** with its bars and pizzeria, continues to pack in crowds from as far away as Vienna (Radlberger Hauptstr. 60, tel. 02742/65521, nightly from 9). You might also try **Bellini** (Mühlweg 67, tel. 02746/66407). The vast Fabrik is a perennial favorite, but otherwise the mortality rate of St. Pölten's clubs and discos is high.

Index

Personal Itinerary

Departure *Date*

Time

Transportation

Arrival *Date*   *Time*

Departure *Date*   *Time*

Transportation

Accommodations

Arrival *Date*   *Time*

Departure *Date*   *Time*

Transportation

Accommodations

Arrival *Date*   *Time*

Departure *Date*   *Time*

Transportation

Accommodations

Personal Itinerary

Arrival *Date* *Time*

Departure *Date* *Time*

Transportation

Accommodations

Arrival *Date* *Time*

Departure *Date* *Time*

Transportation

Accommodations

Arrival *Date* *Time*

Departure *Date* *Time*

Transportation

Accommodations

Arrival *Date* *Time*

Departure *Date* *Time*

Transportation

Accommodations

Personal Itinerary

Arrival *Date*   *Time*

Departure *Date*   *Time*

Transportation

Accommodations

Arrival *Date*   *Time*

Departure *Date*   *Time*

Transportation

Accommodations

Arrival *Date*   *Time*

Departure *Date*   *Time*

Transportation

Accommodations

Arrival *Date*   *Time*

Departure *Date*   *Time*

Transportation

Accommodations

Personal Itinerary

Arrival *Date*   *Time*

Departure *Date*   *Time*

Transportation

Accommodations

Arrival *Date*   *Time*

Departure *Date*   *Time*

Transportation

Accommodations

Arrival *Date*   *Time*

Departure *Date*   *Time*

Transportation

Accommodations

Arrival *Date*   *Time*

Departure *Date*   *Time*

Transportation

Accommodations

Personal Itinerary

Arrival *Date*   *Time*

Departure *Date*   *Time*

Transportation

Accommodations

Arrival *Date*   *Time*

Departure *Date*   *Time*

Transportation

Accommodations

Arrival *Date*   *Time*

Departure *Date*   *Time*

Transportation

Accommodations

Arrival *Date*   *Time*

Departure *Date*   *Time*

Transportation

Accommodations

Personal Itinerary

Arrival *Date*   *Time*

Departure *Date*   *Time*

Transportation

Accommodations

Arrival *Date*   *Time*

Departure *Date*   *Time*

Transportation

Accommodations

Arrival *Date*   *Time*

Departure *Date*   *Time*

Transportation

Accommodations

Arrival *Date*   *Time*

Departure *Date*   *Time*

Transportation

Accommodations

Addresses

Name

Address

Telephone

Name

Address

Telephone

Name

Address

Telephone

Name

Address

Telephone

Name

Address

Telephone

Name

Address

Telephone

Name

Address

Telephone

Name

Address

Telephone

Name

Address

Telephone

Name

Address

Telephone

Name

Address

Telephone

Name

Address

Telephone

Name

Address

Telephone

Name

Address

Telephone

Name

Address

Telephone

Name

Address

Telephone

Addresses

Name	Name
Address	Address
Telephone	Telephone
Name	Name
Address	Address
Telephone	Telephone
Name	Name
Address	Address
Telephone	Telephone
Name	Name
Address	Address
Telephone	Telephone
Name	Name
Address	Address
Telephone	Telephone
Name	Name
Address	Address
Telephone	Telephone
Name	Name
Address	Address
Telephone	Telephone
Name	Name
Address	Address
Telephone	Telephone

Addresses

Name	Name
Address	Address
Telephone	Telephone
Name	Name
Address	Address
Telephone	Telephone
Name	Name
Address	Address
Telephone	Telephone
Name	Name
Address	Address
Telephone	Telephone
Name	Name
Address	Address
Telephone	Telephone
Name	Name
Address	Address
Telephone	Telephone
Name	Name
Address	Address
Telephone	Telephone
Name	Name
Address	Address
Telephone	Telephone

Fodor's Travel Guides

U.S. Guides

Alaska
Arizona
Boston
California
Cape Cod, Martha's
  Vineyard, Nantucket
The Carolinas & the
  Georgia Coast
The Chesapeake
  Region
Chicago
Colorado
Disney World & the
  Orlando Area
Florida
Hawaii

Las Vegas, Reno,
  Tahoe
Los Angeles
Maine, Vermont,
  New Hampshire
Maui
Miami & the
  Keys
National Parks
  of the West
New England
New Mexico
New Orleans
New York City
New York City
  (Pocket Guide)

Pacific North Coast
Philadelphia & the
  Pennsylvania
  Dutch Country
Puerto Rico
  (Pocket Guide)
The Rockies
San Diego
San Francisco
San Francisco
  (Pocket Guide)
The South
Santa Fe, Taos,
  Albuquerque
Seattle &
  Vancouver

Texas
USA
The U. S. & British
  Virgin Islands
The Upper Great
  Lakes Region
Vacations in
  New York State
Vacations on the
  Jersey Shore
Virginia & Maryland
Waikiki
Washington, D.C.
Washington, D.C.
  (Pocket Guide)

Foreign Guides

Acapulco
Amsterdam
Australia
Austria
The Bahamas
The Bahamas
  (Pocket Guide)
Baja & Mexico's Pacific
  Coast Resorts
Barbados
Barcelona, Madrid,
  Seville
Belgium &
  Luxembourg
Berlin
Bermuda
Brazil
Budapest
Budget Europe
Canada
Canada's Atlantic
  Provinces

Cancun, Cozumel,
  Yucatan Peninsula
Caribbean
Central America
China
Czechoslovakia
Eastern Europe
Egypt
Europe
Europe's Great Cities
France
Germany
Great Britain
Greece
The Himalayan
  Countries
Holland
Hong Kong
India
Ireland
Israel
Italy

Italy 's Great Cities
Jamaica
Japan
Kenya, Tanzania,
  Seychelles
Korea
London
London
  (Pocket Guide)
London Companion
Mexico
Mexico City
Montreal &
  Quebec City
Morocco
New Zealand
Norway
Nova Scotia,
  New Brunswick,
  Prince Edward
  Island
Paris

Paris (Pocket Guide)
Portugal
Rome
Scandinavia
Scandinavian Cities
Scotland
Singapore
South America
South Pacific
Southeast Asia
Soviet Union
Spain
Sweden
Switzerland
Sydney
Thailand
Tokyo
Toronto
Turkey
Vienna & the Danube
  Valley
Yugoslavia

Wall Street Journal Guides to Business Travel

Europe
International Cities
Pacific Rim
USA & Canada

Special-Interest Guides

Bed & Breakfast and
  Country Inn Guides:
  Mid-Atlantic Region
New England
The South
The West

Cruises and Ports
  of Call
Healthy Escapes
Fodor's Flashmaps
  New York

Fodor's Flashmaps
  Washington, D.C.
Shopping in Europe
Skiing in the USA &
  Canada

Smart Shopper's
  Guide to London
Sunday in New York
Touring Europe
Touring USA